Freedom's Mirage

FREEDOM'S MIRAGE

Virgil Bennehan's Odyssey from Emancipation to Exile

SYDNEY NATHANS

THE UNIVERSITY OF NORTH CAROLINA PRESS

Chapel Hill

*This book was published with the assistance of the
Z. Smith Reynolds Fund of the University of North Carolina Press.*

© 2024 The University of North Carolina Press

Designed by Jamison Cockerham
Set in Arno, Irby, Fell DW Pica, and Scala Sans
by Jamie McKee, MacKey Composition

Cover art: Victorian trade card from a series of nautical scenes,
1880–1900. Marian S. Carson Collection, Prints and Photographs
Division, Library of Congress, Washington, DC.

Manufactured in the United States of America

LIBRARY OF CONGRESS CATALOGING-IN-PUBLICATION DATA
Names: Nathans, Sydney, author.
Title: Freedom's mirage : Virgil Bennehan's odyssey from
emancipation to exile / Sydney Nathans.
Description: Chapel Hill : The University of North Carolina Press,
[2024] | Includes bibliographical references and index.
Identifiers: LCCN 2024022976 | ISBN 9781469682648 (cloth ;
alk. paper) | ISBN 9781469682655 (pbk. ; alk. paper) |
ISBN 9781469679075 (epub) | ISBN 9781469682662 (pdf)
Subjects: LCSH: Bennehan, Virgil, 1808–1850. | African American
physicians—History—19th century—Biography. | Free African
Americans—History—19th century—Biography. | United States—
Race relations—19th century. | BISAC: HISTORY / African American &
Black | HISTORY / United States / State & Local / South (AL, AR, FL,
GA, KY, LA, MS, NC, SC, TN, VA, WV) | LCGFT: Biographies.
Classification: LCC E185.97.B3327 N38 2024 |
DDC 610.89/96073092 [B]—dc23/eng/20240603
LC record available at https://lccn.loc.gov/2024022976

This book will be made open access within three years of publication
thanks to Path to Open, a program developed in partnership between
JSTOR, the American Council of Learned Societies (ACLS), the University
of Michigan Press, and the University of North Carolina Press to bring
about equitable access and impact for the entire scholarly community,
including authors, researchers, libraries, and university presses around
the world. Learn more at https://about.jstor.org/path-to-open/.

For Judith

A gift to me, a treasure to all

CONTENTS

ILLUSTRATIONS

MAPS

The Exception

Virgil Bennehan's Odyssey began with my own journey.

It was more than forty years ago that I switched. As a graduate student and then young professor, I'd focused on finishing a biography of Daniel Webster, a prominent leader in the years before the Civil War. Already the winds of the profession were shifting from political history and great leaders to social history and ordinary people, and I could feel myself yearning to try my hand at a more "democratic" historical subject.

Fortune smiled. The state of North Carolina was in the process of acquiring a new historic site, just outside Durham, where I'd come in 1966 to teach at Duke University. The proposed historic site was a plantation house, built in 1787, that included four unusual dwellings for enslaved people, constructed in the 1850s. Called Stagville, the original plantation house had formed the beginning of one of the state and region's largest plantation empires, one that by 1860 came to span three states, embrace 30,000 acres, and encompass close to a thousand enslaved workers. As a young historian with an interest in social history I got invited to be a member of the advisory committee on what to do with the incipient site and how to interpret it.

By then I was being drawn to what was the fastest growing and most interesting social history in the field: southern and African American social

Horton Grove. Built in the 1850s at what is now Historic Stagville, each Horton Grove slave dwelling housed four families in slavery times. Archival and oral historians have since illuminated the history of those who dwelled at Horton Grove and others who lived at Stagville, before and after Emancipation. *Photographs Division, Library of Congress, Washington, DC.*

history. If the site had been the plantation dwelling alone, I'd have pitched in but not been particularly engaged. The four cabins for enslaved workers were the magnet. Still standing, they were exceptional, seemingly unique. Each was two stories tall. Each had chimneys on both sides. Each had a wooden exterior and brick interior—"board and batten siding," I came to learn. The structures alone, though they had windows front and back and shutters to keep out the elements, did not open up the story of persons who lived there. This was the story that I (and a host of other historians of the time) was interested in.

Records opened up the story of these enslaved people. The extended family that owned the enslaved workers and the plantation kept records. The builder of Stagville was Richard Bennehan, who with his wife, Mary Amis Bennehan, and his two children, Rebecca and Thomas Bennehan, dwelled at Stagville into the early nineteenth century. In 1803, Rebecca Bennehan married Duncan Cameron, one of the most prominent lawyers in the state, and by the end of the decade, with a gift of land from Richard Bennehan, Cameron shifted from lawyer to planter and had his workers start construction of his own plantation dwelling two miles away, which he came to call Fairntosh. The Camerons' son, Paul Cameron, took over the plantation in

1837 and, over the next twenty-eight years, ran it and added two more plantations out of state. Over the decades, the Bennehans and Camerons kept their correspondence, the letters of overseers, and hundreds of lists of enslaved persons. The correspondence and plantation records totaled 30,000 documents, which family descendants turned over in the 1930s to the newly founded Southern Historical Collection at the University of North Carolina at Chapel Hill.

Those records allowed historians Jean Bradley Anderson to tell the story of the white family and Herbert Gutman ingeniously to decode family connections among the enslaved people on the plantation. Historian George McDaniel supplemented the records with oral interviews with Black descendants to get inside the lives of the post-Emancipation Black occupants of those four two-story dwellings. Their work in the archives and oral history inspired me to pursue two of the plantation's most arresting African American stories, out of which finally came books. *To Free a Family* was about a woman, Mary Walker, who escaped to freedom in 1848 and sought through 1865 to recover the family she had left behind. *A Mind to Stay* explored the fate of 114 persons sent to Alabama in 1844 and portrayed the odyssey of their descendants from the nineteenth century to the present.

In all this—during forty years of work and writing, through hundreds of hours of research and dozens of return trips to the Bennehan-Cameron Family Papers at the Southern Historical Collection—in all this, there was one outlying story, of one outlying person.

His name was Virgil.

Virgil was the first enslaved person whose exact date of birth was recorded in the hundreds of lists of workers and their families kept by the Bennehans and Camerons. The date was December 24, 1808. Virgil was the only enslaved person taught to keep accounts and one of the few taught how to read and write. Virgil was the only enslaved person to become a medical assistant on the plantation. He was taught first by his owner, Thomas Bennehan, whom he accompanied when the owner gave basic medical care to "our black family," as the Bennehans and Camerons referred to their workers. Further training came from physicians who dwelled in the neighborhood and in the nearby village of Hillsborough, doctors who intermittently came to Stagville and Fairntosh to treat serious illnesses.

When Thomas Bennehan wrote his final will in April 1845, he bequeathed all of Stagville's 5,000 acres of land and most of his 330 enslaved workers to his nephew Paul Cameron, with the exception of one family: Virgil's. Virgil—along with his wife, Phoebe, and her niece Margaret and nephew William—was to be freed. The will of 1845 contained two additional provisions. Virgil was to leave the state of North Carolina for either a free state or Liberia. When he left, he was to receive $500. Following Thomas Bennehan's death in June 1847, Virgil put off a decision until April 1848, then hurried to Baltimore to ship out to Liberia. After writing Paul Cameron a long letter from Liberia in May 1848, Virgil came back with his family eight months later. In a "*short* letter" to Paul Cameron in March 1849, Virgil reported his intent to settle his wife, niece, and nephew in Baltimore and head out to California, where gold had been discovered thirteen months before. Then, silence. The last reference in the Cameron records to Virgil came in a letter of 1856 from Paul Cameron to his sister, Margaret. They were just two words, given in passing and without explanation: "Poor Virgil."

To me, as a researcher, Virgil was the plantation's outlier. At the same time, I realized that on the plantation and in his own time, Virgil was the ultimate insider, with a special status on the plantation that set him apart from the exact day he was born to the last mention of him decades later. Trained and trusted as an enslaved young man to keep accounts, groomed as the plantation's physician assistant, freed by his owner's will and death in 1847, transported to Liberia in the spring of 1848 and back in the United States eight months later, declaring his intention to venture to California in early 1849: Virgil's life appeared to accelerate and change drastically in two years' time. And then, after he twice crossed the Atlantic and perhaps trekked the American continent to reach the Pacific, his odyssey ended, shrouded in mystery. "Poor Virgil."

Even as I pursued the fate of Mary Walker and of the 114 persons sent to Alabama, the detective in me stayed on the lookout for clues about Virgil. What set him apart, what led to his being freed, what happened to him in Liberia, why did he come back to America, did he get to California, and if so, what was his fate there? More important, I wrestled continually with a larger question. What did Virgil's story reveal about the African American experience in slavery and freedom?

There were many brief letters about Virgil in the plantation correspondence. Numerous mentions revealed that Virgil was the highly trusted servant of his owner. He possessed the keys to the plantation smokehouse and to the chest of drawers where Thomas Bennehan kept money and important documents.

Virgil presided confidently over the Stagville dwelling while his owner was away. "Virgil does the honors of your house with much propriety," a visitor wrote. But the most frequent references came in conjunction with his medical care of others on the plantation. Most illnesses he treated of his own accord. If Virgil found someone seriously ill, or if his treatment of them with emetics or bleeding didn't bring relief, he would recommend a call to a neighboring trained physician to help with the diagnosis and treatment.

In the entire archive of 30,000 letters, there were only three that Virgil himself wrote. Two were brief reports on plantation conditions. The longest and most self-disclosing was a long handwritten letter that Virgil wrote from Liberia to his former "young Master" and now "friend," Paul Cameron. Written on May 29, 1848, Virgil's letter described his arrival in the country's capital of Monrovia, the reception Virgil received from the highest officials in the capital, and his arrival in the harbor of Bassa and decision to make the village of Bexley the place he would settle. That letter would have to be my mother lode document, from which to extract what I could about Virgil's past, expectations and experience, ambitions and intimations of his future course. There was a second letter of great value in the Cameron papers, this one from Paul Cameron *to* Virgil Bennehan. Letters from literate emigrants in Liberia to their former owners were not unusual. Rare if not unique was Paul Cameron's letter to a former bondman. I found no more letters from Virgil, no attic trunk with more letters about him. I found no descendants, laden with oral testimony about their forebear or with stories of what happened to Virgil, his wife, or her niece and nephew. This was a two-letter project—or so, for a long time, it seemed it would have to be.

I was wrong. There was, figuratively, an attic trunk. Thousands of letters concerning Liberia and its emigrants were held in one repository, the archive of the American Colonization Society. Letters in that vast archive began to connect the dots about Virgil Bennehan's experience in Liberia, why he returned, and what he did after he came back. In the course of pondering all these letters and taking clues and inferences from them, I realized that this was to be a story replete with conjecture, and even with conjuration. Only half in jest did I tell friends that I had embarked on a story "inspired by few events."

It became clear that what set Virgil apart was more than that he became a privileged bondman and a medical practitioner in the world in which he was enslaved. It was that he came to see himself as a "friend" to both the whites in his world and to his own people. White owners and overseers certainly saw him as trustworthy. How did Black people see him? Did they view him as an honest broker and caring medic? Did they see him as a "company doctor," devoted primarily to getting them back to work? Was he perceived as his owner's faithful lackey, a snitch not to be trusted?

When I began to focus on these questions about Virgil, it was 2018. The field to which I had shifted forty years earlier—southern and African American history—had itself undergone seismic changes. To understand this outlying insider's story required wrestling with terms that had been discredited and perspectives that had been summarily dismissed. The very language long used to describe owners and owned is today viewed as cloaking the brutal essence of enslavement. Words pervasive in Virgil's time and prevailing until recently—master, slave, slave owner—have given way to enslaver, enslaved, racial capitalist, and sexual predator. Virgil's world and time was one of plantations and planters, some of whom saw themselves as persons of "good conscience" and who wrote unblushingly of "our black family and our white family." By numerous historians, plantations are now labeled "slave labor camps" and the family metaphor is regarded as language of "self-endearment and cushioned coercion deployed by those with power over vocabulary and people"—or simply disdained as "nonsense." As to Virgil himself, wasn't it quixotic to probe for the possibility of dual loyalty? If he served his enslaver, was he not above all a collaborator, a man obliged to snitch, a bondman who forfeited his own soul as the price of privilege? To portray any of them—Virgil or his enslavers—as "friends" or as "persons of conscience" seemed at best naive and at worst to perpetuate the scorned Lost Cause view of bondage as a world of beneficent whites and loyal Blacks.

Aware of the toxic terrain I was on, I found that others urged me to tread with care. *The exception doesn't change the rule* was the astute counsel of one trusted friend. The detective in me persisted. I needed to know Virgil's story. As I saw it, to explain how Virgil had become an exception, I had to start with the language and perspectives of the white world he had lived in, even at the risk of resuscitating the illusions that others had so cogently challenged and unmasked. At the same time, that good counsel—*the exception doesn't change the rule*—offered me the detachment and central question that I needed. Did the realities of bondage come to envelop even Virgil, as reality had for others in the South elevated—for a time—in the planters' hierarchy? Did the fate of the exception prove the rule?

Freedom's Mirage

1

Toxic Terrain, Medical Calling

How did Virgil become Virgil? Once more, let's start with the date of his birth: December 24, 1808. It is the first exact date of birth recorded in the lists of several thousand persons enslaved on the Bennehan and Cameron plantations. Those lists began in 1776 and continued through 1865. First names and ages were often given, from which one can work back to the year of birth. Some lists gave the name and year of birth. Save for Virgil and a scattered handful of others, however, no lists gave the month and day of birth. It is possible that because Virgil was a Christmas Eve child, his birth and birthday received special notice—and that *he* received immediate notice. If nothing else had transpired in his life, coincidence could account for the listing. More did transpire.

Birth brought the Christmas child into one of the first enslaved families of the Bennehan plantation. His grandparents, Phil and Esther, were born before the American Revolution. They belonged to the estate of Thomas Amis Sr., a small planter in Northampton County in eastern North Carolina, who died in 1764. Thomas Amis's will bequeathed five of his enslaved workers "and their increase" to his eight-year-old daughter, Mary Amis. In 1776,

1

when twenty, Mary Amis wed the thirty-three-year-old merchant Richard Bennehan, who dwelled in Orange County, North Carolina, in the central Piedmont region of the emerging new state. She brought her now increased set of enslaved people with her.[1] Phil, Esther, and two dozen other Amis workers formed the nucleus of a growing labor force that enabled the transition of Mary's husband from merchant to planter. By 1790, Phil and Esther had formed a union, and over the next thirteen years, Esther gave birth to seven children. They called their firstborn child Virgil, quite likely passing on the European name imposed on an African forebear by his first white owner. Their five-year-old son died in 1796. Phil and Esther's second child, Mary, was born in 1793, three years before her brother died. When at age of fifteen she had the first of her children on December 24, 1808, she chose his name in keeping with an early African American tradition. Honoring the memory of her brother, she called him Virgil.[2]

The inventory that listed Mary and her son Virgil gave no name for Virgil's father. Nor when Mary had two more sons—Albert and Solomon—was a father named. When both parents of enslaved children were known, the annual Bennehan plantation lists gave the names of the mother and father and the names of their young. Sometimes the omission of a father's name indicated that the recorder didn't know or wasn't told a father's identity. More often it indicated something else. The father might be an enslaved man who belonged to an adjacent plantation; he might be a white overseer. Or the unnamed father was the owner himself.

As Virgil's life unfolded after his birth in 1808—taught to read and write and keep accounts by age twenty-two, trained as a physician's apprentice by age twenty-six, made a medical caregiver by age thirty, willed free at age thirty-nine—there is no doubt that he was a favored bondman. Did his life advance as it did because he was Thomas Bennehan's son?

Most slaveholders who compelled sex with enslaved women viewed the offspring impersonally. They were simply additions to the labor force. For the few who felt regard for the women or their children, taboos prohibited open acknowledgment—a wife aggrieved by betrayal, lawful descendants who saw enslaved offspring not as siblings but as property and their eventual inheritance, relatives and friends who colluded in denial. The law of every southern state mandated that the status of a child born in bondage followed the condition of the mother. Yet even within these constraints, the owner who cared for his enslaved progeny might secretly or publicly provide special treatment for them while he lived—and mandate their telltale liberation after his death.[3]

Thomas Bennehan's upbringing set the stage for him to be an exception to the rule, a living contradiction: to be an owner who by his lights could empathize with those he enslaved and who could make special provision for an unfree child he fathered. Born in 1782, he and his older sister, Rebecca, grew up on a plantation that their parents called Stagville. Parents and children alike thought of Stagville and its people in familial terms—"our family, white and black." The crops grown in the red clay of the region reinforced the familial outlook. Harvests of tobacco and wheat were far less lucrative than the bonanza crops of sugar and rice and cotton cultivated on richer soils, where it paid to set high quotas and push workers to the limit. In the Piedmont, the planter's crops and livelihood depended on looking after his workers' health. For the Bennehans, sentiment and self-interest aligned to forge a culture of caring.[4]

Even then, like most young masters, Thomas Bennehan might have come of age thinking of the plantation and the people he held in bondage as his rightful possessions and their labor his due. But his view of bondage was shaped by the ethos of postrevolutionary America, a time of debate about the morality of slavery. Thomas Bennehan was in the thick of those heretical discussions in 1796 as a fourteen-year-old student at the recently founded University of North Carolina. So was his cousin Thomas Gale Amis, who joined him at the school, which served as a glorified academy for its young students as well as a fledgling university for older ones. Thomas Gale Amis took those college debates of the mid-1790s seriously and continued his soul-searching for another decade, sharing his deepening doubts about "this injured, unfortunate race" with his Bennehan relative, his "one & only Bosom friend."[5]

Young Amis lived at Stagville for a time but left in despair after he fell in love with his cousin Rebecca and realized that it was an unattainable match. His escape took him to Guadeloupe, where French troops in 1803 had brutally sought to reverse the 1793 French decree of emancipation and where Black rebels in response had torched fields and sugar plantations, leaving the countryside in flames. Thomas Amis's sympathies were entirely with the "unfortunate Sons of Africa." "Mark the event," he wrote Thomas Bennehan. "Having imbibed for a moment the sweet draught of Freed[om]," those who "dared in deed, word, yea *thought* to defend the precious gift are butchered with a cruelty" that would "freeze the blood of all but Devils or Frenchmen. Lord! Is this thy will?" Remaining in the Caribbean, Amis journeyed to Antigua, where in 1805 he found a remarkable sugar plantation where he was told that work got done entirely "without

Graduates with honors, and questions. Thomas Amis and Thomas Bennehan were cousins and classmates at the University of North Carolina in the 1790s, where they participated in intense discussions about the morality of slaveholding. Raleigh Weekly Register, *July 14, 1801.*

chastisement." From the college debates, from Guadeloupe, and from Antigua, Thomas Amis drew lessons about human bondage—but they fell short of liberation. Rather, he urged his Bennehan cousin to recognize that the people he owned "are not brutes, they have sentiments." You and your people will all be rewarded if you "exercise your power with mercy; with-hold the scourge 'till you reflect on their misfortunes." "Treat them as human beings, your interest will become theirs, the sweat shall drop unheeded from their brows & their toil shall not be bitter because they love him who shall enjoy its fruits."[6]

Could slavery and conscience—interest and humanity—be reconciled? On both sides of the Atlantic, at the end of the eighteenth century, the question came to the fore. Orphaned without an inheritance of land or laborers, Thomas Amis could fantasize that with good treatment, his cousin's "interest will become theirs," that unpaid toil "shall not be bitter," and that his enslaved workers could love their enslaver. For others who wrestled with the question, including conscientious British merchants and ship captains involved in the slave trade, the dilemma was real, the struggle agonizing, and the answer less sanguine. For most, the quest was futile.[7]

For Thomas Bennehan, however, the exhortation of his cousin fell on fertile ground. Thomas Bennehan and his sister Rebecca took to heart their cousin's entreaties about the treatment of their "black family," especially when its members were ill. Rebecca Bennehan always found it "truly distressing to witness the sufferings of so many sick and afflicted fellow mortals." So, too, did her brother, "whose particular frame of . . . mind" led to "his own sufferings . . . amid so much sickness."[8] There was a second circumstance that would contribute to young Bennehan's treatment of his enslaved workers and of Virgil as full-fledged "human beings." Thomas Bennehan never married. Unwed, he had no wife or white children to contest any special provisions he made for enslaved persons. He attributed his bachelorhood to a "constitutional coldness"—a social awkwardness and elaborate formality—that doomed his prospects with women of his class and color.[9] A friend equally luckless in love urged his comrade Tom to seek exaltation in faith rather than females. "Let us not labor for that meat which perisheth . . . but for everlasting life." We "are but stewards and must give account of our stewardship . . . and be born again to get to heaven."[10] Not a particularly religious man, Thomas Bennehan had more need of an earthly than a divine mission. Was there a "stewardship" that might allow him to achieve his cousin's summons—to marry interest and humanity? His answer would shape his future and ultimately Virgil's life as well.

When one thinks of the expansion of the plantation South, the direction most familiar is from the eastern South to the west, from land that grew grains and tobacco and rice to soils that produced bonanza crops of sugar and cotton. But in the late eighteenth and early nineteenth centuries, expansion was within the interior. In the case of the Bennehan plantation, the best land for growing grain and tobacco was adjacent to land already owned and near rivers that ran through their possessions. The Bennehan and Cameron holdings grew from just under 900 acres in 1776 to 2,900 acres in 1800 and mushroomed to 7,500 acres by 1815 and to almost 9,000 acres by 1825. Each acquisition brought the clearing of trees, then the draining of wetlands near the rivers, followed by planting and cultivating crops on the reclaimed soil. The harvests of corn and wheat, in turn, needed to be ground at mills that were built or bought by the Bennehans or the Camerons. The process

Richard Bennehan. From 1776 to 1825, Bennehan expanded his plantation from 900 to 9,000 acres, acquiring property adjacent to rivers. Drained lowlands produced rich harvests but bred mosquitoes that infected all with malaria. *Cameron Family Papers, 1757–1978, Southern Historical Collection, Wilson Library, University of North Carolina at Chapel Hill.*

required water to be dammed up into mill ponds, whose controlled flow turned the wheels to grind the grains into cornmeal or flour.[11]

With each accession of low-lying land and each mill fed by ponds of stagnant water, the Bennehan plantation expanded and thrived. So did the breeding grounds for mosquitoes and the parasite that mosquitoes carried, malaria. Unabated expansion created a toxic terrain.

Malaria. The Latin root of the word means "foul air," bad air once thought to be a source of the illness. Though the term "malaria" did exist in 1808, the year that Virgil was born, neither during Virgil's lifetime nor for most of the nineteenth century was there an understanding of the microbe's transmission from the mosquito to human beings. What was understood were the symptoms that followed—severe and sudden chills, high fevers, subsidence of fever in most cases, and increased susceptibility to other diseases by virtue of weakness and debility. The name given to the syndrome of symptoms was "ague," a term that came from the French language, and meant "burning fever." Usually, the shaking chills came and went within forty-eight to seventy-two hours. Other times, the chills worsened, fever lingered, and lassitude followed. In the worst cases, the body turned cold, the hands blue, the brain became congested, and the headaches excruciating—followed by death. The descriptive terms hardly come close to the lived experience of profuse sweating, cold perspiration, a dead pulse, and, above all, uncertainty. In one case reported later, a woman's chill lasted a "full seven hours, her face flushed to a deep purple & then ashen pale," her mind descended to "a state of wild delirium," she cried out that "her head would burst," and the "least ray of light . . . seemed to madden her." Were such symptoms temporary and passing, ones endured for hours, then finally to subside? Were they preludes to yet more ominous stages of illness?[12]

On the Bennehan place, the need to cope with the symptoms of malaria was barely in evidence up through the year of Virgil's birth in 1808. When Thomas Bennehan reported on the health of "our black family" to his father in 1803, he noted that the one sick child was on the mend and "the rest of the family [is] in good health." Five years later, in mid-December 1808, the message was the same. "Jim alone is ill. All others [are] exceedingly healthy."[13] But three months later, in March 1809, Thomas Bennehan himself had become "quite ill and in much pain." His symptoms would continue through the spring and summer of that year and prompted him to leave for respite and recovery to Red Sulphur Springs, Virginia. His father urged him to remain through the last of August for his "health and happiness. May God preserve you."[14] By the end of 1814, father Richard Bennehan himself escaped to Red Sulphur Springs. From its safety he warned his son to stay far away from the lowland opened up for crops. "Let me remind you of the danger of visiting the low grounds, if unfortunately they should be covered with vegetable matter, which will very soon at this season become a Mass of putrefaction fatal to health." The following spring and summer, bilious fever and "ague" prevailed among the enslaved workers and brought "melancholy tidings" of illness and deaths. From then on, it was not a matter of whether chills and fever and disease occurred but of how many people were smitten and how well or poorly they fared. A decade later, with outbreaks widening in scale and lengthening in duration, visiting friends, one a doctor, independently diagnosed the root cause of the plantation's alarming unhealthiness: the erection of "so many mills" and "the extensive clearing of your lowlands."[15]

For Thomas Bennehan, permanent flight was not an option. Nor was the abandonment of clearing and cultivating fertile lowlands or the dependence on mills and mill ponds—or the surrender altogether of the profits and prerogatives that slaveholding brought. Rather, the planter's son, after his recovery in 1809, threw himself into the medical treatment of the enslaved workers made sick by the ubiquitous mosquito breeding grounds created by the plantation's expansion and cultivation.

Thomas Bennehan had found a calling. He became the dedicated provider of medical care for "his people."

That calling became the vehicle by which he could, as he saw it, be a slaveholder and a man of conscience. When a person came down with the first symptoms—fever and chills—Thomas Bennehan went to them and administered medicine. Known to his enslaved people as "Mas Tom," Bennehan decided whether the first chills were moderate and likely to subside or whether the symptoms were more serious. If "very sick," he had the ill person come or be brought to his dwelling, where he placed him or her under close watch in "the kitchen," an outbuilding behind the main house. The kitchen became an improvised intensive care setting, where the ill could be kept under constant observation and given more medicines to abate unrelenting chills. If the condition became "dangerous," Bennehan sent for one of three physicians who dwelled fifteen miles away in the village of Hillsborough. Both the doctor and Bennehan would stay with the patient or patients as long as needed—to see them through the crises or to the end.[16] All remedies were tried. In what was called heroic medicine, Bennehan or doctors administered the emetic ipecac to induce vomiting or the purgatives calomel and cream of tartar powder to force bowel expulsions. Worse cases prompted stronger measures—bleeding or cupping to extract the bile or "bad blood" and to restore humoral balance. We now know that the symptoms and treatments competed for damage done and that the remedies often compounded harm. The only gentle medicine was quinine, a bitter-tasting pill or potion sometimes administered with whiskey, which usually brought temporary relief.[17]

Few patients, Black or white, cared for "the drill," as the heroic medical treatment was called. But all understood that for "Mas Tommy" and the physicians he summoned, no effort would be spared to sustain life. When the treatment worked, as most often it did, the person expressed gratitude.[18] Thomas Bennehan could readily allow himself to believe, as his cousin

Stagville. Built between 1787 and 1799, the Bennehan House at Stagville
was the dwelling of Thomas Bennehan throughout his adult life. Behind
the house was the kitchen, which doubled as an infirmary where the "very
ill" were brought and treated by Virgil and Thomas Bennehan.
Courtesy of North Carolina State Historic Sites, Raleigh.

Thomas Amis had promised, that his enslaved workers willingly worked
and felt affection for the man whose care for them was so palpable, personal,
and tenacious.

The calling took a toll on Thomas Bennehan. When sickness became
widespread, when there seemed to be no containing it, when he began to
lose people despite all his efforts, melancholy set in. His brother-in-law,
Duncan Cameron, who had become a planter at the urging of his father-in-
law, Richard Bennehan, tried to be fatalistic when deaths defeated medical
care and urged resignation to the will of Providence. But Duncan Cameron
knew that Thomas Bennehan took disease and deaths to heart and assured
his sister, Rebecca, that he understood the sensibility and suffering of the
caregiver when his ministrations failed.[19] Others took note of the physical
toll on Thomas Bennehan, urging him to get away from Stagville in the
summertime before he endangered his own health. Observed a friend: "I
think he has tried it long enough to be satisfied, that there is no safety there
for *him*."[20] Each exhortation to escape, and each temporary departure, raised
an insistent question. In his absence, who would care for the people he held
in bondage?

In time, the answer emerged. It would be the child born on Christmas
Eve, 1808, the first person whose exact date of birth was noted among thousands of entries in annual slave registers. It would be Virgil.

Whether Virgil was an unacknowledged son or a most favored servant, there is little question that Thomas Bennehan singled him out for trusted roles. Virgil was taught to read and write, presumably by Bennehan himself. Virgil's spelling was phonetic, but his handwriting, like his owner's cursive script, was florid and robust. Taught to add and subtract, Virgil had an unerring command of numbers and put that skill to good use. By 1831, he was a plantation accountant. He tallied the exact weights of hogs killed at the Christmas season and recorded the precise quantity of pork distributed to the different quarters of people. Virgil possessed the key to the smokehouse, from which meat was distributed each week. He also mastered the manners of an attentive house servant. A visiting friend noted to Thomas Bennehan that Virgil received him and "did the honors of his house with much propriety."[21]

Trusted by Duncan Cameron as well as Thomas Bennehan, Virgil became a regular courier from their plantations to Hillsborough and eventually to Raleigh, still farther away.[22] In November 1828, he brought a letter back from Hillsborough resident Samuel Kollock. The letter contained an offer to sell to Duncan Cameron a fine, industrious enslaved family—whom Kollock was "unwilling to separate"—on "very reasonable terms." Virgil, as he neared twenty, would long since have learned that financially strapped owners routinely turned to Bennehan or Cameron when anxious to sell enslaved families. In part, sellers knew that the brothers-in-law had the wherewithal to buy. More important, sellers who solemnly saw themselves as manifesting "solicitude as to the destiny of [their] slaves" sought out "those said to be good masters" and, when successful, received "grateful manifestations of the Negroes themselves." Virgil did not see the contents of the letter, but as sometimes happened, enslaved family members may have tipped him off. Thomas Bennehan and Duncan Cameron were known as such "Masters of their choice." Couriers could carry multiple messages.

At some point Thomas Bennehan decided to train Virgil as his medical assistant. Likely he first had Virgil accompany him when he visited the sick in their quarters or brought the seriously ill to the makeshift infirmary at Stagville. When doctors came from Hillsborough to care for the gravely ill, he asked them to give medical instruction to Virgil. They taught Virgil the proper medicines to give when fever and chills were routine, when to call for surveillance and close attention, and when to urge a physician's summons. Thomas Bennehan never referred to the medical care that he or Virgil provided as doctoring. They provided what he called "nursing"—akin to

Medical report by Virgil Bennehan. In his medical role, Virgil treated the moderately ill and reported back to Thomas Bennehan, as he did in this medical report from 1839. When Thomas Bennehan was absent from Stagville, Virgil took charge as its resident medic. *Cameron Family Papers, 1757–1978, Southern Historical Collection, Wilson Library, University of North Carolina at Chapel Hill.*

what we might describe as the role of physician's assistant or first medical responder. No later than April 1836, and likely earlier, Virgil was tending to the ill when Thomas Bennehan could not do it himself.

———————————

Virgil had become a trusted medical caregiver. But trusted by whom? Nothing in the letters saved by the planters indicates one way or the other how Virgil's enslaved compatriots felt about him. Virgil himself, however, penned two letters in 1848 that suggest how he viewed himself. Twice in two months he wrote to ask to be remembered to "all his friends." "All his friends" included Old Master, Young Master, and the white mistresses of the plantation. But he also asked to be remembered to four overseers, whom he called his "neighbors," to fourteen specific enslaved friends, and to "a hundred more I could name."[23]

Could an enslaved man be a friend, equally and alike, to his owners, to overseers, and to his fellow workers? The role of physician's assistant in particular carried with it an inherent conflict. Gratitude for life sustained or for health restored could not be separated from awareness that the medic served the owner, who expected a healthy worker to be at *work*. Even more would doubts about allegiance—to the owner or to the owned—fall on a man thought to be the master's son. How could Virgil possibly imagine himself as true to all?

If there is an answer to that question, it requires speculation. Fragments of information suggest that Virgil had a model and a mentor within the enslaved community—that the task of guide fell to Virgil's grandfather. Virgil's mother, Mary, died in 1816, when Virgil was almost eight years old. His grandfather Phillip was fifty-three.[24] For the next two decades, it seems likely that it was the enslaved man Phillip—whose full name was Phillip Meaks—who helped Virgil chart his course and who sought to teach his grandson how to be loyal to all and a turncoat to none.

Two initials—the slimmest of signals—telegraphed Virgil's acknowledgment of the pivotal role that Phillip Meaks played in the upbringing of his grandson. In the longest surviving letter written by Virgil, a two-page letter sent from Liberia in May 1848, Virgil signed his name at the end of the second page. It was the one known occasion when he wrote out his first and last name—Virgil *Bennehan*. Between the first name and surname he added two middle initials: "P. M." For the recipient of the letter, and for himself, "*Virgil P. M. Bennehan*" signified his twofold allegiance. "Bennehan" affirmed his white lineage. "P. M." recognized the legacy of his grandfather.[25]

Phillip Meaks embodied dual loyalty. By the time of Virgil's birth in 1808, Phil—as he was called in plantation correspondence—had become Richard and Thomas Bennehan's most trusted servant. How that trust came to be can be guessed only from a few scraps of evidence that take the story back to 1776. In 1776, Phil was thirteen years old living on the farm owned by the merchant Richard Bennehan, who was not yet the large landowner he would become. Four years older than Phil was an enslaved young man named Charles Thomas or Charles Fry, whom his owner gave the diminutive of Scrub. The colonists of North Carolina, Richard Bennehan among them, were beginning their breakaway from the British Crown, moving from subjects to rebels and revolutionaries. In mid-February 1776, Bennehan was about to depart for a battle 130 miles to the south, near Wilmington, North Carolina. Aware that word was out "that negroes have some thoughts of Freedom," Bennehan ordered the clerk in his store to "make Scrub sleep in the house every night." He needed to be watched lest he use the unrest to escape. Scrub did not leave that week or that year.[26] Instead he bided his time and, when his owner least expected it, disappeared eight years later, on May 15, 1784. Scrub was twenty-five; Phil was twenty-one. Bennehan made efforts to recover Scrub with advertisements in the newspapers of North Carolina and Virginia. Though the owner had always found Scrub to be "remarkably honest and of good behavior," he recognized that Scrub had "great notions of freedom" and would try to get back to Norfolk, Virginia, where he was raised, and to live there as a freeman. Despite the offer of a thirty-dollar reward, retrieval failed.[27]

Phillip Meaks might have learned from Scrub's escape that he, too, could bide his time and make a break for freedom when unexpected. Instead, he chose another course. He chose to make himself indispensable. Phil became adept in the role of caretaker of the equipment for horses—a hosteler who knew harnesses and saddles. He became expert in making "blacking," the polish that kept the leather of equipment and riding boots supple and shiny.[28] Above all, Phil won the trust of the family that owned him, trust that became evident on July 30, 1796, when unknown thieves stole one of the owner's horses. Richard Bennehan asked his nephews, who minded the store, to go after the thieves and to see if they could recover the horse. He instructed the nephews to leave Phil in charge while they went in pursuit. In 1776, Scrub—out of fear of his notions of freedom—had been confined to the store. Two decades later, Phil was assigned to guard the store.[29]

That trust carried over and deepened for the two children of Richard and Mary Bennehan, and especially for their son. Both Rebecca Bennehan, born in 1778, and her brother, Thomas, born in 1782, grew up among the enslaved workers of their father's plantation. Less from their merchant father and more from their mother, who herself had grown up on a small plantation in eastern North Carolina, the Bennehan children learned to think and denominate their enslaved people as part of "our family" and to call them servants rather than slaves.[30] For Thomas Bennehan, coming of age in the 1790s, Phil became a guide to the care of horses and a model for more—for how he and his father could work in tandem and trust with an enslaved man whom they owned. Their bond became evident when persons of the plantation were allowed to gain credits for a time at the Bennehan store. On his own time, Phil made and sold blacking for boots and shoes, which enabled him to become a trader among his own people. When trading with his fellow workers, Phil took on debts and fell behind; Thomas Bennehan bailed him out.[31] The special relationship came to the fore again when a friend of Thomas Bennehan's, mistakenly thinking that Phil had died in 1825, wrote Bennehan that "the loss of such a servant is irreparable. Every day brings forth something to remind you that Phillip is absent."[32] At the same time, Phillip Meaks had family ties within the Black community. Before his wife, Esther, died in 1803, she had borne their seven children. Only two lived long enough to have children themselves, but between them they bore eight grandchildren.[33] Intricate connections with white and Black people became his hallmarks.

If in April 1808, twenty-six-year-old Thomas Bennehan did impose sex on Phillip Meaks's fifteen-year-old daughter Mary, the violation may well have embittered both father and daughter toward the man they had to call "Master." Yet without the power to resist or denounce, they may have yielded to the best bad option open to them and to most entrapped by bondage: to silence resentment and endure compulsion with the hope of a better fate for children and grandchildren.[34]

Phillip Meaks's code of conduct and coexistence offered a model for his grandson Virgil. Almost certainly, he offered counsel as well.

───────────────────────────

Phillip Meaks demonstrated to Virgil how to live in two worlds—the world of service to Thomas Bennehan and the world of trade and trust among his fellow bondmen. The white family, the grandfather could tell and show Virgil, liked to speak and think of their enslaved people as "our black family," none more than "Mas Tommy." Drawing on his own choices, Phillip Meaks could well have counseled his grandson to respond in kind: good servants make good masters. Keep your faith both to our people and to the owner they belonged to. Don't cheat the master; don't tattle on our people. When it became clear that Virgil was slated to go beyond keeping accounts and holding the keys to the smokehouse—that he would train in medicine—the grandfather could readily reiterate his advice. Stick to medicine. Leave the informing to overseers, to drivers, or to snitches among our own people. Phillip Meaks had to know that some would inevitably look on Virgil with suspicion, as a man whose doctoring was provided ultimately to return them to fieldwork and whose loyalty was primarily to his unacknowledged father. He could only tell Virgil that this was the world they were born into and that his role was to do his best and be fair to all. If the grandson played his part,

Gravestone for Lettey, Little River Cemetery. Today a Cultural Heritage Site designated by the County of Durham, the Cameron Grove/Little River Cemetery contains the graves of Black persons who worked at Stagville. Many markers are those of the once enslaved; others are of their free descendants. As was the one for Lettey, most markers were hand inscribed. *Collection of the author.*

he could win the trust of many and vindicate the faith of his father—who in the end would do right by him. Both grandfather and grandson knew what "right" meant. He will set you free.

———————————————

Two markers, in separate cemeteries two and a half miles apart, silently testify to the relationships that tied Thomas Bennehan and Phillip Meaks to each other, and each to the child born on Christmas Eve, 1808. When Richard Bennehan died, his son, Thomas, commissioned a professional headstone, chose its inscription, and had his father buried at the small, white family cemetery at Stagville.

Sacred to the memory of
Richard Bennehan, Esq.

Who departed this life
Dec. 31, 1825
Aged 78 years and 9 months.

When Phillip Meaks died, he was buried in the Little River Cemetery, created for Black people who lived and died on the Bennehan-Cameron plantation. In that separate and secluded graveyard, now covered by overgrowth and pine trees, thirty-six markers have survived. With one exception, all are improvised wooden or stone tablets with hand-carved names and dates of death:

Lettey
DIDE NOV
EMBER 24 1848 Aged 43

For Phillip Meaks's grave, Thomas Bennehan provided a tombstone and an engraved inscription identical to that of his father.

Sacred to the memory of
Phillip Meaks who
departed this Life on
the 22nd June 1837
aged 74 years

In death and distant cemeteries, Virgil's grandfathers received the same mark of respect.[35]

Gravestone for Phillip Meaks, grandfather of Virgil Bennehan, Little River Cemetery. Meaks's gravestone, commissioned by Thomas Bennehan, is the only professional tombstone in Little River Cemetery. *Collection of the author.*

2

The Best Judges

Virgil was not the only protégé of Thomas Bennehan. Born at Stagville on September 25, 1808—three months before Virgil—was Bennehan's nephew Paul Cameron. By the end of the 1830s, the nephew and Virgil would share the role of plantation medic with Thomas Bennehan. Paul Cameron routinely wrote about his partnership with Virgil in diagnosing and treating the ill. "We did this" and "we did that."[1] For his part, when the uncle wrote to his nephew, he offered suggestions rather than instructions about medical care the two men should give. "Of this you and Virgil are the best judges."[2]

For the first two decades of their lives, there was little to suggest that the nephew could imagine such a partnership. Paul Cameron had to come a long way.

Paul Cameron was the son of Thomas Bennehan's sister, Rebecca, and her husband, Duncan Cameron. When they married in 1803, Duncan Cameron was the most prominent lawyer in the Piedmont region of North Carolina. Persuaded to subordinate law to the role of becoming a planter, Cameron received a bequest of land and enslaved persons from his father-in-law, Richard Bennehan, in 1806. In 1810, he commissioned the building of a handsome

Duncan Cameron. Though he steadily enlarged his landholdings, enslaved labor force, and wealth, Cameron found the role of planter "vexatious." In 1834, he moved to Raleigh, became head of the State Bank of North Carolina, and urged his son Paul Cameron to practice law. *Cameron Family Papers, 1757–1978, Southern Historical Collection, Wilson Library, University of North Carolina at Chapel Hill.*

residence on the land deeded to him, a dwelling he called Fairntosh after the ancestral home of Cameron forebears in Scotland. Once ensconced as a planter, he began to encounter the diseases fostered and festering in the lands that he added and cleared. Like his brother-in-law, he threw himself into medical care. Unlike Thomas Bennehan, he found it fundamentally dispiriting. A man accustomed to control, indeed to command, Duncan Cameron learned that malaria and other diseases could neither be controlled nor commanded. Depression set in. In 1816, he wrote a directive to his wife that in the case of his death, she should liquidate the plantation, sell most of the people, and keep only enslaved workers enough to meet her household needs. In what became a recurrent pattern, he recovered, set out to acquire more people and land, and then, when diseases ran rampant once more, suffered renewed emotional breakdowns, each worse than the last. Friends feared for his well-being and urged him to get out. The chance to escape came in 1829, when the failure and near collapse of the State Bank of North Carolina got him summoned as its interim president. He moved to Raleigh and restored confidence in the bank. It was the prelude to a permanent move and the bank presidency in 1834. He left Fairntosh to be run by overseers.[3] For his son Paul, Duncan Cameron drew a lesson. Have nothing to do with being a planter.

Lessons, however, came hard for Paul Cameron. No child to the manor born, growing up amid enslaved servants at the beck and call of their "masters," could escape a sense of entitlement. Paul was no different. Rather than belabor his young son with the need for self-restraint—not merely to expect but to earn the right to command—Duncan Cameron sent twelve-year-old Paul to boarding school in nearby Raleigh. There, along with other boys of his age and class, he would be prepared for college work by the Reverend William McPheeters. The strict taskmaster knew that his equally important job was to teach the privileged young men that they, too, had to submit to rules.

Paul hated it. A friend of his father, William Haywood, had the youngster to dinner in March 1821 and found him on the verge of running away from school and returning home to the plantation. Haywood cautioned Paul. The other boys at school had led him to think that their teacher was a "sour crabbed fellow." Copying them, Paul balked at obedience, got seen as obstinate, and was at loggerheads with the schoolmaster. Haywood counseled Paul to try a different tack. If he conducted himself properly, his teacher "would treat him kindly."[4] Good students made good teachers.

As to Paul's threat to depart school without permission, Haywood warned of serious consequences. "It would certainly disgrace him" and would also humiliate his father. More ominously, "it might be the means of being sent out of the state & to such a distance" from his family and friends as would "prevent his seeing them for one or two years." Paul promised not to be a runaway, not to risk banishment, but rather to remain until he could see his father and present his grievances face-to-face. Haywood wrote Duncan Cameron that he feared that Paul "will not become reconciled." Haywood became the intermediary for an extrication that went according to the code of gentlemen. Haywood presented the teacher with Paul's "request" for removal, one that was "reasonable & urged with moderation." He conveyed that Duncan Cameron felt no dissatisfaction with the attention paid to Paul. Teacher McPheeters understood the ritual of withdrawal without recrimination. He assured intermediary Haywood that he did not think the father "fickle" for yielding to his twelve-year-old son. Obligingly, he added that it "would have been inconvenient for him to have kept Paul longer."[5]

Three years later, on a more public stage, it became clear that lessons remained. Now a sixteen-year-old at the University of North Carolina, Paul Cameron found himself deficient in Greek and hard pressed to catch up with others better tutored. At the same time, he had no doubt about his social place. In his second year at the college, he went to required Sunday chapel and found a first-year student sitting in the place that Paul regarded as his own. When Paul claimed that pew, the young democrat from Tennessee responded that there were no reserved seats. The planter's red-headed son promptly cudgeled the Tennessean, in full view of faculty and fellow students. School rules absolutely forbade fighting—not to mention fighting at chapel—and the violation promptly won Paul a suspension. At that point, Duncan Cameron realized that far more was needed to tame his son's expectation of a right to rule. Again he was dispatched to boarding school—this time out of state. Cameron sent him away to the newly established Partridge Military Academy in Middletown, Connecticut, founded and run by the former superintendent of West Point.[6]

For the enslaved workers on the Cameron and other plantations, the imperative for compliance came early, first from parents and grandparents, then from overseers and owners, with punishment or threat of sale as the ultimate enforcers. For Duncan Cameron's son, the means were utterly different, but in Paul Cameron's case, the need was the same. If he were allowed always to act on impulse and to claim prerogatives, disasters would follow, sooner or later. Duncan Cameron had already sent his older but impaired son Thomas to the Partridge Academy, in hopes that it would provide attentive and patient encouragement for the youngster whose attention span was short and ability to write painfully limited but whose temperament was gentle and whole-souled. The younger son needed sterner treatment and received it. When near the end of 1825, Paul got out of line, Captain Alden Partridge expelled him immediately—and then took him back on his pledge of good conduct.[7] Avoiding any further infringement of regulations, Paul wrote his sister in April 1826 to get him back-channel information about what Partridge—"the old man"—wrote to their father. "I want to know what sort of account he gives of me. I think he begins to have a good opinion. I do my best to gain his good will. I go very straight now." By May 1826, Paul's compliance won praise from the head of the academy. Alden Partridge wrote to Duncan Cameron that his younger son was steadier and more thoughtful than he was a year ago. In language that he knew would gratify the father, Partridge declared that "Paul appears to have become Master of himself."[8] He graduated in good standing and in 1827 matriculated at the new Washington College of Hartford, later to be called Trinity College.

Master of himself, Paul Cameron's next challenge was to become the master of others. His view of those held in bondage by his uncle and his parents revealed that he valued most those he considered "governable." Those who deviated from governability—either by presumption or by open defiance—nettled him.[9] Ironically, the first challenge came from the enslaved man whom his father held in the highest regard and allowed the greatest latitude. Luke was Duncan Cameron's right-hand man—his carriage driver, his courier, his personal servant when Cameron traveled. Away at college, Paul knew that his father's interest in plantation management waxed and waned. It waned when disease ravaged the people, or when crops fell short, or when enslaved workers colluded to labor slowly, or when prices dropped—all events that led Duncan Cameron to lapse into depression. Then came renewed bursts of energy, acquisition of more land and workers and the latest technology.

It was the addition of a tanyard that prompted Paul, away at college in Hartford, to poke fun both at his father's ambition and at his first man Luke. I hear, Paul wrote his older sister Margaret, that father plans a tanyard. What won't he have next? He should call the whole operation "Hodgepodgiana." "He has made Fairntosh a little city and you don't know what you have around you until you think an hour." Then came Paul's jibe at the bondman Luke—and at the absurd idea that even the most valued enslaved man could rise to parity with his owner—or his owner's son. "I expect to see his man Luke declare [Hodgepodgiana] a regular incorporated city and himself

Mayor and sole sovereign. I believe he considers himself next to father even now. I have often laughed to see what he assumed to himself [during] father's absence from home. You recollect our ride to Hillsborough last August [and] how he went on in his grave opinions concerning himself."[10]

Paul preferred instead a servant of humble fidelity who, in his words, "with little mind . . . acted well [her] part," who complied without complaint, and who performed work faithfully—even if the performance was not wholly authentic.[11] He let his imagination about slavery run free in a letter to the young woman he was courting in 1832.

Anne Ruffin was the daughter of Thomas Ruffin, a justice of the North Carolina Supreme Court. Both Anne Ruffin and her father had reservations about the courtship. Thomas Ruffin knew the reputation of Duncan Cameron—lawyer, planter, banker—as an imperious man who could be peremptory and dismissive. The justice told his daughter that if she detected even a whiff of condescension, she must call off the courtship. For her part, Anne Ruffin found her suitor's attentions and eloquence overwhelming. The more he wrote, the more zeal he voiced, the less adequate she felt about reciprocating. Anne Ruffin was not sure she was up to the expectations of Paul Cameron and his family, literary or otherwise. Though Paul wrote her, Anne remained silent.

Paul chose the metaphor of bondage to assure Anne Ruffin that he was undaunted. Who "but a slave would continue to perform services for which he is not rewarded?" A Turkish slave, even if beaten, does not renounce his faith in Allah or fidelity to his master, "though the iron rod of punishment is stained with his blood." So "it is with me: tho' my labor is unrewarded" by a return letter, "still I with all the devotion of a Sultan underling and with far more than his sincerity of heart" cease not to declare my love. It was an exaggerated, not to mention gruesome, but revealing analogy that fantasized bondage, contradictions and all: services unrewarded but loyalty unrenounced; punishment administered but love unceasing; devotion displayed yet sincerity dubious.[12]

When Paul Cameron wrote those words in 1832, there seemed little prospect that he could ever envision himself as a medical partner—or a personal friend—of his uncle's bondman Virgil.

———————————————————————

Nor could he foresee himself as a planter.

The management of enslaved labor was something that Duncan Cameron dearly wished his son would avoid. In the quarter century that the father oversaw and enlarged Fairntosh, Duncan Cameron made a success of it but nonetheless found the planter's life a vexatious one. He hoped that after his son's graduation from college in July 1829, Paul would come home to study law and pursue that profession. Paul dutifully complied. He returned to Fairntosh and undertook the ponderous reading of Blackstone and cognate law books.[13]

His real inclination was no secret to his uncle Thomas. When taking a break from the law books, Paul spent as much time as he could with his uncle, who found his "society a great comfort & enjoyment to me." If the uncle was sick, as he always was in the high season of chills and fever in August, he made sure that for Paul's safety, the nephew "confines himself pretty much [to] the house," where he "nurses me with great affection and attention." With characteristic innocence, Paul's mother wrote her husband in Raleigh that in his father's absence, "our beloved Paul tries to do all in his power to supply your place at home." She "was truly gratified to see what an interest he appears to feel in all our domestic concerns." Duncan Cameron surely felt less delight.[14]

Paul's uncle Thomas knew that Paul complied with law preparation to please his father, but also—and more so—wished to try his hand at managing men, land, and crops. Without undermining the wishes of Duncan Cameron, the uncle—who alone had represented the family at Paul's Washington College commencement in July 1829—made his twenty-two-year-old nephew a gift on January 1, 1831. "From and in consideration, of the natural love and affection, which he hath and bearest, unto his nephew," Thomas Bennehan deeded Paul Cameron 357 acres of land in adjacent Person County. While studying for and then practicing law, Paul would have the chance to test his mettle as the master of enslaved laborers.[15]

It was a gift that would change the nephew's life. Ultimately it changed Virgil's life as well.

In the early 1830s, both Virgil and Paul settled into family life and into the roles charted for them. In 1830, Virgil took a wife. Though marriage among enslaved people was always unofficial and recognized only at the will of the enslaver, on the Bennehan and Cameron places stable unions were encouraged and acknowledged in slave registers. Virgil's wife was named Phoebe. In 1829, Thomas Bennehan had purchased Phoebe, her older sister Nelly, her younger sister Dicey, and Phoebe's nephew William and niece Margaret. He purchased them from the estate of physician John Umstead, who since 1804 had cared for the Bennehans, the Camerons, and their enslaved families.[16] It's possible that Virgil made acquaintance with Phoebe while she was in the doctor's possession. There may have been a deeper connection. Many years later, the daughter of Phoebe's older sister Nelly gave her mother's surname as "Meeks."[17] Was Phillip Meaks the grandfather of Nelly and Phoebe via an off-plantation union with a woman belonging to John Umstead? If so, that would make Virgil and Phoebe second cousins when they became a couple in 1830. Virgil and Phoebe had no children. But Phoebe became a surrogate mother when her sister Nelly died in 1836.[18] Phoebe took over the care of Nelly's two-year-old child Anna and for years thereafter addressed her niece Anna as daughter and signed letters as "Your affectionate Mother."[19]

Husband, household servant, tallyman, medical protégé—Virgil was a young man of settled roles in the early 1830s. Paul Cameron, by contrast, was far from settled. He had dutifully studied for the law and qualified to practice. He won the hand of Anne Ruffin, whom he married in December 1832, and with her moved to the nearby village of Hillsborough, where they set up their household. From Hillsborough, Paul Cameron rode horseback to courthouses in nearby Granville and Person Counties, to pick up crumbs of cases. His lawyer father attempted to downplay the high expectations he had for his son; his lawyer father-in-law touted the excitement of the profession. But the young lawyer knew he was no good at it. His botched attempt at law wounded his ego and led him to suspect that his contemporaries took pleasure at the failure of the privileged son of one of North Carolina's richest, most powerful, and arrogant men. His wife could do little to lift his depressed spirits. The only undertaking that gave him satisfaction was working the small gift of land from his uncle and managing with an overseer the small force of enslaved workers on his 357 acres. That—and the forlorn hope that his father might change his mind and let him take the reins at Fairntosh, which Duncan Cameron had relinquished to overseers and to enslaved Black foremen.[20]

For Paul Cameron and for Virgil, a crisis in 1836 changed everything.

"Despair claims me." So Paul Cameron wrote his uncle Thomas Bennehan on March 23, 1836. For two months, an epidemic of measles had rampaged among the enslaved people at the small quarters in Person County. The nephew had first summoned his uncle in January; the condition of large numbers weakened by measles and pleurisy led the uncle to call at once for a physician. A nearby doctor came and, Paul reported to his father, pledged to stay till danger passed or death "shall end our labors & anxieties." When the physician took leave, Paul remained. He had witnessed the way his uncle cared for the ill, and now he emulated his model. Cameron told his father that he was *"not giving up"*—"great devotion & good nursing may get [them] well." Overwhelmed again in March, the nephew once more called for Thomas Bennehan, who left his own sick people at Stagville to come to the rescue.[21]

A third call for help, in April 1836, brought Virgil to the aid of Paul Cameron's ill workers. When summoned in April, Thomas Bennehan had his hands full. Virgil's grandfather, near the end of a long decline that found him often in delirium or plagued by endless hiccups, needed constant care. Two other aged men required attention. The uncle sent Virgil to assist his nephew, but only for the day. "I cannot spare him of a night"—Bennehan's quaint way of saying he could not spare him overnight—when the three Stagville patients required constant monitoring to see if their symptoms worsened.[22] During that day, however, Paul Cameron saw for the first time what care Virgil gave, what attentiveness he brought to the ill, how he, too, drew on his uncle's model of nursing, and how much Virgil had learned from the physicians who had tutored him. That single day in 1836 began the convergence of the work and lives of the two protégés.

A year later, Paul got his wish. In November 1837, he took over the management of Fairntosh. His father remained the owner, Paul the daily ruler. The son moved from Hillsborough to the main dwelling at Fairntosh with his wife, Anne.[23] Paul's father, Duncan Cameron, and his mother, Rebecca, as well as his six sisters and one impaired brother, resided in the sumptuous mansion Duncan Cameron had built in Raleigh, where he presided over the State Bank of North Carolina. With Paul Cameron's move to Fairntosh, he became the medical caregiver for hundreds of enslaved people under his supervision.

In the meantime, Thomas Bennehan's age and recurrent exposure to the diseases of the plantation obliged him to take ever-lengthening periods away from Stagville. He left the medical care of his people to Virgil. Especially in the summer season, when malaria reached its peak, Bennehan absented himself to Raleigh or sometimes to Buffalo Springs on the Virginia border. When away—for much of 1839, for shorter stints in 1840 and 1841—pangs of guilt stalked him. "I shouldn't be forever in exile from my people"; I "have to get back to them."[24] At the same time, not for a moment did he doubt

Fairntosh. The construction began in 1810 and went on for another dozen years. Fairntosh was the main house where Duncan Cameron and his family dwelled from 1814 to 1834. His son Paul, mediocre at law, longed to take charge. Reluctantly, his father assented, and Paul Cameron moved to Fairntosh in 1837. Like his uncle, Paul had the "very ill" brought to the kitchen for medical care. In this photograph from 1938, the two-story kitchen-infirmary is visible just behind the main house. *Photograph by Frances Benjamin Johnston, 1938,* Carnegie Survey of Architecture of the American South, *Photographs Collection, Library of Congress, Washington, DC.*

or override Virgil's medical judgment. If Virgil reported that most were well, or others sick, or some in need of a doctor's care, his assessments were conclusive.

At least some of the enslaved workers who received the attentions of Thomas Bennehan or of Virgil expressed gratitude for their interventions.[25] At the same time, no more than the Camerons themselves could they welcome the "heroic" treatments meted out to relieve the spikes of fever and chills—treatment that Paul Cameron labeled "the drill." The best description of the sudden onset of chills and the drill that followed came from Paul Cameron's own account of what happened to his own body when he was making his rounds of the sick. "Ague" abruptly brought on chills, followed by high fever, which then caused profuse sweating and led to delirium that left him feeling "staggerish." He made it home and administered the drill to himself.[26] Whether giving the drill to himself or to others, Cameron pursued

Chapter 2

relief by expelling what were thought to be bad humors with emetics. After he administered the ipecac to produce vomiting or calomel to bring on diarrhea, he waited, bucket or bedpan at the ready, until the drug "did its office." Hemorrhaging blood was not uncommon or unwelcome, since it was seen as the release of bile. In extreme cases, Virgil would be asked to blister the patient to draw out ill humors by placing a hot cup on an incision to draw out bad blood.[27] Among the enslaved people, ambivalence ruled about taking the treatment for the burning fever and shaking chills. For some, if neither Paul nor Virgil came around to check, those who needed medical care went to the overseer or sometimes even brought themselves to the makeshift emergency ward at Stagville or to the "kitchen" at Fairntosh. For other workers, symptoms remained unreported rather than endure the remedy. For two of the overseers, the toll of disease and the drill led them to declare the intention to quit at the end of 1848.[28]

By the summer of 1845, Paul Cameron and Virgil addressed each other as medical partners. When Paul got a report of illness at one of the quarters, he did not "order" Virgil to go to that quarter but rather "advised" Virgil to check out the report. When Paul lost a young woman patient, Virgil reassured him that her decline was so rapid that even a physician in the room couldn't have saved her. Both men had come a long way since the day, some nine years before, when Thomas Bennehan had sent Virgil to the rescue of Paul Cameron's ill workers—and to the salvation of the "desperate" nephew himself. That day marked the first step for the two men who, though separated by birth and place, were to become the "best judges" of medical care on the Bennehan and Cameron plantations.

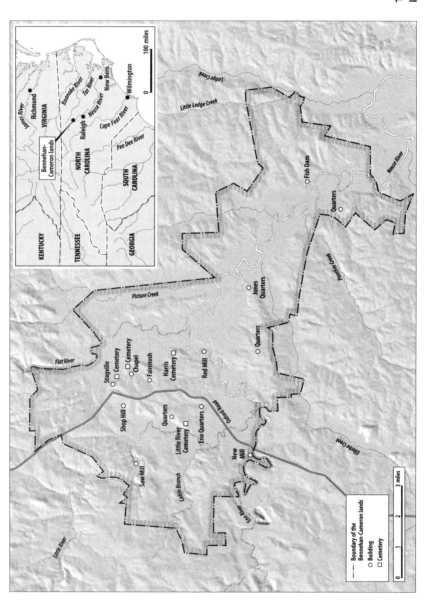

The Bennehan-Cameron lands, 1845.

Boundary of the
Bennehan-Cameron lands
○ Building
□ Cemetery

3

Freedom Bound

Between 1841 and 1845, Thomas Bennehan wrote two wills. Each expressed his wish that upon his death, "my Man Virgil" and Virgil's family should be "freed and emancipated." The wording of the two wills, however, differed in crucial ways. The changed wording—and events in the four-year interval that prompted the change—decisively constrained the freedom that Virgil Bennehan and Paul Cameron would have when the will took effect.

It was February 1841 when Thomas Bennehan sat down to write his will. His latest bout with chronic illness was behind him. But death was in the air. Starting in August 1837 and recurring twice the summer of 1839, three of his beloved nieces had died, slowly and excruciatingly, of tuberculosis—from what was then called consumption. His sister, Rebecca, and brother-in-law, Duncan Cameron, rallied in 1840 to try to save the life of his fourth stricken niece, Anne, taking her and themselves to Charleston to restore her health and spirits, to no avail. She asked to return home to die and, in a room filled with family and gloom, expired on March 22, 1840. Bennehan's sister, Rebecca, though devastated, gradually recovered, consoled by faith and by the beneficence of her daughter's enslaved attendant. The dying daughter had asked her servant Mary Walker to find a famed lay minister to bring her solace and peace, and the freedman Simeon arrived in time to offer Anne comfort and resignation. So thankful had the daughter been for that final grace that Anne expressed a last wish to her parents. Grant Mary Walker her liberty. Her grieving parents obliged. But with a mother and four children still enslaved, Mary Walker declined the offer of freedom.[1]

For the moment restored to good health, Thomas Bennehan decided that it was time to compose a will, and he did so on February 10, 1841. In one way, the task was easy. For all of his fifty-nine years, Thomas Bennehan was closest to his older sister; the two were aligned by affection for each other and by shared regard for those enslaved persons whom without fail they referred to as their "black family." To his "beloved Sister Rebecca Cameron," her brother bequeathed the bulk of his estate—land, persons, stocks and bonds—"with full power to her . . . to dispose of the same among her Children . . . as she may think most expedient & advisable."[2] Even though her husband had sway over the estate by law, Bennehan trusted that Duncan Cameron would defer to his wife and to the sensibility that brother and sister shared when it came to the future of the enslaved people.

For his two protégés Thomas Bennehan chose to make special provisions. One was Virgil, whose birth he had first noted on Christmas Eve, 1808, and whom in the ensuing years he had educated and elevated to the role of medic to his fellow workers. The other was his nephew Paul, whom he had encouraged in the nephew's aspirations to farm rather than practice law and who by the mid-1830s had joined Virgil and Thomas Bennehan as a committed medical practitioner.

Thomas Bennehan's will of 1841 gave to "my Nephew Paul C. Cameron the sum of Twenty-Five Thousand Dollars . . . with this injunction, that he shall have my Man Virgil" and Virgil's wife, Phoebe, and Phoebe's nephew William, "all of whom have been to me faithful Servants, freed & emancipated or should they prefer it removed to Affrica, my wish being that they no longer remain Slaves." When Virgil was liberated, Paul was to pay him "the sum of five Hundred Dollars."[3]

Seemingly straightforward, the will was anything but. Why emancipate Virgil and his family? Why the monetary gift to the nephew? Above all, why the "injunction" that linked the two bequests?

———————————————

The will provided only a brief explanation for the emancipation of Virgil and his family. They had been "faithful Servants." Without question, Virgil had been an exemplary servant, trusted to keep accounts and to safeguard and allocate meat each week to Bennehan's laborers and empowered to provide medical care to the people and to Bennehan himself. Virgil even signed his letters "Your Faithful Servant."[4] Yet it is not difficult to surmise that there were deeper reasons for the grant of freedom. Virgil was the grandson of the Bennehans' earliest and most trusted servant, Phillip Meaks. Although there were numbers of persons who belonged to Bennehan and to the Camerons whom they praised for their fidelity, no others were ever freed. Virgil's liberation certainly would seem still more understandable if he was Thomas Bennehan's son. Liberation was in keeping with what some few slaveholders of "good conscience" did to make final provision for their offspring. Such wills rarely if ever acknowledged a blood relationship to the beneficiary. One can conjecture that such was the case in the 1790s will of Rebecca and Thomas Bennehan's uncle, Thomas Amis Jr. After bequeathing all but two of his enslaved people to his niece, Rebecca, he asked his executor "to embrace the first opportunity" to liberate "his mulatto woman Gracie" and her son Harry.[5] If Harry was his child by Gracie, Thomas Amis's will modeled the undisclosing language that gave cover to what likely was a parental sense of obligation.

As to the bequest of $25,000 to Paul Cameron, clearly there was a bond of affection between the two men. Paul Cameron would later recall that he had always regarded his uncle as "a father and a friend."[6] Thomas Bennehan had been a staunch backer of Paul—gone to his college graduation in lieu of Paul's father, given him his first parcel of land and his first measure of independence from his father's preferences and largesse. He had supported Paul when the nephew gained command of Fairntosh in 1837 and sympathized with Paul when within a year he realized the limits of that role—to wit, that he was and never would be more than a caretaker for his inheritance of a grain plantation. By 1838, Thomas Bennehan knew that Paul Cameron had greater ambitions. He wanted to strike out on his own, to add to his inheritance, to prove his worth by acquiring far richer land in the west to grow cotton, the South's most remunerative crop. Paul won his father's reluctant assent and agreement to bankroll a buy if the son found the right place. As of the Bennehan will of February 1841, however, Paul's western reconnaissance in person and then inquiries by letter had turned up nothing.[7] If Paul found no western land by the time of Bennehan's death, $25,000 would enable him to make a purchase on his own, without becoming yet more beholden to his father.

Thomas Bennehan could have made the provisions for his two protégés independent of each other. Instead, he linked the bequests. His will allocated

$25,000 to Paul, "with this injunction" that he shall have Virgil "freed and emancipated." Why the "injunction"?

The unrealized plan of a friend had given Thomas Bennehan firsthand knowledge of the potential gap between the desire to emancipate and its accomplishment. Early in the nineteenth century, John Umstead was the neighboring physician to whom the Camerons always turned when they or their people needed urgent medical help. In the 1820s, Umstead and his wife themselves became ill. As their health began to fail, they were cared for by their enslaved servant Dicey. In 1828, widowed and without heirs, physician Umstead arranged for the sale of all but three of his many enslaved persons to Thomas Bennehan and composed a last will and testament.[8] The document expressed his wish that his faithful servant Dicey and her two daughters be freed. "In special trust and confidence," Umstead bequeathed Dicey and her children to Thomas Bennehan and another friend, Catlett Campbell, with the wish that they take legal steps to have the threesome liberated.[9] The law of North Carolina was about to change to require that any newly emancipated person be compelled to leave the state. But in 1829, the law still allowed that a person willed free could remain on two conditions. One was that he or she be credited with supplying not just faithful but "exemplary and meritorious" service to her benefactor. The other was that the will's executors guarantee that the freed person could support herself or himself and that they post a bond they would forfeit if the freed person became a burden on the community.[10]

Entrusted with the mission of their friend, Thomas Bennehan and Catlett Campbell acted to see through his goal. To the judges of the Orange County Superior Court, designated to rule on manumissions, they reiterated the doctor's extreme and repeatedly expressed anxiety that the liberation of Dicey and her increase be carried out. As required by law, they affirmed that Dicey's emancipation was more than a reward for ordinary service. Her ministrations to the Umsteads were "unusually & highly meritorious." She "exhibited that watchful anxiety & tender solicitude of a friend, rather than the ordinary attentions of a slave." They concluded with an appeal to the conscience of the judges. "*Every consideration of humanity*" argued for granting Umstead's "earnest wishes" to free Dicey and her family.[11]

Though the case didn't come to court until 1831, when the law had changed to require exile for the emancipated, their appeal won Dicey's freedom and that of her daughters. They could stay in place. For her, they put up the required bond. The daughters were another matter. Emeline and Harriet were both children. Their mother could not earn enough to support them and herself. Umstead anticipated the difficulty and so added a fallback wish. If the girls remained in temporary bondage, the "proceeds of their labor shall be to the use and benefit of aforesaid slaves and to no other."[12] It was a proviso more aspirational than enforceable. In the meantime, the young girls would remain in the custody of Thomas Bennehan and Catlett Campbell.

It is not clear whether any of the three men—John Umstead or his two executors—anticipated what happened by the time that Thomas Bennehan wrote his own will in 1841. The two girls had grown to become young women and mothers; freeing all the "increase" of Dicey meant liberating her adult daughters and their children as well. Moreover, the changed law mandated unequivocally that all those freed must leave the state. Were the two executors prepared to free the mothers and their children? Were Emeline and Harriet prepared to part from other family members and from friends they had made since 1829? "*Every consideration*" and what constituted "*humanity*" had gotten complicated. Trusted to carry out Umstead's wishes, both men felt the weight of what they'd not felt able to do.[13]

As he composed his own will in February 1841, Thomas Bennehan drew a lesson from the loopholes and limits of the Umstead will. For the liberation of Virgil, Paul was to be his uncle's agent, as Bennehan had been for his friend John Umstead. But gone was the language of wish, entreaty, anxiety, and trust. Paul Cameron was to receive his uncle's bequest with the "injunction" that he free Virgil and his family. An "injunction" was a directive, an emphatic authorization, an imperative just short of a command. The injunction declared Thomas Bennehan's firm expectation, with rewards for both protégés. Paul would gain $25,000 and enhanced independence. Virgil and his family would receive $500 and liberation from bondage.

After Thomas Bennehan wrote his will in 1841, for the most part his health stayed steady. To keep it so, he retreated much of each summer to Raleigh and to the household of the Camerons to escape the throes of "ague," turning medical care over to Virgil. What obliged him to redo his will was the death of his sister, Rebecca. Despair over the loss of her four daughters, and her own subsequent illness, finally caught up with Rebecca Bennehan Cameron, and at the age of sixty-five she died in Raleigh in November 1843. With his sister gone, the brother had to make his own disposition of his property—his thousands of dollars in stocks and bonds, his 12,000 acres of land in adjacent Orange and Wake Counties, and the 330 enslaved persons in his possession. After delaying the necessary updating for a year and a half, Thomas Bennehan wrote a revised will on April 28, 1845.

Thomas Bennehan could have left the arrangements for Virgil and Paul Cameron intact as they were in 1841. When he composed his new will in 1845, however, he made changes. In the new will, he bequeathed not money but land to his nephew Paul. Instead of $25,000, Paul was to receive the entirety of his uncle's landholdings in Orange County, the Stagville and adjacent Little River plantations, amounting to 5,000 acres. The inheritance again was tied to Virgil's emancipation. But no longer was the link expressed as an "injunction," without consequences if unfulfilled. The vast bequest was granted "on this condition & which is fully understood by him" that Paul Cameron liberate Virgil and his family: his wife, Phoebe, her nephew William, and now her young niece Margaret. The choice of destination—removal to one of the free states of the North or to Africa—was no longer up to Virgil but rather delegated to the will's two executors, Duncan Cameron and Paul Cameron. Paul remained obliged to "pay to Virgil or invest for his use the sum of $500." The rest of the estate—the other land and the 330 enslaved persons that Bennehan owned—was to be divided among heirs by the executors, trying as far as possible to keep families together.[14]

Not only did the language of the final will go beyond the "special trust and confidence" of the John Umstead will of 1829. It went beyond the "injunction" of Thomas Bennehan's own will of 1841. If Paul did not satisfy the "condition" of the new will of 1845, the nephew would lose his 5,000-acre inheritance, and Virgil would forfeit his freedom. The new link was ironclad.

"*On this condition . . .*" Nothing in the correspondence of either the uncle or his nephew indicates an erosion of the affection and bond between them. The cushioning clause—"*and which is fully understood by him*"—suggests that the uncle had gone over his reasons with Paul and intended no intimation of mistrust. Might Thomas Bennehan have thought that Virgil would decline liberation? Nothing explicit in 1845 suggests that possibility. Yet Thomas Bennehan had to know that on rare occasions, such as that of Mary Walker and perhaps that of Dicey's daughters Emeline and Harriet, enslaved persons who were promised manumission chose to stay in bondage with their family members rather than accept freedom with exile. Virgil had two brothers and an elderly aunt at Stagville and, as he saw it, hundreds of friends.[15] Surely it had to occur to Thomas Bennehan that Virgil, at the very top of his owner's plantation hierarchy, might hesitate to swap gilded bondage at Stagville for removal to an unknown destination where he had no friends, no work, and four people to support. There may also have been reason to think that the medical partnership of the two protégés might lead them to wish to continue together. If so, why not allow that choice—which an "injunction" would have permitted—rather than block it with a "condition" that constrained them both.

One can only conjecture. Thomas Bennehan might well have understood that the deference and authority accorded to Virgil came in part, perhaps in large part, out of deference to his owner. Overseers accepted Virgil's doctoring, for the enslaved people and even for themselves, not just because of his skill but because of the master who had him trained and made him the owner's surrogate. No matter how attentive Virgil was, no matter how willing a friend to all he wished and thought himself to be, he was still the sovereign's protégé. When Thomas Bennehan was gone, would his authority still enable and protect Virgil?

There was the more delicate question of who might be Virgil's protector after the departure of Thomas Bennehan. Bennehan could never say and perhaps never expected that Virgil would lose the confidence of his nephew Paul Cameron or of his brother-in-law, Duncan Cameron. Not in the ordinary course of things, not with either Cameron at his best. At the same time, Bennehan had observed both Camerons in times of foul temper. Both were subject to severe depression. Both reacted harshly if they felt crossed or thwarted.[16] If Virgil ever came under suspicion that he was not wholly dependable, his privileged status could evaporate fast.

As Bennehan might have seen it, something more fundamental than the volatile Cameron temperaments put Virgil at risk. Between the writing of the wills of 1841 and 1845, there was a seismic change in the world of Stagville and Fairntosh. Since 1838, Paul Cameron had hankered to start a cotton plantation in the western part of the South. In November 1844, he made the move. With his father's backing and a force of 114 of his father's enslaved workers, Paul Cameron journeyed to Greensboro, Alabama. There, on the recommendation of a relative, he bought an already-cultivated plantation of 1,674 acres for $29,305.[17] Thomas Bennehan had long known of Paul's ambition to break free—to add to the family fortune rather than to tend it, to reap the rewards of the richest soil and the most profitable crop of the South rather than be limited to the income from harvests of wheat and corn. The move itself did not put a breach between the nephew and his uncle.

The break was different. Since the founding of Stagville in the 1770s and the beginning of Fairntosh in 1810, its owners had for the most part abided by an unstated pact. They bought but, except in rare instances, did not sell their enslaved people. As a twentieth-century descendant put it, "They stole your labor but they kept you together." Well aware of the trade-off of family preservation in return for unpaid labor, Paul Cameron knew that his Alabama venture fractured the unspoken pact. He was removing 114 people from their home and kin in Piedmont North Carolina to a place 400 miles away in western Alabama. When he chose the "emigrants to go west," he tried to select persons in family groups. Inevitably, he made separations. Needing mostly younger workers, he parted offspring from parents, siblings and cousins from each other. At the time and long after, he perceived himself as proceeding in a humane manner.[18] But members of the "black family" saw him differently. By the people of Cameron's Fairntosh plantation, Paul Cameron became perceived as an agent of betrayal—a "young and reckless master," in the words of one enslaved woman.[19]

Is it far-fetched to imagine that Thomas Bennehan saw peril in the future from Virgil's close association with Paul Cameron? As long as Thomas Bennehan lived, he remained Virgil's patron and protector at Stagville and a buffer against Virgil's identification with Paul, who was sovereign at Fairntosh. But when Paul Cameron inherited Stagville and became ruler of both domains, the perception of Paul as "young and reckless" could spell danger for Virgil. Virgil could no longer be a friend to all if allied to Paul. The two allegiances were incompatible. There was little way to take vengeance on the young master. There would be ways to sabotage his collaborator. The disaffected might act out their anger—and bring Virgil down—by sowing distrust between the protégés.

There is no knowing whether any or all of these considerations went through Thomas Bennehan's mind as he wrote his final will in April 1845. Whatever the complex of motives, he made clear the outcome he wanted. He wanted Virgil and his family freed. He understood that liberation meant exile. He put Paul Cameron in charge of fulfilling his mandate. And he made the stakes as high as he could for his nephew—to see to it that Virgil was liberated or lose the Stagville plantation in Orange County.

All concerned understood that it was Thomas Bennehan's intention to have Virgil and his wife, Phoebe, freed. It seems likely that it was at Phoebe's behest that the will of 1841 liberated her nephew William and that the will of 1845 added the aunt's younger niece Margaret. What is doubtful is whether

D. Cameron
Slaves sent to Alabama.

men	Boys	women	Girls
1 Charles	1 Thomas	1 Agg	1 Winny
2 Lundy	2 Gustavus	2 Rosetta	2 Leaky
3 Milton	3 John.	3 Martha	3 Milly.
4 Joney	4 Juba	4 Peggy	4 Chaney
5 Little Joe	5 Jacob	5 Nicey	5 Dicey
6 Orrin	6 Lewis	6 Riley	6 Liza
7 Jack	7 Japhet	7 Molly	7 Betsey
8 Jim Hargis	8 Dave	8 Mary	8 Barbary
9 Nathaniel	9 Simon	9 Fanny	9 Anne
10 Prince	10 Alexander	10 Milly	10 Jincey
11 William	11 Anderson	11 Lucky	
12 Carolina	12 Eaton	12 Nancy	
13 Willie	13 Wesley.	13 Patty	
14 Peter		14 Sally	
15 Anderson		15 Lizy	
16 Tom		16 Eliza	
17 Nelson		17 Becky	
18 Eno Edmund		18 Chaney	
19 Old Peter		19 Molly	
20 John L		20 Sylla	
21 Dave L		21 Sally	
22 Lewis.		22 Nancy	
23 Jiney Taylor		23 Delphia	
24 Green		24 Lizzy	
25 Paul.			

Men 25
Boy 10
Women 24
Girls 10.
Children 26.

Slave list. Frustrated by the limited profits of Piedmont North Carolina crops of wheat, corn, and tobacco, Paul Cameron desired to expand into cotton, the South's far more lucrative crop, which grew best farther west. In 1844, he sent 114 enslaved persons to Alabama, 400 miles away, to labor on a cotton plantation. His choices separated kin and friends. *Cameron Family Papers, 1757–1978, Southern Historical Collection, Wilson Library, University of North Carolina at Chapel Hill.*

any of them knew the requirements of the final will—or knew that its terms locked them in.

Thomas Bennehan's death throes began in March 1847. Day and night at Stagville his two protégés took turns tending him. His breathing became difficult; his feet and legs became swollen; sleep became elusive. To lance the ill humors, Virgil blistered Thomas three separate times. Virgil understands "his condition as well as myself," Paul reported to his father, and "has been to his master a faithful and *tender* nurse."[20] Thomas Bennehan rallied one last time, and in May he shifted to Raleigh for care at the capacious Duncan Cameron residence. He relinquished all medical oversight at Stagville to Virgil. In his weakened state, he knew he would only be an encumbrance. As ever, he held out hope to come back, perhaps in July. He never returned.[21] Death claimed him in Raleigh on June 24, 1847. He was sixty-five years old.

A month later, on July 25, 1847, Paul Cameron began a plantation report to his father that started with praise for Virgil. Virgil "has all of his sick at Stagville" and is "as in times gone by attentive and kind to them." Then he shifted to the subject of Virgil's future. "I don't know a more useful man in his condition in life—and his *destiny* and *residence* will be made and controlled entirely by your advice."[22] His remark suggested that Paul was speaking for both Virgil and himself and that both men "fully understood" that the will of 1845 designated the Cameron executors to decide which removal was "most to their interest & happiness"—to "some of our free states, or to Africa." But then came a startling disclosure. It revealed that neither man had in fact seen Thomas Bennehan's final will or knew the mandate it imposed on both of them.

Virgil's "inclination is to remain where he is and to be near me."[23]

"*His inclination is to remain where he is and to be near me.*" Virgil and Paul Cameron both believed in July 1847 that Virgil had a third option open to him: to decline manumission altogether, remain on the plantation, and "be near me." Paul Cameron was conveying and seemingly endorsing an overture from Virgil to both him and his father. "I don't know a more useful man in his condition in life" who is "as in times gone by attentive and kind" to his patients. Virgil left the decision up to Duncan Cameron. "Should you advise otherwise he will go from us." Not until the final will was later opened and read did either protégé or Duncan Cameron know that Thomas Bennehan had bound them all.

What Thomas Bennehan could not have anticipated when he wrote his will was the turn of events that forged a bond between the protégés that went beyond their medical partnership. The unexpected events—and that bond—brought Virgil to the point of declaring to Paul Cameron his readiness to forego freedom, for himself and his family, and "to be near me."

What drew the two men closer at the end of 1845 was the failure of Paul Cameron's venture at a western cotton plantation. Indebted to his father for almost $30,000 to buy the secondhand place and to supply the enslaved labor force to work it, the son suspected right away that he'd been duped by a relative—the uncle of his wife—into buying poor land. He held the suspicions to himself on his return from Alabama in the spring of 1845, though he couldn't disguise his glumness.[24] When he arrived back in Alabama in November 1845, he was appalled at the contrast between the anemic cotton crop grown on his place and the abounding crops of neighbors. Now quite certain that he'd been deceived, he unleashed his grief and anger in a torrent of November and December letters mailed home to his father. His relative had secretly profited from the knowing sale of inferior land. "I regard myself as a deluded man, blinded by misplaced confidence and unsuspecting friendship." "Woe that I had any connection with my wife's family. . . . I regard myself not only as a dupe but a *victim*." "No one has a better right to exclaim 'save me from my friends.'" He felt humiliated and isolated by his own credulity. "I am sometimes without confidence in my fellow man & then give it as I would a hungry man bread." "If ever a poor fellow needed all the consolations of letters from *friends*, it is me. I fear 1,2, & 3 will be almost as many numbers as I should need to *number my friends in this world*."[25]

When Paul Cameron unburdened his sense of betrayal to his father, however, Duncan Cameron rebuked him. The father demanded that he speak and write no more of it. Family comity demanded silence and suppression. "I hope you are mistaken." But if not, "what good does it do to indulge . . . so unpleasant a subject"? Let us agree "for *your own sake* to dismiss it from your mind" and to trust all to Providence. To "do so, is alike the dictate of policy and *duty*." When Paul persisted in his lamentations, his father demanded—in the name of "the happiness of *all* connected with you"—that "you should *dismiss* the subject from your mind. . . . I will say nothing further of so repugnant a topic."[26]

The son obeyed his father and knew that there was no other family member to confide in. "I have never written my uncle because I should indulge in my griefs—& better not to say what I certainly should say." Each and all of his relatives—his uncle, his wife, his father-in-law, his brother-in-law—had close or blood relations with the man he felt had deceived him. To whom else could he disclose "the troubles of a devoted son"? To whom else could he reveal that he had "been wronged, grossly wronged"? To whom else could he express his regret that he had *wasted* his father's means and made himself "an object of *derision*"?[27] There was only one person to turn to.

Paul Cameron confided in Virgil. A later letter, written in August 1848, signaled that Paul told Virgil exactly what happened in Alabama and offered advice that he wished he had received himself: "Don't waste your means on foolish purchases."[28] Cameron further revealed to Virgil his plan to redeem himself—to find better land and send still more people to the Deep South as soon as he found the right place.[29] As a "young master," Paul Cameron could not invite Virgil as an enslaved servant to reciprocate confidences in 1847. Both men understood the limits of what Paul could ask or Virgil divulge. But when circumstances and distance later allowed, he did urge Virgil to open up to him. "Tell me what you feel and what you suffer." Both men could discern the coded import and inflection of that delayed invitation. "Tell me what *you* feel and what *you* suffer." Asymmetrical though it was, the opening of Paul's repressed emotions created a bond between the two men that went beyond their collaboration as medics. By the summer of 1848, the protégés addressed each other as "friend."[30]

With so much going for him at Stagville—a medical practice exceptional for an enslaved man, perceived friendships with owner and owned alike—little wonder that Virgil made his startling declaration on July 25, 1847. His "inclination is to remain where he is and to be near me."[31]

Chapter 3

4

Patrons Galore

In mid-May 1847, Virgil Bennehan was an enslaved man on the Stagville plantation in charge of medical supervision of his fellow bondmen and -women, taking the place of his owner and father during Thomas Bennehan's final illness. A year later, on May 16, 1848, he and his family arrived by ship in the harbor of Monrovia, Liberia, with 134 emigrants from Virginia and two free persons of color from the Midwest. The next day he became the only emigrant allowed to disembark from the *Liberia Packet*, to set foot in the capital of the country, to receive a guided tour of the city, and to be welcomed personally by the elite of the Black republic. During the three days that followed, he met with the country's secretary of state, the author of the Liberian declaration of independence, and the physician brother of the president at the president's residence—honors reserved exclusively for him and for two free persons of color who had come to scout Liberia for followers back home. Virgil never knew of the interventions of others that elevated him from exile to emissary. Nor did he know that those interventions bound his fate to the plans of new rulers: the white American sponsors and the nominal Black leaders of Liberia. Least of all could he foresee in May 1848 that he would be a prime witness when those plans went disastrously awry.

Thomas Bennehan's will of 1845 had barred the option that Virgil preferred after his owner died—to forfeit his freedom and to remain on the Stagville plantation and by Paul Cameron. For Virgil and his family, the will mandated both freedom and departure: removal to a free state or to Liberia. The will of 1845 also named Duncan Cameron, and not Virgil himself, as the person to choose his destination.

Duncan Cameron was in no hurry to hasten Virgil's exit. He understood that the law of North Carolina required any manumitted person to leave the state within sixty days of being willed free. But the rule came into play only when the will was probated. Cameron held off probating the will. He knew that the summer months were the sickliest on the plantation; both his son and the enslaved people needed Virgil's medical presence for one more season. The postponement allowed Virgil and his wife, Phoebe, a foretaste of freedom and a time for early farewells. They were permitted to take a carriage to nearby Hillsborough to "visit their friends" and spent the evening and overnight with the aged white physician James Webb, who had mentored and then worked with Virgil for almost two decades.[1] Some weeks later, Virgil went to Raleigh for a visit and for goodbyes to friends there. For the rest of the year, Virgil remained the primary provider of medical care at Stagville, attending the sick as he always had, Paul reported admiringly, with "care and affection."[2]

For Duncan Cameron, there was another reason to delay a decision. He left the state shortly after Thomas Bennehan died in Raleigh in June 1847 and remained away throughout the summer. He was away when son Paul wrote that Virgil left his "*destiny* and *residence*" entirely up to Duncan Cameron. The Cameron patriarch was in Philadelphia.[3] With his older daughter Margaret, he was in the city for a second successive summer to seek a medical diagnosis and cure for the illness of his younger daughter Mildred. Traumatized by the deaths from tuberculosis of four sisters between 1837 and 1840 and further stunned by the passing of her mother in 1843, Mildred had developed sudden spasms and intermittent paralysis. Physicians in Raleigh found no physical causes and shied from labeling it hypochondria. So Cameron turned to doctors at Philadelphia's Jefferson College of Medicine, who found ways to give Mildred relief but not release from her symptoms. Frustrated but absorbed by the inconclusive medical quest, Cameron felt no compulsion to get Virgil's destination settled.[4]

The summers in Philadelphia might have opened Duncan Cameron to considering that city as Virgil's destination. But most free persons of color whom Cameron had contact with were in service—domestics, house servants, waiters, carters, hucksters. Those were not roles he would wish for Virgil. Doubtless he could see that a few were well off—Black artisans, ministers, a dentist or two, some in businesses. Virgil's work on the plantation, however, was medical. Was there a chance he might pursue medicine in the northern city? Given Cameron's encounters with the white physicians who sought to help his daughter, he was not overwhelmed by their ability. Nor did it seem likely that any of them would help train Virgil—whose patients on the plantation had ailments such as malaria and tuberculosis and typhoid—to deal with different diseases that prevailed in the city. Not just at the Jefferson College of Medicine, with its large contingent of southern medical students, but farther north as well, Black colleagues were unwelcome.[5] Could Virgil find persons of color as his patients, who would trust a Black medic, an uncredentialed man from the South, and pay him for his services? It would have been reasonable for Duncan Cameron to judge that Virgil would not be able to carry on as a doctor, in Philadelphia or elsewhere in the North.

What of Liberia?

In December 1816, a group of white leaders founded the American Colonization Society and starting in 1820s, by treaties, payments, and force, created Liberia on the western coast of Africa as a colony for manumitted bondmen and -women. On July 26, 1847, Black "colonists" of Liberia declared their independence to the world and proclaimed themselves a nation—the first Black republic on the African continent. With mixed feelings, leaders of the American Colonization Society endorsed Liberian independence. However, the ACS still controlled the locations and funded the first six months of food, shelter, and medical care for manumitted people sent to the country.[6]

For his part, though Duncan Cameron had affiliated with the American Colonization Society in the 1830s and been elected president of its Raleigh Auxiliary in 1834, his leadership had lapsed near the end of the decade. But in 1839, Cameron became involved in a legal case that brought Liberia back to his attention. The case was that of a group of enslaved persons freed by the will of John Rex, a northern artisan who had moved to Raleigh, made good money, and bequeathed freedom and funds to those of his bondmen and -women who agreed to go to Liberia. John Rex's will gave a portion of his legacy toward the creation of a hospital. When white heirs and hospital advocates sought to channel almost all the money to the hospital, Cameron sued on behalf of the Rex ex-slaves and won the case. The money nonetheless remained tied up by further maneuvers.[7] In the meantime, however, Cameron had urged the Rex people to emigrate with the implicit promise that their inheritance would be forthcoming and on his assurance that they would be contented in Liberia.

It was an 1839 letter from one of those emigrants that might have given Cameron pause about Liberia as an ideal destiny for Virgil Bennehan and his family. Freed Rex woman Malinda Rex wrote emphatically that she was "not satisfied." "I have not found nothing as they said and never will. Dear Sir if you had known this place was as poor as it is you would not [have] consented for us to come here. If I had known myself when you was telling me I would not have been so willing to come but I thought I could get along like I could [in Raleigh] but I find it to the contrary."[8]

What made matters worse was the peremptory decision by the white governor of Liberia, still an ACS colony in 1839, to force the issue of the overdue payment to the Rex people. Unless their money came, an imperious Thomas Buchanan told the emigrants, we "must pay for our provision," rather than receive any allowance from the ACS. Duncan Cameron surely understood, wrote a distressed Malinda Rex, that "if we have to pay all our expenses it will consume all." Though "you are a great way off from us, I hope you will not suffer this to be. You are all my dependence."[9]

How in good conscience could Cameron propose Liberia as Virgil's new home?

No correspondence between father and son revealed how Duncan Cameron thought through the choice delegated to him by both his brother-in-law's will and by Virgil himself. But if Duncan Cameron did feel uncertainty, it was dispelled in the fall of 1847 by what must have seemed a providential coincidence. The coincidence brought Virgil to the attention of the head of the American Colonization Society and would link Virgil to his most ambitious goals for 1848.

In 1847, the Camerons resided in a boardinghouse on Sansom Street in Philadelphia, a location that made them neighbors of the wealthiest and most powerful leader of the Young Men's Colonization Society of Pennsylvania. A seventh-generation Quaker, Elliot Cresson believed that the best place for persons of color, whether free in the North or manumitted persons from the South, was Liberia. He tried his best to win over Black Philadelphians, to no avail. Almost all opposed deportation. Cresson hoped that they might come around in time, especially as conditions for them in the North stagnated or worsened. In the meantime, he concentrated on a project within Liberia that had been the focus of his philanthropy and that of colonization colleagues in Pennsylvania and New York since 1834.[10]

The Cresson project of 1834, a settlement located sixty miles south of the Liberian capital of Monrovia, was an experiment designed to prove that an emigrant colony committed to temperance and pacificism could coexist peacefully with the local people. Named Port Cresson to honor its American benefactor, the settlement was founded in the region controlled by the Bassa and Kru peoples, the indigenous inhabitants of what colonists called Bassa County. The mission of Port Cresson was to prove that newly freed persons could thrive in Africa—and among Africans—on Quaker principles. Quaker emissaries took care to acquire the settlement's initial 700 acres of land by purchase from a local monarch, King Joe Harris, not fathoming that land ownership as understood by Americans was foreign to indigenous West Africans. Land could only be held in trust by a ruling lineage for their entire population; private ownership of land was taboo.[11] The Quaker founders may have hoped to transmit a culture of tolerance to their first Port Cresson immigrants and to avoid the "cultural arrogance toward all things African"—differences in dress and language and society—that led many self-styled *Liberians* to regard uncivilized *natives* as subjects or adversaries, repositories of "a deep darkness of witchcraft, superstition, and heathenism." The founders were encouraged by reports from earlier settlers that the Bassa people were "'averse to war'" and that King Joe Harris not only welcomed schools for his people but even sent his son to the United States to "'learn book.'"[12]

If peaceful coexistence was the founders' hope, it was not to be. At Port Cresson, conflict was assured from the start. The Quaker settlement's other mission was to establish a beachhead for disrupting the traffic in slaves. Two centuries before the ACS and its first emigrants settled in 1822, Europeans and the transatlantic human trade had transformed warfare and intensified competition among indigenous Africans. Wealth, prestige, and military advantage went to coastal leaders who thrived as middlemen in the slave trade between the coast and interior. Rival African leaders and their communities were elevated above others by weapons, ammunition, and payment from European slavers. After the British and American abolition of the slave trade by 1808, the purchasers were mostly Spanish captains who took the captives to Brazil and Cuba. Perhaps unknown to its founders, Port Cresson was set

Lithograph of Bassa Cove, 1836. The project of Quaker Elliot Cresson and of the Pennsylvania Colonization Society, Port Cresson was a settlement in Liberia designed to operate on Quaker principles of pacifism, temperance, and antislavery. A brief truce with indigenous leaders gave way to war in 1834, when the self-disarmed settlement was attacked and vanquished. This idealized sketch, with three tranquil Africans in the foreground, was commissioned to promote support for a revived settlement called Bassa Cove.
American Colonization Society Papers, Library of Congress, Washington, DC.

in territory that was "a central trading depot" for the slave trade; leaders among the Bassa and the Kru peoples were among Liberia's "most notorious slavers."[13]

To his regret, King Joe Harris learned that Spanish slavers would not trade near a settlement of Americans, for fear of interference by British or US patrols. With a Quaker leader at Port Cresson who adamantly refused to arm the newly freed Virginians in his care and a Bassa king belatedly convinced that the newcomers would jeopardize his livelihood and diminish his power, the stage was set for deadly confrontation. Six months after the settlers' arrival in December 1834, forces of King Joe Harris attacked the unarmed village, burned its dwellings, and killed twenty-two emigrants, followed by the desertion of all its survivors. In Monrovia, ACS leaders mobilized 120 settlers to retaliate. They attacked the monarch and, with the help of Harris's rival kings, defeated and dethroned him, forcing him to concede more land, to abandon the human trade, and to build a new settlement nearby called Bassa Cove.[14]

Pacifism had failed. The Bassa region became part of what one historian calls a "single, ongoing war over African lands and trade." For white ACS leaders in America and the Black colonial elite they installed in Liberia, a sense of divine right as well as self-defense justified domination and dispossession. In Bassa, for a time, overt conflict gave way to a wary truce. The newly established village of Bassa Cove became a fresh recipient of manumitted people but remained an anemic outpost, little supported by the ACS and repeatedly subverted by the Africans around it.[15] In the mid-1840s, Elliot Cresson and his wealthy allies pressed the ACS to make the restoration of a viable American presence in Bassa County a priority and to send new emigrants to revive the settlement. In October 1846, he won. The board of the American Colonization Society pledged to send the next large cohort of emigrants to Bassa.[16]

Duncan Cameron had come to know Elliot Cresson both as a neighbor and perhaps as a member of the Philadelphia mercantile community, among whom Cameron took refuge away from watching his daughter suffer and her doctors flounder. When Cameron told Cresson about Virgil and the choice ahead, Cresson immediately saw Virgil as a capital asset for Liberia—and for the Bassa project.[17] On behalf of Duncan Cameron, Virgil Bennehan, and Bassa, the Philadelphia philanthropist took it upon himself to write to the head of the American Colonization Society, William McLain. McLain was a white Washington clergyman and former agent of the ACS who in 1844 was appointed its secretary and chief administrative officer. Few matched his zeal for the colonization cause or his conviction that for all persons of color—free in the North or manumitted from the South—Liberia was a place where they would flourish and could be an instrument for the far vaster project of ending slavery in Africa. On November 6, 1847, Cresson wrote to William McLain to present Virgil Bennehan's credentials and to urge the ACS head to include Virgil and his family on the next ship of emigrants to Liberia. "My venerable friend Judge Cameron tells me that his bro-in-law Mr. Benham [sic] left four slaves of estimable character for Liberia, well provided for, who are all anxious to go out at first opp[ortunity]. Two are young adults—the male a good mechanic—shoemaker, I believe, the other, with his wife, is a capital practical M. D. & having an aptitude for practice for years with all the domestic wants, except surgical cases. He speaks highly of all. I requested him to address you."[18]

The recommendation for Virgil was included between reminders that both Cresson and Cameron represented funds desperately needed by the

William McLain. When McLain assumed leadership of the American Colonization Society in 1844, emigration to Liberia and donations for its support had plummeted. McLain successfully promoted a revival of emigration. But contributions fell far short of the increase needed to pay for transport, food, and shelter for the rising number of emigrants. *American Colonization Society Papers, Library of Congress, Washington, DC.*

Chapter 4

American Colonization Society to pay for a surge of persons manumitted for transport to Liberia. Cresson's letter began with a reiteration of "hope that you may direct your next emigrants to Bassa" and the nearby village of Bexley, along with his expectation that doing so would induce Episcopalians to establish and bankroll a "mission station asylum for their own slaves" at Bexley. It concluded by reminding McLain that Duncan Cameron was the key person in North Carolina seeking release of the rest of the Rex inheritance for the ACS. "If you have not yet [received] the Rex legacy, he deems the case now stripped of the former judicial difficulties." The letter made clear that both of Virgil's patrons—Cameron and Cresson—were men of consequence and cash.[19]

William McLain understood immediately that the inclusion of Virgil on the next voyage, useful for Liberia, would benefit ACS fundraising. McLain expected to hear from Duncan Cameron immediately after Cresson had paved the way. When he heard nothing, he wrote Cresson asking when he could expect to receive a letter from Virgil's sponsor? Cresson replied that he was sure that his friend would communicate soon. "I presume the reason was the uncertainty whether his people could be made ready for the next voyage. If so, he will say so. He spoke very highly of them. He thinks you will have no further difficulty getting the Rex money."[20]

Duncan Cameron may indeed have been waiting for word of the next ship to depart for Liberia from the port closest to Raleigh: the port of Baltimore. All had thought that departure would be early in 1848. But the *Liberia Packet*, expected imminently to return from Liberia to pick up new passengers, was delayed, out so long that all feared it was lost at sea. In fact, it was not a storm but "the calms"—the absence of wind to fill its sails—that slowed the *Packet*'s journey across the Atlantic from the normal time of thirty-five days to sixty-two days instead. Uncertainty reigned until word came at the end of March that the ship was back and would now depart from Baltimore in early April. Duncan Cameron saw the notice in the Washington *National Intelligencer*: "All interested parties should show up by April 11." Suddenly there was a premium on time.[21]

Duncan Cameron had decided for himself that Liberia was best. But out of respect for his late brother-in-law and for Virgil, he wanted Virgil to make the choice. Tell Virgil, Cameron wrote to his son Paul, that if he is to elect Liberia, he needs to decide now. The choice is his; I lean to Liberia.[22] Virgil assented. Meanwhile, Duncan Cameron rushed a letter to William McLain, asking if he could place Virgil, his wife, and her niece and nephew on the *Packet*. Cameron detailed Virgil's credentials, adding to what Cresson had written in November. Virgil Bennehan "is highly intelligent—reads and writes—understands arithmetic. And has, as much by training as by direct experience acquired a respectable share of practical knowledge of medicine." He added that there were funds sufficient to pay his family's way and to cover all expenses in Liberia. Cameron signaled his connection with Elliot Cresson indirectly, by adding that "their destination will be to Bassa Cove," Cresson's pet project.[23] For McLain's benefit, Cameron offered a credential of his own. He omitted mention of his role in seeking payment of the frozen bequest to the Rex people already in Liberia. Instead, he wrote that McLain's fellow Washingtonian Joseph Gales was a longtime friend and knows "me well." William McLain knew that Joseph Gales Jr. was the publisher of the *National Intelligencer*, one of the most powerful newspapers in the country and a reliable advocate for colonization.[24]

From Elliot Cresson's letter and now from Duncan Cameron's request, William McLain could have no doubt that Virgil was supported by men of consequence. Nonetheless, McLain replied that the ship due to sail from Baltimore in April was full and asked whether Virgil Bennehan and his family could postpone their departure until the next scheduled sailing in the fall.[25] A year before, the head of the ACS would have welcomed four passengers on the next boat out. Manumissions had declined since the 1830s and by 1847 had dribbled down to almost nothing. By the mid-1840s, the ACS was on the verge of terminating a voyage for lack of recruits.[26] Default would have cratered confidence in its mission and capacity, among both southerners considering manumissions and northern donors on whom the society depended for funds. In response to the crisis, McLain had toured the South to restore confidence among planters and redoubled efforts in the North to win donations.[27] His efforts to revive manumissions to Liberia proved to be a resounding success, the campaign for contributions far less so. The result was that suddenly the ACS was flooded with applicants but short of funds to support them for their first six months in Liberia.[28]

"And still they come!" That was the phrase coined by William McLain's counterpart in Baltimore, James Hall. A young doctor who had gone to Liberia in 1831 to be the colonial physician for the ACS, he subsequently became the agent and manager for the settlement sponsored by the Maryland Colonization Society. Sickness forced his return to the United States in 1836. He remained affiliated with the Maryland Colonization Society and in 1845 became a stockholder and manager of the newly constructed vessel, the *Liberia Packet*. Hall's primary task was finding places for passengers on the *Packet* and securing payment of their fares. Those four words—*"and still*

they come"—applied in particular to the *Liberia Packet's* scheduled departure from Baltimore in April 1848. The *Packet* already had committed places to 134 passengers from Virginia and was slated to sail next to Savannah, Georgia, to pick up 80 more, which would fill its berths to the limit of 214 men, women, and children. From Savannah it would depart for Africa. When McLain asked Duncan Cameron if the four Bennehans could wait, the ACS agent was in a bind.[29]

Duncan Cameron rarely took no for an answer, and he knew that in Virgil Bennehan's case, waiting until fall could create difficulty. Probate for Thomas Bennehan's will had taken place in November 1847. The law now required the manumitted Bennehans to leave soon. Though Duncan Cameron expressed no fear that anyone would hold him or the Bennehans to the letter of the law, he nonetheless turned to pressure. He telegrammed North Carolina congressman A. H. Venable. Venable knew that Cameron was one of the most important men in the state—head of the state bank, friend of state supreme court justices, owner of hundreds of enslaved people. Cameron in turn may have known that the congressman was important to McLain, who sought legislative support for American diplomatic recognition of Liberia as a nation, so far withheld. Can you tell McLain that I need to hear from him and that it is imperative for Virgil and his family to be on that ship now, not on another ship months from now? Venable immediately did as Cameron asked.[30]

It was now abundantly clear that Virgil Bennehan was the protégé, directly or by proxy, of four powerful patrons: Elliot Cresson, Joseph Gales, Congressman A. H. Venable, and Duncan Cameron himself. Wisely, William McLain capitulated. McLain telegrammed to Cameron that if you can have the family here by April 11, they'll have a place on the *Liberia Packet.* McLain's decision was made easier, as he explained in a follow-up letter to Cameron, by the abrupt cancellation of the Savannah stop, aborted because of a suspected outbreak of smallpox among the awaiting passengers. Now Virgil and his family would be in comfort among 138 emigrants and not jammed into a shipload of 214.[31]

William McLain hoped that the inclusion of Virgil and his family on the April voyage to Liberia would satisfy all his sponsors. He would soon discern that he needed to go a step further.

William McLain had another goal of paramount importance for 1848, a goal that Virgil Bennehan should have suited perfectly. The ACS head thought the time had come when Liberia could attract a "better class of emigrant."

The better class would be "more intelligent" than the mass of those sent from the South, whom McLain privately referred to as "very ignorant"—denied education, accustomed to obedience yet, once in Liberia, reluctant any longer to "slave" at fieldwork. Numerate, literate, a physician by training and experience, Virgil Bennehan certainly matched McLain's criteria. But by the end of 1847, McLain had his eye not on the better class among those manumitted from the South but on free persons of color from the Midwest.[32]

"Oh how important that these *Spies* should bring back a good report" about the "Republic of Liberia!" So William McLain had written in December 1847 to Joseph J. Roberts, the former governor of the ACS colony and now the first president of Liberia. The "*Spies*" were to be men of color from the free states who would visit Liberia and return home with favorable reports—testimony that would recruit other free persons of color to emigrate to the newly independent country.[33] Until Liberia declared its independence in July 1847, it was a colony in Africa created and governed by the white-controlled American Colonization Society. Most free Black people and all white and Black abolitionists had scorned the colony. To them, it was the pawn of white sponsors, whom adversaries saw as a motley alliance of those who wished to rid the North of free Black people—seen as dregs and dependents—and to relieve the South of manumitted slaves, seen as paupers or potential incendiaries. To its opponents, colonization falsely eased the conscience of its advocates, who ignored the reality in the South that while a few were freed, slavery grew exponentially and the reality in the North that free Black people viewed America and not Africa as their homeland.[34] But with Liberians themselves now governing a self-proclaimed independent nation, McLain and others believed that the ACS could attract "more intelligent" Black individuals from the Midwest and the North who would recognize the unique chance to build a country and to gain in Liberia the freedoms denied them in the United States.

Changing circumstances in the Midwest produced two men of color whom McLain saw as his ideal "spies." The United States' war with Mexico that began in 1846 brought victory and the annexation of the northern two-thirds of Mexico in 1848. Bitter controversy ensued over whether slavery would be allowed in the vast new territory. In the North, a "Free Soil" movement emerged to bar the extension of bondage—and to keep all the annexed land for white farmers and white workers. Adamantly opposed by the South, the movement paralyzed the Congress and roiled the politics of the country. In the Midwest, the Free Soil movement had a whipsaw effect. In Ohio, it brought a push to lift myriad restrictions on the rights on free persons of color; in Illinois and Indiana, it prompted a backlash to add a new barrier. Already barred from the right to vote, to sit on juries, to testify against white people, to attend public schools, free Black people now confronted a proposal to ban all further Black immigration into the state. Black persons who entered in violation of the proposed law would be punished by a fine, imprisonment, or indentured servitude amounting to reenslavement.

During the summer of 1847, while Virgil was making his farewells in North Carolina, a convention met in Springfield, Illinois, to revise the state's constitution. An overwhelming majority of delegates supported a constitutional amendment to prohibit Black immigration into the state. Tabled for fear that the courts or the Congress would reject the new constitution with that amendment, the ban's supporters opted instead for a statewide referendum in 1848. The Black Baptist Association of the state, meeting in Alton, Illinois, in August 1847, anticipated the outcome of the vote, which indeed produced resounding support for the ban when 70 percent of Illinois voters later endorsed the referendum.[35] At the conference, the association authorized a delegate to go to Liberia to see what the chances were for Black people to be free and to thrive there.

The Alton conference named Samuel Ball as the delegate. Samuel Ball was a thirty-seven-year-old barber from Springfield, Illinois, who had come to Illinois from Virginia in 1835. Literate, astute, devout, he had become an elder and leader of the Black Baptist denomination in the state and had written a catechism for Black Baptists in the 1840s. In Springfield, like all Black barbers, his clients were white and included the governor, a supporter of colonization. Ball's mission received letters of endorsement from the governor and Illinois secretary of state; other colonizationists raised funds for his travel and to support his family while he scouted Liberia.[36] Samuel Ball had a personal stake in the outcome. Widowed in 1844, he had remarried and started a second family.[37] For his wife and young children, as much as for other persons of color, might Liberia offer a better life than the constrained future they faced in Illinois?

The other recruiter on whom McLain pinned his hopes was Moses W. Walker, who dwelled just outside of Steubenville in eastern Ohio.[38] A cooper by trade who worked in a community with a large number of Quakers, free Black Moses W. Walker for some time had sided staunchly with abolitionism and opposed colonization. A sometime lay preacher and a man who on his own was studying medicine, Walker concluded late in 1847 that abolition offered no hope for persons of color, enslaved or free. On the first of December 1847, he appeared in the study of Steubenville's Presbyterian minister,

Steubenville
Ohio –

Rev. Mr. McClain

Dear Sir;

Unknown to you in person I take the liberty of addressing you on a subject of common interest to the Col. Cause. For some years past I have been acquainted with Moses W. Walker – a Coloured Man shrewd intelligent, pious & of very fine appearance. He has been much duped by the abolitionist – & averse to thinking of Liberia & has been filled with prejudice towards an enterprize which now is persuaded opens the only way at present practicable for the elevation of his injured race.

I was highly gratified by a call from him at my study to day. His object was to tell me he had dismissed his prejudices & wanted information. I gave him some twenty numbers of your publications. –

Letter recommending Moses W. Walker for Liberia. When Virginia-born leaders in Liberia declared their independence in 1847, William McLain sought free Black "spies" to visit the country in hopes of positive accounts of the Black-run republic. Later that year, Ohio minister Henry Comingo reported the conversion of free Black Moses W. Walker to colonization and his readiness to go to Liberia and report back. *American Colonization Society Papers, Library of Congress, Washington, DC.*

a colonization advocate whom he had known for some years. He told the Reverend Henry Comingo that "he sees [that] abolition sympathy won't prevail & he voluntarily turns to me [as one] regarded by [abolitionists] as a perverse colonizationist." Twenty-six-year-old Walker declared himself converted to colonization as "the only way at present . . . for the elevation of his injured race." With the zeal of a convert, Walker proposed to go out on the next voyage of the *Liberia Packet*, remain a few months, and return and report to those who like him were hitherto "duped by the abolitionist." The Steubenville minister immediately gave Walker twenty issues of the *Liberia Herald* and sent Walker's proposal to ACS leader William McLain. Comingo described Moses Walker as a fluent speaker and preacher, a "colored man of shrewd intelligence & of very fine appearance," who "has the confidence & esteem of a large mass of the colored people in Eastern Ohio." If Moses Walker's reconnaissance went well, "he could not only go with his family, but induce a great many who would believe him to embark likewise." McLain had found his second "spy."[39]

The two men were McLain's protégés, on whose behalf he would write to Liberian officials and American Colonization Society employees. Leaders and ACS agents in the country were to show the investigators the best of Liberia.[40] As far as Virgil Bennehan was concerned, it seemed sufficient for the ACS head to accommodate him and his patrons by granting Virgil's family a place on the *Liberia Packet*, with no need for more special treatment. When Virgil arrived in Baltimore four days before the *Packet's* departure, that plan changed.

Once word came from William McLain that the Bennehan family must arrive in Baltimore by April 11, all made haste to gather belongings and say final farewells. Freed along with Virgil and Phoebe Bennehan were Phoebe's niece Margaret, nicknamed Peg, and her nephew William, called "Toast" by the Camerons. Peg and Toast said goodbye to their cousins. Phoebe took leave of her many other nieces and nephews. Most painful for Phoebe was parting from her niece Anna, the daughter of Phoebe's older sister Nelly— whom Phoebe had reared after Nelly died when Anna was two years old. For his part, Virgil hurriedly said goodbye to his younger brothers Albert and Solomon and to his elderly aunt Mima. Both Virgil and Phoebe had time to pay a last visit to the Little River Cemetery, the burial ground for Black workers from Stagville and Fairntosh, and the final resting place for Virgil's grandfather Phillip Meaks and Phoebe's sister Nelly.

Paul Cameron took charge of the departure. He placed the four passengers and himself on a carriage to Raleigh, where the five of them boarded a train for Norfolk, Virginia. At Norfolk, they took a ship to Baltimore and arrived there on April 7, four days before the scheduled sailing of the *Liberia Packet* on April 11. Cameron found lodging for the Bennehan foursome at a respectable boardinghouse run by a free Black carpenter, Patrick Hamilton, then got a place for himself at a hotel in town and wasted no time in going to the office of the American Colonization Society in the Post Office Building in the center of Baltimore. There he found ACS agents William McLain and James Hall making last-minute arrangements.[41] He likely took it on himself to smooth any feathers ruffled by his father's pressure and impressed on them once more Virgil's credentials. Virgil Bennehan was a special catch for the American Colonization Society and for Liberia.

Might Virgil be too special? An alarm went off when the ACS officers met the next day with Virgil Bennehan and Paul Cameron together. It became evident that Virgil had the medical experience and poise that the Camerons had described and that he and Paul Cameron shared a special bond. What was missing was zeal. Quite rightly they detected, as Virgil wrote to Paul two days later, that his "heart [w]as too full" to voice his full feelings about the impending departure.[42] The agents were not unaccustomed to emigrants who were anxious and some angry at being forced into exile as the price of their freedom.[43] For most emigrants, however, those reservations didn't matter. Once in Liberia they were locked in, without resources to return even if they wished.

What happened at the meeting made it clear that Virgil was in no such bind. Paul Cameron first paid $240 to McLain for the transport and for the first six months of care in Liberia for Virgil and his family. McLain signed the receipt. Then Paul handed to Virgil an additional amount of money to take with him—$620 in gold. Duncan Cameron had decided to match the $500 bequest to Virgil from Thomas Bennehan with another $500 of his own. In this way he could feel assured that Virgil would not meet the fate of Malinda Rex, who faced degradation without money in Liberia. Possibly some of the $1,000 total had gone toward providing Virgil with medical supplies. Virgil signed a receipt for the $620 in gold, and McLain added his signature as a witness to the transaction.[44] Virgil would ship out as the richest passenger on the *Packet* and one of the wealthiest emigrants ever sent to Liberia.

At that moment it became clear that if Virgil wasn't converted to Liberia, he could bring himself and his family back. For Bassa and for the patrons who backed Virgil, it was important for him to be satisfied. Deep down, time

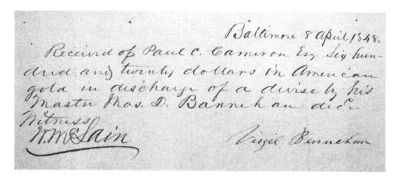

Receipt for gold. This receipt for $620 in gold meant that satisfying Virgil Bennehan required more than a berth on the *Liberia Packet*, for if dissatisfied, he could afford his fare back. William McLain instructed the ship's captain to have Virgil Bennehan join the two free Black "spies" to be feted by Liberian officials. *Cameron Family Papers, 1757–1978, Southern Historical Collection, Wilson Library, University of North Carolina at Chapel Hill.*

would later reveal, William McLain and James Hall recoiled at having to extend more favors to a man who seemed so privileged already. Nonetheless McLain resisted the impulse and lacked the luxury of writing off Virgil as a man too coddled to appreciate what Liberia had to offer. Instead he recognized that it was important to treat Virgil, along with the two "spies" from the Midwest, as a recruit.

McLain decided to incorporate Virgil into the plan he had made for the two free men of color. The three of them, and only the three of them, would be allowed off the ship after its arrival in the harbor of Monrovia, Liberia's capital. Even though the *Packet* would be anchored for four days within sight of Monrovia, McLain ordered the captain to keep all the other emigrants on the ship. Experience had shown that if allowed to disembark and spend time in Monrovia, many passengers would refuse to reboard for distant outposts elsewhere. With so much at stake, William McLain made Virgil Bennehan the exception. On shore, the three men were to get the royal treatment and to be wooed by Liberia's leaders. Virgil Bennehan was to meet the elite of his new country, so he could see himself as one of them—and be won over.[45]

Powerful patrons, his medical credentials, and an endowment that gave Virgil the option to return placed Virgil "above the regular class of emigrants" and set the stage for what the ACS handlers hoped would be his embrace of a future in Liberia.

5

I Am Not Certain

After thirty-two days at sea, Virgil and the *Liberia Packet* arrived at the harbor of Monrovia, the capital of Liberia, on May 16, 1848. The next day, Virgil, the two free men from the Midwest, and the ship captain James Goodmanson went onshore to the capital for a tour of the public buildings, schools, and churches. In the three days that followed, Virgil and the midwesterners met and dined with four leaders of Liberia, sailed twenty miles upriver from the city, and scouted the country's richest farmland. Reboarding the *Liberia Packet* on May 21, Virgil arrived at Bassa Cove on May 23. At the end of the month, after two weeks in Liberia, Virgil wrote a long letter to Paul Cameron. "My Dear young Master & friend," he began. In two crowded pages, he described his elaborate welcome, the kindness of all his hosts, and his warm reception in Bassa. Nonetheless, Virgil confided, "I don't know whether I shall remain here or not." Liberia "is a very fine country for some people but I am afraid it will not suit me. I may become satisfied with it but it is doubtful at present." "I may . . . return to America. I am not certain."[1]

Virgil may well have been unmoored by the marked contrast between what he encountered in Monrovia and what he found in the small settlements

Letter from Liberia. In May 1848, Virgil Bennehan wrote a long letter to Paul Cameron, named the dignitaries he met in the capital, and praised the richness of land and farms that he saw around Monrovia. His letter contrasted Monrovia sharply with poverty-plagued Bassa Cove and Bexley, settlements where he disembarked to reside. *Cameron Family Papers, 1757–1978, Southern Historical Collection, Wilson Library, University of North Carolina at Chapel Hill.*

Chapter 5

at Bassa, sixty miles to the south of the capital. The Monrovian residence of "Rev. Mr. [Hilary] Teage," the author of the Liberian declaration of independence and Virgil's first host for "dinner in the American style," was among the most impressive of the capital. It had porticos back and front, closed-in windows, and large and airy rooms. No less distinctive was the dwelling of the country's head of state, with tapestry carpets, oil paintings on the walls, and embroidered curtains.[2] President J. J. Roberts was out of the country pursuing diplomatic recognition of Liberia from England, France, and the United States. At "the president's house," Virgil had breakfast instead with "the President's Brother," American-trained physician "Dr. [Henry J.] Roberts." Virgil and physician Henry Roberts likely talked for a time about medical treatment in Liberia. After a "tea in the evening" with leading merchant "Col. [Beverly Page] Yates," Virgil met for a final dinner and a long conversation at the home of "Gen[eral] [John N.] Lewis."[3]

John Lewis, titled General from earlier service in the colony's militia, was now Liberia's secretary of state; he also doubled as the highest-ranking employee of the American Colonization Society. "Much pleased" with Virgil during their long conversation of "several hours at my house," John Lewis encouraged Virgil to settle in Bexley, the Bassa village eight miles inland from the harbor town at Bassa Cove. In what would prove to be a discretely incomplete explanation, Lewis noted that a longtime resident of Bexley was Judge John Day, a fellow signer of the Liberian declaration of independence and the missionary brother of the most famous free Black furniture-maker of North Carolina, Thomas Day. Lewis rightly guessed that craftsman Thomas Day, who lived and worked twenty-five miles from Stagville, was well known to Virgil. Lewis immediately wrote Judge Day that Virgil would be coming to see him and declared flatly that Virgil's "intention is to live at Bexley."[4]

The titles Virgil provided for each of his hosts—the Reverend Mr. Teage, Colonel Yates, Doctor Roberts, General and Secretary of State Lewis—conveyed unmistakably to the Camerons that Virgil had been received as a gentleman by leaders of the new nation. The titles that Virgil *omitted* suggested something else, namely that though now a former bondman, he didn't want the "young Master" to think him suddenly above his station. Virgil's letter home did not reveal how he himself was addressed—as Doctor Bennehan— or that his midwestern companions were called Reverend and Elder, and that indeed all Americans of color arriving in Liberia were then and thereafter titled Mister or Miss. The formerly enslaved never again were addressed as "boy" or "girl" or only by their first names. That symbolic and startling shift in itself won the allegiance of many emigrants to the Black republic.[5] And

President's house, Monrovia. Joseph J. Roberts, a free Black emigrant from Virginia, was the last governor of colonial Liberia and became the first president of the country in 1847. His brother Henry Roberts trained as a physician in Vermont and returned to Liberia late in 1847. In May 1848, Virgil met with physician Henry Roberts at the president's dwelling. *American Colonization Society Papers, Library of Congress, Washington, DC.*

yet though Virgil revealed no prefix for himself, his signature hinted that he felt the elevated stature that came with the country. At the end of the letter, Virgil signed a full name rather than just his first name and added two middle initials, P. M. The signature acknowledged both his father Thomas Bennehan and his grandfather Phillip Meaks. *Virgil P. M. Bennehan* was a first for him.[6]

In contrast to Monrovia, Virgil's arrival at Bassa Cove began inauspiciously and continued to disappoint. A huge sandbar and strong crosscurrents prevented ships from sailing all the way to the dock. Finding the "bar very bad indeed," Virgil reported, the *Packet* had to disgorge "the emigrants" (as Virgil referred to his fellow passengers) on a "beach and let them walk to Bassa." To get the passenger cargo to port, it was unloaded onto a small boat over the sandbar. Virgil's vessel immediately overturned, drenching the family's clothing and bedding "as wet as water could make them and like to [have] lost them at that." Taking John Lewis's advice, Virgil went eight miles up the river from the Cove to scout Bexley, where he found the land on both sides of the river "very rich indeed." But he had not come to Liberia to farm—Virgil wanted to practice medicine. Immediately he found that at

Bassa Cove and Bexley, "Everybody wants doctors but none can pay them." "I find practice enough in this place, but no pay," he wrote to Paul Cameron on May 29. "Money in Africa is out of the question. . . . I have at this time 5 patients and the five is not worth $5."[7]

It's not clear whether Virgil understood then or later why money was short. After an interlude without warfare in the mid-1840s, chiefs of the Bassa, Kru, and other communities detected an upsurge of new immigrants. They foresaw further encroachment on their lands, new disputes over sovereignty, and additional economic constriction of their direct commodity trade with British and French merchant vessels. They responded by curbing their trade with the settlers, orchestrating thefts, and urging their people to withdraw from menial labor for the "'mericans." Newcomers like Virgil understandably could not discern the ominous first signs of renewed hostilities to come. Those longer in Liberia chose to dwell in denial.[8]

Virgil acknowledged that there was another way to make a living in Liberia. Farming "is The Best Business in This Country." With considerable understatement, he noted that "land and labor is very cheap," with land selling from $0.25 to $1 an acre. Possessing $620 in gold, Virgil readily saw he could afford to farm. "But I cannot go into that business yet," he wrote. Perhaps he didn't need to explain to Paul Cameron that at home, he and his wife had tended a garden plot, and little more. He might have added that the main crops he had seen in Liberia were unfamiliar. Rice, cassava, ginger, arrowroot, orange and other fruit trees were not grown on the Piedmont plantation of tobacco and grains. And he could have added further that mules, oxen, horses, cows, and hogs—the livestock that sustained the work and people of the plantation South—were little in evidence in Liberia.

Little wonder that after only two weeks in Liberia, Virgil reiterated, "It is a very fine country but I don't think it will suit me at present."[9]

Virgil's letter home reported more than what did not suit him. The final paragraph of his letter revealed how profoundly he still identified with the world he had left. "Remember me to all," he began. Repeating that phrase five times, Virgil named twenty-eight people, casting light on the community of persons to whom he felt most connected. "Remember me" to "old Master" and Duncan Cameron's daughters "Miss Margaret and Miss Mildred," and followed with Paul Cameron's wife "Miss Ann and the children." "Remember me" to "all my colored friends," starting with "My brothers and aunt and their children." Many of the other fifteen "colored friends" that he

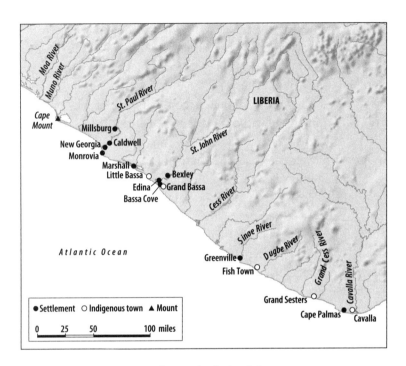

Settlements in Liberia, 1848.

named, like Virgil himself, were persons elevated by Thomas Bennehan or the Camerons to special roles on the plantation—David Bell the gardener at the Cameron mansion in Raleigh, Daniel Watson the foreman at Stagville, Ben Umstead the carriage driver, Henry Dixon the cooper, Pats (Patsey) the cook and house servant, young Phil the hog-minder, Ovid the blacksmith, Demetry (Dempsy) the wagoner, and four plantation elders—fifty-seven-year-old Grace, sixty-two-year-old Charity, sixty-four-year-old Ben Parks, and sixty-three-year-old Luke, who also was a carriage driver in Raleigh.[10] When Virgil called the names of the white overseers of the plantation, he addressed them not as overseers or as "Mister" but as "my old neighbors." "Remember me" to E. Tilly, John Ray, "my friend William Harris," Mark Tate, Samuel and William Piper and their families. He did confer titles on the last two friends he listed. "Remember me to Mr. Green and . . . Mr. Fendall," the first the white Episcopal minister the Reverend William Mercer Green, who served the Camerons and preached occasionally to their enslaved people, and the second Mr. Fendall Southerland, for years the senior overseer at Stagville. "I could call 100 more names," Virgil added. Tell "them all how day for me."[11] Virgil's list highlighted the community that he still felt allegiance to—white and Black, free and enslaved, owners and overseers. They were "all my friends." Virgil was not the only deported person to feel less attachment to Liberia than to the people of his past.

"Regarding my remaining in Africa," Virgil wrote, "I hope in my next [letter] to have something to write you."

No next letter arrived from Virgil. But two months after his reiteration of doubt on May 29, a strikingly different report came to ACS head William McLain. "Dr. Bennehan has bought an extensive piece of land . . . which he intends developing, so soon as his own strength will recover." He "has lost none of his family, and the other emigrants who went up to Bexley with him are doing well, as regards recovering from the fever."

So reported the free Black merchant and American Colonization Society official in charge of the Bassa settlement, Stephen Benson. Writing to ACS head William McLain on July 24, 1848, Benson added, "I think Dr. Benne-han will prove a desirable acquisition to this country. I think, so far as I am acquainted with him, he is of the right metal [mettle], possessing indepen-dency of mind and patriotic fortitude to brave all difficulties." The Bassa official included the Bennehan news as the high point of an upbeat letter, meant not only for William McLain's eyes but for publication in the ACS monthly publication, the *African Repository*.[12]

Did Virgil Bennehan actually change his mind? It's unlikely that Benson knew of the patrons who wanted assurance that Liberia had satisfied Virgil. What Benson did know was that McLain and *African Repository* readers put a premium on good news. Stephen Benson's preface—"so far as I am acquainted with him"—suggested that Virgil in Bexley had kept his distance from Benson in Bassa and that Benson was projecting Virgil's disposition toward the country. But Benson's report contained more than speculation that Virgil intended to stay. The solid evidence was that Virgil had bought and planned to develop "an extensive piece of land."

What might have happened in the two-month interval? It is possible that Virgil was influenced by a former bondman from Virginia, who was among the 100 or so emigrants already settled in Bexley. Freed by a professor at Washington College in Lexington, Virginia, Samuel Harris and his family had arrived in Bexley eighteen months before Virgil. But according to the ACS agent in Lexington trying to recruit other free Black persons to Liberia, Samuel Harris had written discouraging letters back to his friends, report-ing a "hard time" and many deaths.[13] By mid-1849, however, Samuel Harris

Stephen Benson. The leading merchant and agent of the American Colonization Society at Bassa Cove welcomed Virgil Bennehan's family and the 134 Virginia emigrants who would bolster the outpost. Benson reported at the end of July 1848 that "Dr. Bennehan" had purchased "an extensive piece of land" to develop after he acclimated to the African fever. *American Colonization Society Papers, Library of Congress, Washington, DC.*

had reversed himself. Writing now directly to William McLain, the head of the American Colonization Society, Harris acknowledged that "if persons come out here they must make up their minds first that they will meet with difficulties and troubles," as Harris did. But if they have faith, it will see them through. A Christian must "expect to meet with trial. When I come out, I met with troubles" and wished "myself back again." But on reflection "I have made myself satisfied. Now you could not get me and my family to come back to the United States to live again." He reported that he had a beautiful farm of ten acres on the St. John River, a fine crop of arrowroot and ginger, and that his wife raised ducks and chickens, her stock growing from 6 to 50 to 100. "We have fried chicken and a roast duck whenever we feel like." Harris was even prepared to travel back to Virginia "to tell the people in Lexington all about it." If his conversion began during the first two months of Virgil's stay, Harris may have helped Virgil start to see things differently. Virgil's family members may also have weighed in. At Stagville, Virgil's wife, Phoebe, her niece Margaret, and her nephew William experienced nothing like Virgil's privileges. They would have appreciated the gains that Liberia brought for Harris's wife and children. No longer in service, working for themselves, reaping what they sowed, addressed as Miss and Mister, able to raise ducks and chickens, Polly Harris and the Harris children felt "Blessed" by "the mercy of God."[14] Phoebe Bennehan and her niece and nephew could surely have understood why.

Or it may be that Virgil, who had come with $620 in gold, had second thoughts about undertaking the "best business" of farming in a place where "very rich" land sold for $0.25 to $1 an acre and where indigenous people labored for $2 to $3 a month. The interval of June and July would have given Virgil time to reconsider his initial reservations. A buy of an "extensive piece of land" would have made him a large farmer. Five to eight acres was the limit of what most emigrants could acquire and clear. But in years past, a few emigrants who came with significant means did develop large holdings and produced successful commercial crops. Residents of Bexley could certainly have told Virgil about Louis Sheridan, a well-to-do free Black man who arrived from North Carolina in 1838. With wealth he'd accumulated in North Carolina, Sheridan had purchased 570 acres. Paid African workers cleared and cultivated a coffee plantation of 45 acres on his land. Until his death in 1844, Sheridan had thrived, despite bitter disputes with Liberian authorities and intermittent desertions of his workers.[15] Virgil may even have imagined enlisting the collaboration of the handful of Virginia shipmates who followed him to Bexley to be under his medical care, which Virgil continued to provide for what little he could get.

Society agent Stephen Benson concluded his report at the end of July on an optimistic note. Most of the emigrants who came two months before had survived the intense first round of malarial fevers that came after arrival in Liberia. At Bassa Cove, those healthy enough were out clearing their small plots of land; at Bexley, Doctor Bennehan had ambitious plans for when he regained full strength. The agent may have accurately glimpsed a seismic shift that warranted his confidence that "Dr. Bennehan will prove a desirable acquisition to this country." Perhaps after all of Virgil's initial doubts, the North Carolina emigrant had arrived at a different vision of himself in Liberia, one that moved him past the possibilities that bounded his life in America.

What neither Stephen Benson nor Virgil P. M. Bennehan could foresee at the end of July 1848 was that, within weeks, they and Bassa would be at the center of the worst Liberian disaster of the 1840s.

6

The Height of Folly

When Virgil boarded the *Liberia Packet* in Baltimore on April 11, 1848, he knew only that he was bound for Bassa after his arrival in Africa. A year before, the ACS head agent William McLain had made the decision to focus on the repopulation of Bassa. That goal served many purposes. It appeased Elliot Cresson and the Pennsylvania patrons who wanted the settlement resurrected after a decade of decimating disasters. It responded to the appeals of residents in Bassa whose small numbers made them vulnerable should hostilities resume with the Bassa and Kru peoples surrounding them. It allowed McLain to envision that Bassa "could be made into a commercial place," to complement the port in Monrovia.[1]

Neither Virgil Bennehan nor the other emigrants knew why Bassa was their destination. Nor did he or they have any inkling that their fate in Liberia hinged on a gamble.

William McLain had long since dismissed any medical challenge that might stand in the way of his plan: the dangers involved in what was called "acclimation." He knew that emigrants sent to Liberia would suffer from the African fever. The fever would hit them within the first three weeks of their arrival. Severe headaches, chills, and lassitude would follow. After the first attack, the fever would subside, seemingly for good, only to return again and again in a cycle that would last six months and sometimes more. Called the "ague" in both America and Africa, it was very different from what Virgil and others had endured at home. Spread by mosquitoes from body to body, the African strain of malaria was far more lethal than the parasite species in the southern United States. "Ague" in America debilitated; African fever in Liberia killed. In the 1830s, close to half of all emigrants died from the parasite infection.[2]

But by the mid-1840s, when William McLain took the helm of the American Colonization Society, he and other ACS officials had convinced themselves that heavy mortality was a thing of the past.[3] To northern minister A. B. McCorkle, who inquired about fatalities in Liberia, McLain responded in early December 1847 that over the past few years, only 5 percent of emigrants had died. A week later, he told Virginia sponsor Anne Rice, who intended to place a freed family on the *Packet*, that, of recent passengers, "only one has died." With "ordinary prudence" by emigrants, acclimation posed little danger.[4] And indeed, the same opinion was shared by the presiding colonial physician employed by the ACS. American-trained white physician Dr. J. W. Lugenbeel had worked out a protocol to minimize deaths. His protocol was rest, surveillance, quinine, and immediate care for the ill. If arriving passengers were properly housed in "one or two long houses" where a single doctor could attend to the symptoms of each person and where all were obliged to rest and be supervised, then more would live than die. Only those already infirm or old or very young were likely to perish.[5]

When William McLain and his Baltimore associate James Hall made the decision to send the entire shipload of emigrants to Bassa, the officials didn't bother to ask about Bassa's medical preparations. Instead, McLain's question focused on the prospects for creating a better port there, which might elide the problem of the sandbar and allow the opening of a new harbor. On February 2, 1848, McLain wrote to physician Dr. Lugenbeel and to his most trusted employee in Monrovia, John Lewis. Only in passing did he inquire about the readiness of Bassa for more emigrants; he highlighted instead his commercial idea. The inquiries arrived five weeks later in Monrovia. Both men answered unequivocally—and focused exclusively on health. Bassa was not medically prepared for new emigrants. Persons sent there could only be housed in separate thatched huts, rented from Bassa villagers. Arrivals could not be clustered together. No trained physicians were there—just two men, nominally doctors, who had no experience dealing with the large number of persons intended for Bassa.[6] Last, there was the question of the season. The worst time to send people to Liberia was the rainy season, which began in May and lasted until October. Experience rather than an understanding of the role of mosquitoes dictated that the drier season was the healthiest time to come. Both men posted letters with their opposition to the Bassa plan. Waiting late to reply, John Lewis declared that although the goal was worthy, proper housing was inadequate. He recommended rerouting Bassa emigrants to a different location. Physician Lugenbeel, writing back immediately on March 15, was more categorical. To send emigrants to Bassa in its unready condition would be the "height of folly."[7]

In the past, when they deemed it wise or unavoidable, Liberian officials on the ground had overruled instructions from the ACS leader in Washington. In January 1848, Joseph J. Roberts, the president of Liberia, had yielded to passengers who had disembarked temporarily in Monrovia and then refused to leave, deciding to take their chances in the overcrowded city rather than reboard for a settlement more remote and rural. Later that year, John Lewis had ruled against another destination, deemed too insecure for settlers. Of McLain's Bassa directive, Lewis again proposed to route the newcomers to a safer location. He added, however, "Should you insist, I will comply."[8]

By the time of the scheduled departure of Virgil and the Virginians in April 1848, McLain and Hall had not received the replies of their trusted Liberian employees. The ACS heads nevertheless made a crucial decision that would fundamentally shape the experience of Virgil Bennehan and the Virginia emigrants in Liberia. They decided to go ahead with the Bassa plan and to guarantee its execution. To president Joseph J. Roberts, agent John Lewis, and physician J. W. Lugenbeel, McLain wrote the same command. All emigrants on the *Liberia Packet* must land at Bassa, and nowhere else. Falsely he claimed that the "unconditional" instruction to settle all at Bassa came from the former owners of the manumitted people. The ACS was obliged to follow that wish, with no alterations. The order was irrevocable. "You have *no discretion*."[9]

On the eve of the *Packet*'s departure, McLain conveyed the orders to the Liberian officials in writing and orally to the ship captain. In his letter to Dr. Lugenbeel, McLain added, "I trust that you or Dr. Roberts will go down with [the emigrants] on the *Packet*." McLain did not explain how either doctor could abandon patients already in his care to journey sixty miles south, adding lamely, "I know it may be difficult," but "it cannot be avoided." He left it to Lugenbeel somehow to work it out.[10]

After the *Liberia Packet* departed from Baltimore, the warnings from Liberia arrived. William McLain was on notice. His irrevocable plan for Bassa had put the lives of Virgil Bennehan and the Virginia emigrants at risk.

When *Packet* captain James Goodmanson conveyed Virgil on shore at Monrovia on May 17, he brought the letters of instruction to John Lewis and J. W. Lugenbeel, the highest-ranking ACS employees in Liberia. Recognizing that the Bassa directive was ironclad, they complied. Both now commended the decision. Reinforcements would lift the spirits of settlers already at Bassa, Lewis observed, and put hostile chiefs on notice that Liberia intended to hold the outpost. At the same time, Lewis noted that McLain had not said how to manage if neither ACS physician felt able to leave his existing patients to attend the newcomers. Lewis said he would ask Stephen Benson if he could find "medical advice" on site.[11]

J. W. Lugenbeel praised *half* the decision. It was wise to bar more settlers from Monrovia. That said, when it came to McLain's wish that either he or Henry Roberts attend the Bassa emigrants, Lugenbeel found excuses. He had learned that Stephen Benson planned to divide the emigrants between the village of Bassa on the coast and Bexley, eight miles inland. Of course, Lugenbeel could not shuttle between them and follow his protocol, which prescribed that all be housed and treated in one place. As to Henry Roberts, he would recommend that he go down, but he didn't see how Roberts could be spared from tending those already in his care. Lugenbeel did not note that McLain's proposal was flawed to begin with, requiring two doctors to oversee three far-flung sites; nor did the senior physician say that he had no intention of giving orders to the president's younger brother. Rather, he circuitously stated that "it is probable that Dr. Roberts may go down." Lugenbeel scratched through the entire sentence that followed: "But I shall not officially direct him." Rather, he concluded that he would "request" that Dr. Roberts go to Bassa if he could "prudently leave his laborious and responsible charge" of patients in Monrovia. His evasion meant that Bassa would have no trained physician primed in the protocol of how to minimize deaths.[12]

Virgil Bennehan, in his excursion on shore at Monrovia in May, had met with both John Lewis and Henry Roberts. Both withheld as much as they disclosed to him. His conversation with John Lewis lasted several hours. Naturally, Lewis did not reveal to his guest his view that sending emigrants to an unprepared Bassa was profoundly unwise. The closest Lewis came to giving Virgil an alert was to suggest that Virgil settle his family, not in Bassa, but inland at the village of Bexley, which Lewis privately presumed was just far enough from the swampy coast to reduce exposure to the acclimating fever. Virgil also met with Henry Roberts, the president's brother. Henry Roberts had recently returned from medical training in the United States. It is likely that Virgil received some counsel from physician Roberts about what he would be up against in dealing with the African fever. What the newly minted doctor did not tell Virgil was that he had opened the trunk of medicines designated for Bassa and removed almost all the medicines for use by his own patients in Monrovia. Roberts left a fraction for Stephen Benson and kept the manifest, so there was no way to determine what or how much was missing. Nor did Roberts reveal that he would not accompany the new emigrants to Bassa, then or later.[13]

When Virgil and the two free Black "delegates" returned from the city to the *Packet*, they found a shipload of discontented people. While the privileged trio had toured Monrovia, the Virginians had remained within sight of the capital but confined to the ship. If this was a taste of freedom in Africa, it was bitter. When finally on shore at Bassa, the agent in charge, Stephen Benson, had directed half the group to go inland to Bexley. Captives in bondage, kept shipbound for four days within sight of Monrovia, they had taken their last orders. Almost all decided to stay in Bassa, and no threat or command from Benson could dissuade them. A handful decided to follow Virgil Bennehan to Bexley, impressed with his medical care on board the *Packet*. Their decision would save their lives.[14]

In the meantime, grateful to have the promised reinforcements for Bassa, Stephen Benson repeatedly put the best face on things. Even without one of the two ACS physicians, he felt that the newcomers could make do with the "medical advice" on site. He turned first to Dr. J. M. Moore, a self-taught practitioner who possessed enough quinine and other medicines to make up for the shipment hijacked by Henry Roberts. Otherwise, Benson reported, the emigrants would have "suffered inexpressibly." When some began to die in early June, agent Benson and Dr. J. M. Moore summoned W. W. Davis, a Bassa practitioner dismissed for shortcomings some years before.[15]

With deaths rising, the "folly" predicted by J. W. Lugenbeel seemed to be underway, as eight, then ten, then a total of eighteen emigrants succumbed to the fever in the first month. But Benson and the physicians pulled back from declaring an epidemic when a nurse noted that one of the first to die was a woman who had venereal disease. It turned out that all the victims were women and all afflicted with "the venereal," as they called it. Abruptly, the deaths stopped. Physician Davis reported that the rest of the emigrants were convalescing. In the meantime, Benson had encouraged the Virginians to clear their fields as soon as their first symptoms subsided rather than remain at rest until the next round. To him the danger had passed. At the end of June 1848, the ACS agent in Bassa declared that "the worst is over." A month later, on July 24, he happily reported that after early discontent, most newcomers expressed the "greatest satisfaction" with Liberia and their prospects ahead.[16]

––––––––––––––––––––––––––––––––––––––

Then it all began to unravel. Unseasonable cold had delayed the reinfection of the Virginians. The falciparum malaria parasite carried by the mosquito required a temperature of sixty-six degrees Fahrenheit or more to survive. For the months of June and July, as one Virginia emigrant wrote home, it had been so cold that he had to wear winter garb all the time and to have a nighttime fire going in his small, unventilated hut, producing not just heat but smoke, which kept mosquitoes at bay. When normal temperatures above seventy returned in August, the mosquitoes bearing lethal parasites again flourished, their base in coastal swamps replenished by torrential rain that fell three times a day.[17] The Virginia emigrants rapidly fell ill. The optimistic reports from Benson and the doctors at the end of July proved premature.

In August 1848, the "worst" began in earnest. The flaws at Bassa, identified in the spring, now bore down on the emigrants. Without one or two long houses constructed to concentrate and treat the ill, the Virginians were dispersed to rented huts and encouraged to work their fields rather than conserve their strength when not fevered. Without a credentialed physician in Bassa, the sick were attended by two local practitioners, one dismissed eight years before for drunkenness and the other primarily a pharmacist. As cases multiplied and worsened, confidence in the Bassa medics disappeared.[18] By the end of the month, the Virginians began to die in droves.

The rising death toll in the village of Bassa was no secret to Virgil and to the few Virginians who went with him to Bexley, inland from the coast. When Virgil needed more medicines for his family and his patients, he went to the Bassa commissary that Benson ran. What desolation he didn't see for himself, he learned from family members whose Bassa relatives were afflicted. Illness did not spare Virgil, his family, or the Bexley emigrants. The difference was that in his village, all in his care survived.[19] Circumstances favored the North Carolina medic. He had to manage only a handful of patients. His long experience at treating the ill at the Stagville plantation transferred well to Bexley, where it mirrored the surveillance model worked out by ACS physician J. W. Lugenbeel. Virgil kept his patients under careful observation. He treated their symptoms immediately. He exuded reassurance that each would live. Had half the 134 Virginians agreed to settle in Bexley, as agent Stephen Benson had demanded to no avail, likely Virgil, too, would have been overwhelmed, as were his medical counterparts at Bassa. Scale and his skill spared every person on Virgil's watch.

The soaring number and sheer agony of the dying stunned Virgil and the Virginians. At home in North Carolina, neither Virgil nor Paul Cameron had ever seen or allowed deaths of the magnitude Virgil witnessed in Liberia. As the tragedy unfolded in August, Virgil almost certainly learned from older villagers that the Bassa catastrophe of 1848 was not its first. Twice earlier in the decade, once in 1840 and again in 1843, similar disasters had occurred. A survivor of previous outbreaks assured Virgil that widespread suffering was a thing of the past.[20] Now it recurred on a far larger scale.

Eyewitnesses to the fatalities of the 1840s had relayed accounts of those horrors. Walter Jayne, a white missionary and typesetter from New York, was living in Monrovia when reports came in about the mounting death toll to fever at Bassa and Bexley in the summer of 1840. In his journal, he entered a graphic description of the havoc, a forerunner of what Virgil and the Virginians encountered in 1848.

> July 8. Today I learned that 39 of the emigrants at Bassa had died!! I was informed that whether they had good medical treatment or not, one thing was certain, they were not properly nursed—not properly attended to; [and] in two instances for certain, (and probably there were many others) the corpses had been found dead so long as to have become so stiff as not to be able to put the shrouds upon them. . . . More die from want of proper attention than from the fever. . . . The managers of this death-producing society ought to be exposed.
>
> August 9. . . . about 43 of the late emigrants have died—of 120 about ⅓ have paid the debt of nature—and that too in less than five months after their first arrival!! [The ship *Salada*] . . . landed her passengers at Bassa about [March] 25th. Thus is human life sacrificed. . . . *I have been told* it is in part for want of proper attendance and nourishment . . . so says Rev. Mr. Eden who was at Bassa when they landed and then sometime subsequent.
>
> September 2. Last evening a public meeting was held . . . to make provision for the poor and dying who were suffering for medical

aid, which they were now deprived of, in consequence of Gov. B[uchanan's] discharging Mr. [W. W.] Davis whom he employed as colonial physician.

Walter Jayne didn't have to rely on reports from Bassa to describe the cruel unfolding of the African fever that preceded death. He witnessed the symptoms firsthand as they felled his fellow missionaries. The first round of fever enervated for days on end and left its victims weak and feeble. One compatriot, a white physician, became "troubled in mind." A second attack brought chills, vomiting, and bladder hemorrhages. Another comrade lost appetite, suffered stiffened joints, shortness of breath; his fingers turned purple. Hopelessly depressed, he lapsed into "universal lassitude" before finally he died.[21]

Three years later the witness was Louis Sheridan, the wealthy free Black emigrant who had come from North Carolina in 1838 and established a coffee plantation just outside of Bexley. Sheridan knew that newcomers should be sent to Liberia in its cool and drier months and never in the wet, warm months, when they were most exposed to the lethal fever. When a group *did* arrive in Bexley in May 1843, he expected high casualties. He was nonetheless aghast at the toll which took one of every four lives. To him, it was "a distressing spectacle to behold such havoc of lives connected with the acclimating process." Were it not for his unchanged conviction that Liberia was still the best place for manumitted people, "nothing on earth would reconcile me to" their deaths.[22]

When in Monrovia in May 1848, Virgil's tour of public buildings and meetings with government officials insulated him from the street talk of ordinary Liberians, who viewed Bassa as a deathtrap. Rumors of heavy mortality in the entire country may well have reached the Virginian emigrants before they left. Such apprehensions were common among free Black people considering Liberia, among manumitted people consigned to go there—and were a recurrent claim by opponents of colonization.[23] If Virgil had also heard the rumors, he could have dismissed them through June and July, when all of his Bexley patients and most emigrants settled in Bassa had survived. The horrors of August and the two months that followed made him a believer—and an angry one.

But angry at what and at whom? Had Virgil known the sequence of events, there were targets all around: William McLain's tardy request for an opinion about whether Bassa was ready for new emigrants; the ACS leader's decision to dispatch all settlers to Bassa before he heard back; the compliance of Liberian agents to submit to orders despite their better judgment; the theft of medicines by the brother of the Liberian president; the excuses that left Bassa without a trained doctor to care for the newcomers. Virgil knew none of this. He directed his fury instead at the entire country.

As he soured on Liberia, Virgil came to see its seeming advantages in a different light. In May, he had written home about the richness of the land and the prosperous farms, and after early uncertainty, he had apparently decided to try his hand at farming. But as the rains of the summer continued, a 180 inches coming in downpours and even tornadoes, he saw newly cleared land reclaimed by overgrowth.[24] Virgil could observe from the outset that farm animals of the South—mules and horses and cattle—could not survive in Liberia. All succumbed in Africa to sleeping sickness carried by the tsetse fly. Nonetheless, he judged that the low wages of indigenous workers—two to three dollars a month—made it feasible to clear and plow an "extensive" parcel of land without draft animals. In Bassa, however, those workers were intimidated by increasingly aggressive community leaders, who called on them to withdraw their labor on pain of death. That command was part of a cold war in Bassa that proved to be a prelude to overt conflict, which came at the end of 1848.[25] The mounting deaths, the incessant rains, the cold war—all led Virgil to reverse his initial judgments about land, labor, and health in Liberia. The country was a grave for hopes and humans alike.

By September 1848, Virgil Bennehan was biding his time. He knew that for two more months, he would have the prepaid support of the American Colonization Society—provisions of food and medicine and housing. He knew that in the fall, the *Liberia Packet* would return to Bassa. Following protocol, he let the Bassa ACS agent Stephen Benson know that he planned to sail back to the United States with his family, just for a short visit. So Benson reported to William McLain in November 1848, but he added that informants in Bexley doubted that Virgil planned to come back; the agent doubted it, too. By then the two men were estranged. No longer did Benson praise Dr. Bennehan's "patriotic fortitude" and "independency of mind," as he had in July. When Virgil sought payment of fifty dollars for the care of patients he had treated in Bexley, the agent refused. It was true, Benson conceded to his superior William McLain, that none at Bexley had died. But Virgil had not been authorized to doctor emigrants on behalf of the ACS; what was more, he billed for service to his own family. Benson offered Virgil half the amount, on the condition that Virgil sign a receipt for "payment in full." If Virgil wanted the other twenty-five dollars, Benson told him to see William McLain in Washington and make his case.[26]

Stephen Benson was right. Virgil had no intention of coming back to Liberia. He would indeed make his case in America. But the denied twenty-five dollars would be the least of his grievances.

By the time the *Liberia Packet* arrived at Bassa at the end of October 1848, to pick up cargo and passengers to take back to the United States, the tally of the dead in the benighted village was complete and catastrophic. As the *Packet* made stops at other ports and finally in Monrovia, those who learned about the dimensions of death in Bassa strained to find words to describe the calamity. Society agent John Lewis, forced in May to comply with his employer's directive to send emigrants to a destination unprepared to receive them, lamented Bassa's "unprecedented mortality." Physician J. W. Lugenbeel, who likewise deferred to orders despite earlier warnings of "*folly*," nonetheless seemed stunned at the "enormously great mortality" that fulfilled his prediction of disaster. When the *Packet* made its last call in Monrovia and set sail for the return voyage to Baltimore, it carried the news in their confidential letters to William McLain.[27]

The *Liberia Packet* carried more than confidential letters. It also carried four eyewitnesses to the calamity. They had no intention of holding back what they'd seen. Foremost among them was Virgil Bennehan.

7

The Messenger

William McLain, in his Washington office in August 1848, was unaware of the cascade of deaths beginning that month in Bassa. He had other worries. "We are out of money!" The American Colonization Society, he wrote to his Baltimore colleague James Hall, had never been this "*hard* up." Emigrants there were aplenty, awaiting the next ship in Baltimore, lined up to depart in Savannah, holding in Virginia for the date of their deportation. What fell drastically short were donations. The ACS was $8,000 in debt.[1] Where was the money to cover the ACS commitment to pay for the emigrants' transatlantic voyage and six months of support in Liberia?

On August 4, a telegram raised McLain's hopes. From Baltimore, James Hall telegraphed that the *Liberia Packet* had returned from Liberia. McLain was "anxious for our letters, & very anxious to know what *she brings*." He was looking for good cargo and good news. The good cargo would be imports from Liberia—palm oil, camwood, coffee, arrowroot—that the ACS might sell in America to add needed income to its coffers. The good news would be word that the directive of emigrants to Bassa, which McLain by then knew to be a gamble with their health, was a success. If almost all were weathering the African fever, then sponsors of the emigrants, patrons invested in the Bassa outpost, and other donors would reward the ACS with contributions.[2]

While McLain awaited delivery of the letters to his office in Washington, he had a different challenge to deal with. One of the main claims made for Liberia was that its leaders fought to stamp out slave dealing in the country and surrounding region. That argument was upended by an article in the *New York Herald*, which published the allegation of a former ACS employee that Joseph J. Roberts, the governor of the colony until 1847 and now president of the country, had engaged in the slave trade. An ACS agent in Portland anxiously wrote McLain to ask him to respond to the charge. Base "*Slander*," McLain replied. "You can answer that *slander* about Roberts and others [allegedly] in the slave trade by saying on my authority 'that it is an *enormous lie!*'" Quite the contrary: Roberts and Liberia remained at the forefront of rooting out slavery, in Liberia and elsewhere in Africa.[3]

The Portland agent also sought reassurance from McLain on another matter—mortality in Liberia. He raised the question of mortality indirectly, by focusing on the story of an "old African woman" and her descendants sent to Bassa on the April 11 voyage of the *Liberia Packet*. Was she and were they still alive? McLain replied on August 8, before he received the latest letters from Bassa. The ACS head seized the chance to trumpet once more what he believed was Liberia's strong suit—astonishingly low mortality. "The Old African woman and her sixty children sailed in the Liberia Packet April 11. She and children had all been sick, but not one of them died." You may challenge the annals of the world to produce any other colony where the mortality has been as small or as many survived, including the early settlements at Jamestown and Plymouth, which endured many more deaths. "You are safe in doing that."[4]

Soon after McLain posted his reply to the agent in Portland, the letters from the *Liberia Packet* arrived.

———————————————————

The *Liberia Packet* that docked in Baltimore on August 4 had made the Atlantic crossing in twenty-six days and contained the latest reports about the fate of the Virginia emigrants sent to Bassa. The news was mixed. The medical summary came not from a trained ACS physician, as McLain had wished, but from a local medical practitioner, W. W. Davis. Writing on June 17, six weeks after the emigrants' arrival, physician Davis recounted that 18 of the 134 Virginia emigrants had died. The first practitioner assigned to their care was doctor Moore, who had summoned Davis's help when the numbers of ill multiplied. Moore had discovered that the victims were women with venereal disease. The physicians left it to inference that "the venereal" had made the women more vulnerable to the African fever—an inference that gains plausibility if the women were pregnant as well. None knew then about the malaria parasite carried by the mosquito nor that illness and pregnancy lowered resistance to infection. Stephen Benson, the head of ACS affairs in Bassa, added his report at the end of June, the last written before the *Packet* departed. Benson offered a lower count of the dead—fourteen, not eighteen—and, while regretting any losses, intimated that all who came without venereal disease survived the African fever well.[5]

Perhaps under normal circumstances, William McLain might have taken these reports, overall, as confirmation of his confident response to the agent in Portland. But McLain now possessed the belated warnings of his chief physician and of his most senior employee in Liberia that sending emigrants to an unprepared Bassa put their health at risk. McLain already had learned that Henry Roberts, the other official ACS physician and the president's brother, had taken the medicines meant for the Virginians' care. Now the letters of June and July brought more ominous news. Neither American-trained ACS physician had gone to Bassa to attend the Virginians. And that instead of urging rest after bouts of fever, the protocol that Lugenbeel followed to conserve the strength of his patients, Stephen Benson had commended those who went out to work. Could McLain trust that the deaths of fourteen to eighteen already diseased women would cap the mortality at Bassa? Or were there many more deaths to come?

It is not clear when William McLain received a subsequent, reassuring letter from Stephen Benson written on July 24. "The worst is over," Benson declared. Whether or not McLain had Benson's letter in hand at the start of September 1848, he was not reassured.

On September 2, McLain suspended further emigration to Bassa.[6]

The *Packet* that arrived on August 4 at least promised the fulfillment of McLain's other special mission of the spring of 1848. The ship brought home the two free persons of color from the Midwest whom McLain hoped would return with favorable reports of Liberia and entice followers back home to emigrate. If Samuel Ball of Illinois and Moses Walker of Ohio endorsed colonization, McLain believed, Liberia stood to gain a "better class of emigrant." Stressing the stakes involved, McLain had written to Liberian leaders, including the president, asking that all show the two "spies" the best of the country. The *Packet* that brought back Samuel Ball and Moses Walker carried a welcome message from two leaders who saw them off in Monrovia. "Neither will have a hard word to say about Liberia."[7]

Samuel Ball made his first report on Liberia to a meeting of colonization supporters in New York City a week after his arrival. It was all that William McLain had hoped for. Ball declared that the country had fertile land for farming, good health for those who followed the right precautions, and the chance for emigrants to gain what was denied to persons of color in America—the right to vote, to hold office, to educate their children. Ball pledged "to interest his brethren in Illinois and take with him a large emigration."[8] McLain had every expectation that on his return to Illinois, Ball would carry the same message to the Black Baptist Association of the state, which had chosen him to survey Liberia on their behalf.

Had William McLain or Virgil Bennehan been at the meeting of the association that received Samuel Ball in Alton, Illinois, on August 25, 1848, they would have witnessed the rapture that greeted him on his safe return. The Black Baptist assembly welcomed Ball with "much feeling, . . . the shaking of hands, . . . tears shed for joy, and praises to God" for his safe passage home. Eagerness to learn his assessment had intensified since his embarkation in April. While he was in Liberia, the white citizens of Illinois had voted on a referendum to ban further Black emigration into the state. Seventy percent of the voters had approved the ban: 78 percent in the county that included Ball's hometown of Springfield. The vote fell short of a legislative act. But added to the so-called Black Laws of the state that denied the vote, office holding, public education, and jury service to free persons of color, the referendum sent a resounding message that persons of color were unwanted in Illinois.[9]

Samuel Ball began his address in Alton as he had in New York City, detailing the many strengths of Liberia. It had soil as fertile and productive as any on earth. Fruits and crops of the country abounded. The African fever was not dangerous when the patient had adequate medical attention, good lodging, nursing, and nourishment. But then he paused. He looked out at the Black Baptists who had entrusted him as their emissary. His listeners on alert, he resumed. *Let the truth be told.*[10]

The truth was that a small clique of merchants and political leaders controlled the country. Living in fine dwellings, dining on sumptuous foods, having on hand the best wines, waited on by native servants, they ruled as a Black aristocracy. Liberia was no democracy. Settlers from America could vote and serve on juries; nonetheless, entry into the ruling class was foreclosed. He gave the example of an emigrant who began as a doorman at the legislature but, when proposed for office, was denied entry. The "leading men" would "not suffer the man who waited on them one year to sit by their sides the next." As to African peoples of Liberia, colonization promised religion and uplift. In fact, almost all were consigned to servant and subordinate roles. When he asked about their schooling, Ball was told that Africans "were heathens and not considered worthy." Viewing the "natives" as "their inferiors," colonists told Ball that it "would not do to treat them better." If "you did it would make them insolent and saucy, and . . . they would rise up and cut their throats"—a sentiment not unlike that of enslavers in the United States about the danger of Black literacy.[11]

Most damning of all, Liberia was a hellhole for those who came without money, as most did. To be sure, the American Colonization Society supported emigrants for their first six months. But funding ended before many were well. If they wanted to work, they had to compete with African-born laborers paid two to three dollars a month. The impoverished faced indifference. He told the story of a child sent out to beg for a chicken for his family who came back empty-handed after an entire day in Monrovia.[12] Ball brought his verdict home with two wrenching accounts. One was what happened to a family sent out from nearby Coles County, Illinois, the year before. The wife in Anthony Bryant's family, threatened with enslavement, had preserved her freedom in a notorious court case. But white friends, who feared for her safety, funded the family's migration to Liberia. Samuel Ball found Bryant penniless and desperate for him to carry him and his little boy back to Illinois. The other account was of a man so eager to exit Liberia that he asked to be reenslaved if that would secure his family's return. Samuel Ball's conclusion: For those with "intelligence and means, there is no better country." But for those who came without their own resources, as most did, they risked descent into hopeless poverty. "I consider it one of the worst countries he can go to."[13]

"*Would I emigrate to Liberia?*" Ball asked. It was not a hypothetical question. Widowed several years before, the thirty-seven-year-old Springfield barber had remarried and had a young family. Thinking of their future as well as his own, he answered. He would go, but only on certain conditions. He would go only with others who came with sufficient resources to rely on after their six months of acclimation. They would acquire and settle in their own colony, separate from the reach of the aristocracy that ruled the Black republic.[14] In their genuine democracy, they would work for the education and fair treatment of all people, African and American. On those terms alone

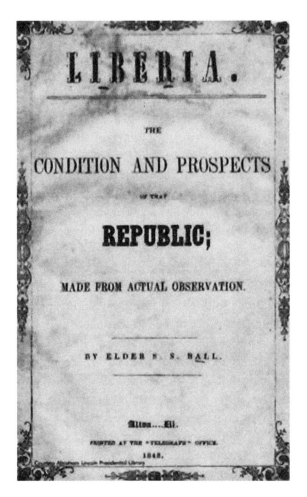

Report on Liberia by Samuel S. Ball. A Black barber and a Baptist Elder from Springfield, Illinois, Ball was one of two delegates who visited Liberia in 1848 and whom William McLain hoped would bring back positive reports to induce northern Black people to emigrate. On his return in August 1848, Samuel Ball commended Liberia's material resources but condemned the country's rulers as a Black aristocracy that neglected poor emigrants and subordinated indigenous Africans. It was the "worst country" for a poor man.
Rare Book Collection, Abraham Lincoln Presidential Library, Springfield, Illinois.

would he migrate and encourage others to do so. Only then might they flourish without white American or Black Liberian rulers holding them down.[15]

Samuel Ball's address to the gathering at Alton was soon published and distributed. Antislavery newspapers, adamant opponents of colonization, reprinted its most damning conclusions. When the pamphlet reached William McLain, he ruefully conceded that Samuel Ball's mission and message had done more harm than good. McLain turned away from the "delegate system" to gain good reports on Liberia.[16]

McLain could take some consolation that his other "spy," Moses Walker of eastern Ohio, had returned a zealot who regarded the Black-ruled republic as little short of a miracle. Even before he left, Walker had read and absorbed the message of the most militant advocate of Black self-rule, Hilary Teage, author of the Liberian Declaration of Independence and editor of the *Liberia Herald*. Only in their own country, Teage had written, could persons of color escape the unrelenting degradation of living among white persons who thought them inferior and did all they could to keep them so. Only in their own country could they have and speak their minds without worry of being thought impudent or dangerous. Moses Walker met Hilary Teage on the second day of the Monrovia tour arranged for the two "delegates" and for Virgil Bennehan. While the North Carolinian only made mention of a pleasant reception, the Ohio delegate found the inspiration he came looking for. On the days and nights of his travels that followed, Walker found more. Though a barrel-maker by trade, Walker aspired to be a minister as well as a medic. In Liberia, he found and relished opportunities to preach at every stop to emigrants and indigenous people alike. Back home in America, Walker declared that Liberia was "'the only hope of the colored man, both here and in Africa.'" Liberia proved that "'the *black man too*, is actually capable of self-government.'" For Walker, as he later put it, Liberia was "magic."[17]

Moses Walker's zeal, however, turned out to be as much a liability as an asset. At least that was the report of McLain's white ACS agent and fund raiser in Ohio, who went to Steubenville on August 31, 1848, to hear the first address that Walker made on his return to an audience of white supporters of colonization. The first thing the agent noted was that the speaker was unwell. In Liberia, Walker had spent nights with hosts in villages; he had contracted the African fever and had returned enfeebled. Now back in Ohio, he addressed the white listeners with passion but spat blood as he did so. His praise for the country echoed Hilary Teage—Liberia alone offered escape from the insuperable barriers, soul-crushing humiliation, and "'interminable degradation'" that white people inflicted on persons of color in America and

Africa. The speech appalled the ACS agent and, he reported, alienated the white people of good will who came to the meeting. "In manner and message," the address did much "mischief." Moses Walker's manner and message would have to be domesticated before he could be useful to the colonization cause. Until then, Moses Walker's fervor did less good than harm.[18]

His faith in the "delegate system" shaken, his hope for attracting the "better class of emigrant" undermined, his plans for Bassa in limbo, William McLain ended 1848 shadowed by setbacks. Worse was to come in January with the arrival of the *Liberia Packet*. The ship brought the return of Virgil Bennehan and three Virginia survivors of the worst mortality of the decade in Liberia. They had not gone out as spies or delegates. Led by the North Carolinian, they came back as determined messengers.[19]

Dr. James Hall, agent for the Maryland Colonization Society and McLain's main contact in Baltimore, was ill and in bed when he got the word. On January 18, 1849, the *Liberia Packet* had returned safely from Liberia, arriving the night before, in the solid travel time of thirty-one days. Normally James Hall would have hastened from his office to the harbor, to welcome the captain, passengers, and cargo back to Baltimore. On this day and for the next two, however, he was immobilized, too sick to leave his house. At home in bed, unwelcome news came. Virgil Bennehan, three Bassa survivors, and even the captain of the *Packet* were wasting no time in spreading their account of the calamity at Bassa Cove.[20]

In Baltimore, the "rantings of the Chambliss [people] and the NC doctor have played the devil with us here," James Hall wrote to William McLain on February 1. Hall didn't specify to whom the "NC Doctor" was talking— perhaps to the free Black carpenter who had boarded him while he waited to depart back in April; perhaps to others awaiting the next ship to Africa; perhaps even to free Black people in Baltimore dead-set against colonization. Virgil Bennehan's report was shocking: *eighty-five persons* had perished at Bassa, almost two-thirds of those sent six months before. The three Virginia survivors joined in sounding the alarm. They immediately communicated to John Chambliss, the executor who had sent seventy-three people to Bassa, that most had died. Waiting for his response, they joined in spreading the news in Baltimore. As if the testimony of the once-enslaved returnees wasn't bad enough, the dismayed ship captain confirmed the high death toll. Publicly Captain James Goodmanson made known that of the 134 Virginians he had taken to Liberia in April 1848, 80 were dead.[21]

Had he been well, James Hall explained to William McLain, he would have acted immediately to counter the claims, calm the Chambliss ex-slaves, discredit Virgil Bennehan, and muzzle Captain James Goodmanson. Unable to intervene at once, Hall urged McLain to come from Washington to help control the damage. They should start with the captain: he should be "*removed*" from his job. Already, word of the deaths had led the *Packet's* two ship's carpenters to disappear, carpenters needed to sail with the vessel in case of leaks and damages. As to the Chambliss trio, in person McLain might be able to placate them. McLain certainly needed to write Chambliss to calm him down, conveying his deep regret for the inexplicable and unprecedented loss of life. Unless McLain took action, persons in Virginia, always the largest source of manumitted people, would pull back from plans to send more to Liberia. To forestall harmful reports in the future, Hall proposed a draconian preventative. They should "bring home no more in the packet unless they have been out 2 years."[22]

William McLain set about the work of curbing the damage. To John Chambliss, he wrote of his "grief for the melancholy fate of those who died" and candidly acknowledged the "drawback that so many deaths are to the Society. The like has not occurred for years past, & it will be years before we can recover" from it.[23] Reassurance was important as well to northern backers of colonization, whose donations were imperative as the number of manumitted people rose. Abolitionists in the North had already confronted the ACS with relentless critiques of colonization's "real" motives—to deport all free Black people from the country and to dampen antislavery with the paltry liberation of a few instead of emancipation for all. Now the news from Bassa gave enemies another bullet. "Awful!!!" wrote John Pinney, the hand-picked agent of the New York Colonization Society. The doctor at Bassa was "allowed to murder 80 emigrants!" He "deserved to be *hung*." "It is too bad." To defuse the anger, McLain took the line that Bassa was a singular case. He used his editorial control of the American Colonization Society's publication, the *African Repository*, to commission a positive account of the good health and medical care of emigrants. McLain's friends at newspapers in Baltimore and Washington kept silent about what really happened.[24]

The danger that remained was word of mouth. In Virginia, the loose cannon was John Chambliss. The apologetic and "grieving" letters about "this great affliction" from William McLain and James Hall failed to mollify him. Chambliss listened instead to the three Bassa survivors and, when he did, exploded. "Mr. Chambliss is much excited & says that if what people who have returned [and reported] is true," colonization "is only another name for murder!"—"deliberate, wholesale murder!"—"& he will investigate the case and expose it to the world!" Soon after their return to Virginia, the three repatriates made their final statement about Liberia. They asked to be reenslaved.[25]

One other witness to the deaths at Bassa needed to be contained: "Dr. Banahan." Along with John Chambliss, "Dr. Banahan" was "circulating the most extravagant stories" about Liberia, stories that William McLain feared will "greatly injure our prospects in this country." Despite the damage done in Baltimore, McLain thought that he might meet with Virgil Bennehan in Washington, either to confront or to appease him. "Dr. Banahan passed [through] this city, but did not call to see me."[26] William McLain learned why. Virgil Bennehan was on his way back to North Carolina. He intended to carry his report home.

By early February, with his family, Virgil Bennehan was back in North Carolina.

How he made it back is unknown. By the first months of 1849, agitation had intensified in the South over the escape of enslaved persons to the North. Infuriated by the indifference or outright hostility of northerners to the reclaiming of fugitives from bondage, southerners were further provoked by feats of the most daring captives, who smuggled themselves out of bondage and had their triumphs celebrated by abolitionists. Despite the rising tensions, Virgil likely returned the same way he came—by ship and then by rail. He was going *south*. For all observers knew, he was on his owner's business, and not wantonly violating the laws of Virginia and North Carolina, that no enslaved person freed from bondage could return to or remain in either state for more than twenty days.

Once in North Carolina, his destination was Raleigh, where he had to know that he might face a mixed reception. Persons in Raleigh, white and Black, knew Virgil Bennehan. They associated him with Thomas Bennehan and with the Camerons, father and son. Virgil could reasonably believe that white friends of the Camerons, though surprised to see him back, would continue to regard him as a proper man who knew his place. Yet some in Raleigh—and Virgil himself—surely recalled what happened to free Black Lunsford Lane when he returned to Raleigh in 1842 after moving to the North and acquiring his freedom seven years before. Lane came back to raise funds for the liberation of his wife and children. He and his quest nominally had the approval of the best men of the city. But rumor circulated among

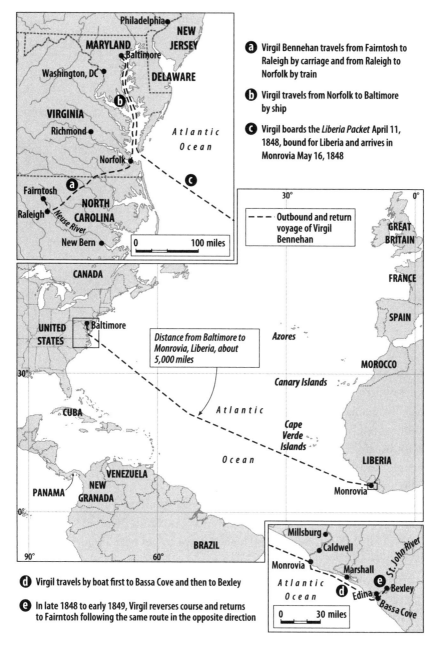

Virgil Bennehan's transatlantic journeys, 1848–1849.

artisans and workers of Raleigh that Lunsford Lane, when in the North, had not only received funds from antislavery backers but slandered the South in the process. Lunsford Lane became the lightning rod for class resentments. He was abducted, tarred and feathered, and then, to his surprise, released. His captors told him that his seizure was not about him but a message to the mighty who thought they could exempt him from the law—the law that no manumitted man could return for long to the state.[27]

Virgil Bennehan decided to run the risk of return. His mission was not to appeal for money, or to seek the release of anyone else from bondage, or to embody the tainted kindness of northern philanthropists. He had a different mission. It was to tell the truth about colonization. Tell the truth to whom? He most certainly did not arrive with the incendiary goal of informing enslaved persons that they should balk if freed on the condition that they go to Liberia. William McLain knew Virgil's audience. The "NC doctor" intended to warn white people of "good feelings"—such as the owner who liberated Virgil's family—about Liberia. McLain acted quickly to undercut the man and his message.

In the 1840s, the American Colonization Society employed agents in different parts of the country to promote Liberia. They were to raise money, usually in small meetings in churches or public places. They were to alert William McLain of potential recruits for emigration—in the North and Midwest among exasperated free persons of color, in the South among white people ready to manumit enslaved people. It was uphill work, and agents, who worked for a small salary and a portion of funds they raised, boosted their spirits and income by passing along the best news and numbers they had. The society's agent in North Carolina was Henry Brown.

William McLain turned to Henry Brown to counter Virgil Bennehan. Writing from Washington in the first week of February, McLain informed the agent that "a family by whom Mr. Cameron sent to Liberia last A[pril] has returned and gone to Raleigh. He says many bad things about Liberia. He will doubtless do much injury." Brown was to undermine him, starting with his character. "Allowances are to be made for him. He has been petted all his life & thinks of himself quite as important a personage as he really is!" Well aware of the shocking numbers and "most extravagant stories" that Virgil had circulated in Baltimore, McLain provided agent Brown with a different version of events, one that placed blame for so many deaths on the panic of the victims. Not eighty-five but "*sixty-four* of the company in which he went out, have died. There has not been such great mortality in years. It is a very great affliction. No good reasons can be given for it. The disease got among them & they became alarmed, & it seemed as if they would all die. This however is a *solitary* instance in the last ten years."[28]

Agent Henry Brown obliged his employer, spread the society's narrative, and a week later reassured McLain that no one in Raleigh took Virgil Bennehan seriously. "I think you need have no particular fear of any impression that he will make on the whites around him, though it may be to some extent unfavorable on the blacks. His character there is well understood. Having spent his life in gentlemen's parlors, he could not bear the idea of laboring in the Sun."[29]

Henry Brown spoke too soon. A week after the reassurance, William McLain received an urgent letter that revealed that Virgil Bennehan had far more impact—and made a far more sweeping critique of Liberia—than the North Carolina agent disclosed.

John Newlin was a Quaker who dwelled in the western edge of Orange County, North Carolina, at a crossroads settlement called Lindley's Store. His farm was fifty miles west of Raleigh and thirty-eight miles from the Cameron plantation in the eastern part of Orange County. A trustworthy and conscientious Quaker, Newlin had become the executor of the dying wish and verbal trust of a friend and fellow Quaker who decided to emancipate her enslaved workers upon her death, on the condition that they be sent to Liberia or to a free state. Those were the same terms that freed Virgil Bennehan and his family. The Bennehan will, however, had made the bequest of other property *contingent* on the manumission of Virgil. The will and trust of John Newlin's friend had not. Hence, there was no penalty imposed on relatives who decided to contest the will, which they did for eleven years. A lawyer as well as a Quaker, Newlin fought for the freedom of the forty people in the courts. In 1849, the case was still in court, but victory seemed close for Newlin and the people.[30] Newlin had decided on Liberia as their destination and was making provisional arrangements when Virgil Bennehan came back to North Carolina in early 1849 with an indictment of the entire Liberian enterprise. A distressed John Newlin sought help from ACS head William McLain.

> Virgel Benehan [*sic*] with several other slaves were willed by Thomas
> D. Benehan to be free. . . . They shipped to Africa perhaps last Spring

John Newlin. Newlin was a Quaker lawyer in North Carolina who had custody of forty-some emancipated persons he hoped to send to Liberia. Shaken by Virgil Bennehan's return to the state in 1849 and his denunciation of Liberia as a deathtrap, John Newlin appealed to William McLain to rebut Virgil's claims. McLain dismissed Virgil Bennehan as a malcontent too "petted" in bondage to labor in Liberia.
Courtesy of the State Archives of North Carolina, Raleigh.

or Summer. I understand that Virgel has some learning and [is] a man of some smartness. I understand that Virgel and all the others freed by TD Benehan returned to the U. States this fall past much dissatisfied with the Country and says that the People are very Poor have nothing and can raise nothing the land is so Poor that many [are] almost in a state of starvation and that [Liberian] President Roberts himself is engaged in the Slave trade and that eighty-five of the emigrants he sailed with had died. This information I have [learned] here from high authority.

Newlin's "high authority" reported that Virgil Bennehan's warning had made an impact. "Southern men mostly look to the dark side of Colonization in Africa. Virgel's tales from what I hear are readily believed."[31]

If the report from Raleigh was accurate, Virgil Bennehan had gone well beyond damning Liberia as a deathtrap—and had reversed many of his first impressions of the country. "Poor land" was not how Virgil described Liberia ten days after his arrival. At the end of May 1848, he wrote Paul Cameron of the rich soil and flourishing crops he saw on farms adjacent to the great rivers of the country. In the six months that followed, he had seen what the torrential downpours of the rainy season did to the crops and the soil. Tropical overgrowth reclaimed cleared land; farmers had to clear, farm, and then fight back the overgrowth by hand and hoe, without the aid of mules or oxen or horses. In his letter, Virgil had reported "poor people" in his small village of Bexley, most without more than a dollar for his medical care. What he would discover in months to come was that money was short everywhere. Many emigrants turned to trade and soon became mired in the uncertainties of a barter economy. They had to acquire trade goods from a patron at home and needed African traders willing to bargain. Collapse came on both sides, especially in Bassa. There the Bassa African people pulled back from trade as a ploy and prelude to open war to drive out the "white people," as they called the American émigrés.[32]

Even settlers who came with money, as did Virgil, found themselves forced to spend it on goods at hugely inflated prices and when unable to replenish their means, they fell into debt and some to beggary. The persons who most reliably had an income in Bassa were agents of organizations back home—employees of the American Colonization Society or of missionary societies back in America. Those agents, in turn, promised to economize every penny allocated to them.

Virgil Bennehan's testimony about Liberia was chilling. Poor land, poor people, a deathtrap—the picture was enough to give pause to any freed person with a choice of destinations or to a white person such as Quaker John Newlin, trying to make a responsible decision on behalf of the manumitted people in his charge. But Virgil did not stop there. Colonizationists claimed as part of their mission the redemption of Africa and Africans from the slave trade. Not so, contended Virgil Bennehan. He passed along the rumor, making the rounds in England and the United States, that Joseph J. Roberts, the former governor of Liberia when a colony and now the first president of the republic, had engaged in the slave trade. Abolitionists quickly picked up on the story and used it to blast the pious claim of colonizationists that they were the true liberators—liberators of *Africans* from bondage.[33] For Virgil Bennehan to embrace the slave-trade charge was the ultimate indictment of colonization.

No wonder that John Newlin pressed the head of the American Colonization Society for a denial of all that Virgil Bennehan asserted. "Is there no evidence of sufficient authority to be obtained in truth that will counteract Virgel's [sic] statements?" William McLain obliged. "Virgil's statements are of the most extravagant nature. All that he says about the poorness of the people, the soil, etc is totally without foundation & is contradicted by the letters of officers in our Navy and other persons who have visited Liberia." It was true that "of the company on which he went, 149 in all, about 64 died," wrote McLain, inflating the number sent and minimizing the number who died. "This is a larger portion than has died of any other company for twenty years. If that many died of all companies, I would abandon the enterprise at once. We cannot give any good reason for so many deaths among [them]. It is one of the strange providences that sometimes occur." McLain dismissed John Newlin's worry that Virgil Bennehan had swayed anyone of note. He repeated the reassurance of "our agent Mr. Brown who had lately been at Raleigh," who doubted that Virgil could make "any impression . . . on the whites around here. His character there is well understood." A man who had never labored "in the Sun," of course Virgil saw the land as poor—too poor for the likes of him to work. Virgil Bennehan's disillusionment was that of a spoiled man.[34]

John Newlin was grateful for the reassurance that no white people had taken Virgil seriously. But damage was done, and he knew it. Society agent Henry Brown was right. White people were not Virgil's only listeners. In December 1850, the Quaker's legal case won and the manumitted people free to go, they refused, however, to leave for Liberia. Against his better judgment but unable to persuade them otherwise, John Newlin escorted them to Ohio.[35] A year later, yet another catastrophic loss of lives in Bassa—when 60 of 149 emigrants died—vindicated Virgil and not McLain about the danger of death. Unable any longer to dismiss the anger of settlers on site—why not just "*cut their throats before they left*"?—or to suppress newspaper reports of the ACS's "'murderous work'" in sending people to Bassa's still-lethal environment, William McLain halted emigration to Bassa.[36]

8

A Broken Bond

His mission in North Carolina completed in February 1849, Virgil Bennehan might have reversed course and returned to the North. Years later, Paul Cameron offered his version of what happened next: "A family of negroes devised to him by a friend 'for emancipation,' whom he settled in Liberia under the Care of the American Colonization Society, providing them with house and food for twelve months, and one thousand dollars in gold ... [returned] from Africa and presented themselves at his door in Orange county, *begging him to take them back.*"[1]

There is every reason to question this account. It came in the 1870s, in a conversation between Paul Cameron and another former slaveholder, John H. Wheeler, who reported it in his book *Reminiscences and Memoirs of ... Eminent North Carolinians* (1888). Both men regarded themselves as benevolent masters in slavery times. Both felt betrayed when their former bondmen scorned their good treatment and repaid it with ingratitude. For John Wheeler, the man who interviewed Paul Cameron for his book, the sting of rejection had been humiliating, and occurred twice. A former state treasurer of North Carolina, Wheeler had been named US ambassador to Nicaragua at the moment that the Central American country had briefly been commandeered by a southern military adventurer, William Walker.

Paul Cameron. Twenty-some years after Virgil Bennehan returned to North
Carolina in 1849, Cameron claimed that Virgil and his family had appeared
at Fairntosh and begged to be taken back into bondage. For Cameron,
Virgil's pleading offered proof that slavery under his rule was benign.
*Cameron Family Papers, 1757–1978, Southern Historical Collection,
Wilson Library, University of North Carolina at Chapel Hill.*

John Wheeler had brought his personal servant and her children with him to
Philadelphia, planning there to ship out to Nicaragua. At that moment, Jane
Johnson got word to members of the Philadelphia Underground Railroad
that she was forcibly being taken out of the country. A party of antislavery
men boarded the ship, seized Jane Johnson and her children, took them on
shore, and sped them out of the city. A trial of her rescuers ensued, in which
Wheeler claimed that his servant was taken against her will: her supposed
saviors were kidnappers. At that moment, Jane Johnson came out of hiding,

appeared in the courtroom, and testified against her former owner and his claim. Wheeler won the case against the lead rescuer but lost the enslaved woman and her family—all in a very public trial.[2]

Recently discovered is that a second woman from Wheeler's household escaped as well and made her way north. She composed a scathing quasi-fictional account of bondage under Wheeler's rule under the pseudonym of Hannah Crafts, but Wheeler was spared a second public embarrassment. The manuscript was not found and published until 2002 as the first novel written by an enslaved woman—*The Bondwoman's Narrative*—and her identity uncovered only in 2013.[3]

When he interviewed Paul Cameron in the 1870s, John Wheeler was looking for validation that bondage was beneficent, the mirror opposite of its depiction by self-proclaimed liberators, whether before or after the Civil War. Paul Cameron needed little incentive to oblige. A few years earlier, in a memorandum of April 1865 meant for the eyes of an occupying Union commander, Cameron had described himself as the benign owner of 800 people who were always provided for—in sickness or in health, in childhood or old age, whether fit to labor or not.[4] In his conversation with Wheeler in 1870, Cameron made no mention of a thirty-month insurgency of his workers after Emancipation, which finally led him to expel all Black laborers at the end of 1867. Rather, all parted "with kindly feeling."[5] Nothing ever altered his belief that bondage under Cameron rule was better than freedom. Proof positive was Virgil Bennehan's return from Liberia and supposed appearance at his door, "*begging him to take them back.*" It was a story, Wheeler added, that Paul Cameron recited "with some zest."[6]

Was there any truth at all to the tale?

It is clear that Virgil Bennehan did return to North Carolina in early February 1849. Did he ask Paul Cameron to take him and his family back into slavery—and if he did ask, was it as Paul Cameron framed the account, a blanket vindication of bondage? Clearly enslavement for *Virgil* had been exceptional. He had been the house servant of his owner, Thomas Bennehan. He had kept plantation accounts, possessed keys to the smokehouse, had access if needed to Thomas Bennehan's personal documents, and above all, had become a medic on the plantation. He rode freely among the quarters of people, dispensing care when needed and calling for help if required. If Virgil did ask to return, it was as the plantation medic, with the unique latitude he'd possessed.

There were different reasons that Virgil's family might have concurred with a request to return. His wife, Phoebe, niece Margaret, and nephew William all had been part of a group of people sold to Thomas Bennehan by the estate of John Umstead in 1829. When freed and sent to Liberia in 1848, they had left behind relatives—nieces and nephews, siblings and cousins. In their six months in Liberia, they and Virgil had borne witness to deaths of dozens who had sailed with them on the *Liberia Packet* and doubtless learned of other emigrants who'd perished in Bassa in years past. Virgil's family had survived the first six months of African fever. But if they sailed again to Liberia, how long would it be before the virulent fever recurred, as it always did? Had they been in Baltimore longer while waiting passage to Liberia in April 1848, they might have pressed Virgil to remain there. But the short stay among free and enslaved people in Baltimore had been a blur. For the Bennehans, coming back to the Cameron plantation was a return to home and family.

It is certainly plausible that Virgil and his family may have wished to *visit* their former home place. Numbers of persons sent to Liberia longed for one more chance to see those dear to them.[7] But to *stay*?

When Virgil Bennehan decided to return to America, he surely wondered whether he might be welcomed back to the plantation on which he'd spent his first forty years. His quandary may have been settled by a coincidence that had to seem providential. The ship that arrived in Bassa in November 1848 was the *Liberia Packet*, the same vessel with the same captain that had brought him from Baltimore that spring. Quite likely Captain James Goodmanson was startled to see Virgil Bennehan and his family boarding for a trip back to the United States. Only six months before, he had escorted Virgil to meet Liberia's premier leaders in Monrovia and spent several full days showing off the public buildings and finest residences of the capital. Virgil would soon confide to the captain about what had happened in Bassa in the intervening months. But before that, Captain Goodmanson had a surprise for Virgil. It was a letter to him from North Carolina, dated August 8, 1848. The letter was from Paul Cameron.

Cameron had sent the letter care of William McLain at his office in Washington. Not knowing for certain where Virgil had settled in Liberia, Cameron asked the head of the American Colonization Society to forward it to "my old friend Virgil." McLain promised to do so by the *Liberia Packet*, departing in early September. Normally completed in just over a month, the ship's voyage took fifty days, as the captain dealt with a leak on the vessel that forced a tedious journey across the Atlantic. It was late October when the *Packet* finally arrived.[8] When Cameron wrote to Virgil on August 8, the planter had not yet received Virgil's earlier letter to him, sent on May 29. Virgil's letter had made clear that although "good for sum," Liberia was not for him. He would likely be coming back. One can only surmise that Paul Cameron's letter to Virgil Bennehan, received as he boarded the *Packet*, stirred a powerful yearning for home.

To "My old friend Virgil," Cameron wrote, "Here alone in my old Home in Orange, I seat myself to write you not knowing that my letter will ever be received in your distant and far off home. But it shall be no fault of mine that you do not sometimes hear from your old home and old friends in due time."[9]

Home. Old friends. If Virgil had any doubts that he once had a home and still had friends in North Carolina, the providential letter from Paul Cameron provided reassurance. "Your friends in this neighborhood [and] at Raleigh and elsewhere have frequently asked after you." Other remarks in the Cameron letter, unquestionably well intended, were the mirror opposite of how Virgil felt and painfully reinforced Virgil's decision to exit Liberia. Cameron characterized Virgil Bennehan's voyage to Africa—an exile forced by the law of North Carolina—as turning "your back on the land of your birth—to see us never again." Cameron eagerly looked forward to Virgil's "telling me how you are likely to be pleased with your new home." When he wrote, Cameron could not know how displeased Virgil was. Cameron particularly wanted to learn "that you have or can find employment," having yet to learn that "Dr. Bennehan" had a practice but could make no living from it. Then, as in their former times together as plantation medics, Cameron provided a roll call of names and illnesses. "Mina & family—chills," John, sick enough to be "brought up to the house"; Ben Sears—suddenly dead of congested chills, attended by Cameron and a doctor without success; Cameron's father, sisters, wife, and children in good health.[10]

As Virgil read and reread Paul Cameron's words while recrossing the Atlantic Ocean, one can imagine the rekindling of ties to his birthplace and a renewed connection to the man who wrote him so warmly. "You have no friend this side of the grave who will be more interested in hearing that you are happy and comfortable." You have "in all matters be[en] faithful, and true, just and honest, and . . . must be respected and make friends." Deal "with me in candor and tell me what you feel and what you suffer." Should "you ever see Stagville again, I trust you will find it has not in any respect gone down in my hands." Cameron signed the letter, "With best wishes, Your friend, Paul Cameron."[11]

If Virgil Bennehan did present himself and his family at the plantation dwelling's door in Orange County and did ask Paul Cameron *to take them back*," he was responding to repeated expressions of friendship. There was reason to hope that friendship and loyalty might open the way.

Virgil and Paul Cameron both knew the law of North Carolina. Once formally freed, any manumitted ex-slave had to leave the state within sixty days. If the person stayed or sought to return—presumably permanently— the freed person was to be reenslaved. Voluntary reenslavement in North Carolina required an act of the state legislature.[12] Could reenslavement be done unofficially? Paul Cameron knew that powerful as his family was, the Camerons could not defy the law to provide an unsanctioned haven for Virgil. To be sure, the Camerons had a large plantation; the few white workers on it were in their employ; and, in Virgil's view, the overseers were his neighbors and friends. But the plantation was not an enclave where the Camerons answered only to themselves. That lesson they had learned from an episode involving Paul Cameron's impaired brother, Thomas. Thomas Cameron had an altercation with some rough-edged white persons in the neighborhood. Against the advice of his brother and uncle, Thomas had insisted on bringing an offender to trial—and won. The victory was Pyrrhic. Within months, a Cameron barn was burned, and Thomas Cameron was shot and wounded while riding his horse. Courts were not the only enforcers of the law.

Formal reenslavement by act of the state legislature was a rarely pursued step. Even if successful, there was no assurance that the legal option would stay the tongues of those who presumed that Virgil Bennehan owed his privileges and his liberation to the parentage of Thomas Bennehan and that the link between Paul Cameron and Virgil Bennehan might be more than that of master and servant. However Paul Cameron might go about reenslaving Virgil and his family, there would be rumors.

There was one more issue, which neither man could talk about. If Virgil Bennehan did indeed propose a return for himself and his family in February 1849, he likely saw himself as the same man who'd left ten months before. But was he? He'd spent half a year in a country nominally run by Black leaders. There he'd been called "Doctor Bennehan," and other male emigrants had been addressed as "Mister." His wife, niece, and nephew had witnessed those courtesies, forbidden back home. At risk to himself, his family, and perhaps even to the standing of the Camerons, Virgil had come back to North Carolina and presumed that white people would welcome the warnings of an ex-slave. Had Virgil Bennehan seen too much, learned too much, acted too boldly to be viewed as the judicious man he always was? If allowed to stay, he and his wife and family might be grateful at the outset. Having encountered free Black people in the North and in Liberia, would the Bennehans stay subservient? More than he knew or could admit, had Virgil Bennehan returned a different man—and no longer a safe one?

Loyal as Virgil was, the law was designed to do what Cameron now felt obliged to do. Keep the distance between white and Black, a barrier between Master and Friend. To Virgil's request to return—later portrayed as a plea—the young master said no. Paul Cameron may well have taken care to explain his decision to Virgil: regrettably, reluctantly, he was bound by law and custom, neighbors and peers, to turn him down.

There is, however, reason to think that there was a different tone in the exchange between the two men—more rebuke than regret—a tone that broke the bond between them, a tone that severed forever Virgil Bennehan's tie to home.

On the day that Paul Cameron wrote his letter to Virgil Bennehan, August 8, 1848, he and others in his family had no reason to question the fidelity of Virgil or of any favored servant of the Camerons. On that exact day, 400 miles away in Philadelphia, that faith shattered. Mary Walker was an enslaved caregiver who had for successive summers accompanied Paul Cameron's two sisters and father to Philadelphia for the medical treatment of his younger sister. Mildred Cameron had fallen ill in 1844, traumatized by the slow deaths of four older sisters to consumption. Survivor's guilt came to plague her with convulsive spasms and fluctuating paralysis; with her father, Duncan Cameron, and oldest sister, Margaret, she journeyed to Philadelphia for medical care. Repeated stays and attentive doctors brought relief but no cure. Caregiver Mary Walker had reassuringly professed her disdain for free Black people of the North. But late in the summer of 1848, Mary Walker and Duncan Cameron had a quarrel that he took as insubordination. He pledged to punish her on their return to North Carolina by sending her to the Deep South, exiling her from her family. On August 8, 1848, Mary Walker disappeared into the city.[13] Her escape would cast doubt on the loyalty of all.

In the political world, such flights ultimately led to the southern demand for a new fugitive slave law and to stiffening northern Black and white resistance to that demand. Less well known is the impact of escape on slave owners and the enslaved people left behind. Virgil Bennehan unsuspectingly

Deposition about Mary Walker's escape. Enslaved servant Mary Walker accompanied Duncan Cameron and his invalid daughter to Philadelphia for medical treatment in the 1840s. After a quarrel, Cameron declared that he would exile her to the Deep South. She fled. Free Black Nicholas Boston described the dispute in a deposition in 1850. Her flight eroded Paul Cameron's faith in the fidelity of trusted servants.
Ellis Gray Loring Papers, Schlesinger Library, Radcliffe Institute, Harvard University, Cambridge, Massachusetts.

encountered that shock wave when he returned to the Cameron plantation in February 1849.

When it came to trust, Paul Cameron was volatile. When he felt deceived, as in the episode with his misguided purchase of exhausted land in Alabama, his rage knew no bounds. "How or why I could have been so blind is past my finding out. No child was ever so deluded." "God help me," he confessed to his father on that occasion, "I am sometimes without the confidence in my fellow man & then I give it as I would a hungry man bread."[14]

To Paul Cameron, Mary Walker's flight in August 1848 was a betrayal. In response, he replaced faith in the fidelity of the "black family," once un-questioned, with all-embracing suspicion. He cast the greatest doubt on the loyalty of the most privileged. He made his distrust explicit when his two sisters returned to Philadelphia for medical care and required a proper servant to tend to their needs. He suggested that it might "be well for them to have a servant from Home"—then instantly clarified what he meant. *Not* "one of our own slaves for I should not know which one of them to trust. But a good servant might be looked up about Raleigh." He most certainly would not recommend "one of those city Negroes," a free person of color. Freedom subverted fidelity, as he believed living among free Black people had corrupted Mary Walker. "They will have the 'liberty of going out' and will take 'the liberty of picking & stealing' and the higher 'liberty of being impudent.'" It "makes me *mad* to think that my sisters can't have what they want and need, when they have so many at Home."[15]

When Virgil Bennehan returned to North Carolina in February 1849, he had no idea how profoundly Mary Walker's defection had hardened the feelings of the man who had written to him so warmly six months before. Nor was there any way for Virgil to know that emotions in the Cameron family itself were fraying. For Duncan Cameron, the toll of his daughter's prolonged paralysis and the repeated failure to alleviate it had brought on a nervous breakdown. Suffering "*greatly* from nervous excitement," the senior Cameron revealed to his son that he could no longer concentrate and must resign from his long-held post in Raleigh as president of the State Bank of North Carolina. His close friend, Supreme Court Justice Frederick Nash, who by custom took dinner with Cameron every Sunday, confided to his wife that his shattered friend had become a ghost of himself. "The old com-manding figure is gone."[16] Just before Virgil Bennehan arrived back in North Carolina, the distressed father proposed that he move back to Fairntosh to be under the care of his son and daughter-in-law. Paul Cameron responded peremptorily. "*My* first wish is to see you once more yourself & I will do anything to accomplish it." But the son, his "mind divided with duty to you, sisters, wife and little ones," summarily rejected the idea of placing his father in their home. The abrasive tone of the rebuff reflected the son's strain in seeing his once-commanding father in free fall and brought an apology of sorts. You may "think I have a very strange way of exhibiting my affection and devotion. You may think me blunt and rough but you will never question my fidelity." Contritely, Cameron confessed that "I can't think with proper composure about any matter. It is said to be the darkest before the day! This has been a long and dark day with your son."[17]

If Paul Cameron refused Virgil in the same "blunt and rough" manner he used to deny the request of his parent, Virgil Bennehan would have had every reason to be startled. This was the person who six months before had affirmed him as always "faithful and true, just and honest." This was the friend who had invited him to "deal with me in candor and tell me what you feel and what you suffer." Before he left the Cameron plantation, Virgil and his wife would learn about Mary Walker and the shadow of doubt her escape had cast on all.[18] Was he, too, no longer "faithful and trusted"? Was he under *suspicion*?

It was the last time the two men ever spoke.

Cast out of North Carolina, where was Virgil to go?

When a ship was readying to leave the harbor in Baltimore for another voyage to Liberia, William McLain always made the trip from his ACS office in Washington to the society's office in Baltimore. There he joined with James Hall, the manager of the *Liberia Packet*. Starting in 1846 and for the next half-dozen years, Hall tended the affairs of gathering in newly freed people for the *Packet's* departure, hiring crews, and paying the ship's stockholders and expenses from now always insufficient ACS collections. When separated by the thirty-mile distance from Washington to Baltimore, McLain and Hall corresponded every day. Face-to-face in the third week of February 1849, on the eve of another voyage of the *Liberia Packet*, the two men suspended their daily exchange of letters.[19]

William McLain had arrived in Baltimore with much on his mind besides getting the shipload of exiles on board and out of port. He was still engaged in damage control about the deaths at Bassa Cove and in repelling the *slander*—as he characterized it—that Liberia's president had once engaged in the slave trade. At least, he believed, he had put to rest the allegations of

Virgil Bennehan, who had sought to poison interest in Liberia in the capital city of North Carolina. William McLain relied on the report from Henry Brown, his North Carolina agent, which dismissed Virgil Bennehan as a spoiled slave whose assertions carried no weight. But before arriving in Baltimore, he had received John Newlin's letter to the contrary. McLain planned to respond as soon as he returned to Washington from the *Liberia Packet*'s departure at the end of February 1849.

By the time he was back in the capital and composed his reply of March 6 to John Newlin, the North Carolina Quaker alarmed by Virgil's denunciation of Liberia, William McLain had what he believed to be conclusive evidence that Virgil Bennehan's charges were those of a schemer rather than an altruist. The ACS head wrote that Virgil Bennehan had come back to Baltimore just before the sailing of the *Liberia Packet* and had sought out McLain in the city. Astoundingly, Virgil Bennehan had declared his readiness to return to Liberia. "Dr. Bennehan" proposed that the American Colonization Society employ him as a salaried society physician and pay him $600 a year for his services. To William McLain, the offer exposed Virgil Bennehan's "extravagant stories" for what they were: a ruse to extort a job in a country he had denounced as a deathtrap.[20]

Was William McLain's account credible? If Virgil had made the proposition to either ACS agent when they were *apart*—William McLain in Washington or James Hall in Baltimore—they certainly would have written about it, as they corresponded in detail about everything else. But the two agents were together in Baltimore when Virgil purportedly spoke to McLain. No letters between them ever mentioned the unexpected bid. It is possible that McLain fabricated the account further to discredit Virgil. The ACS head was not above duplicity when it suited his purpose. But the details of the arrangement lent it credence. Virgil knew from his experience in Liberia that individual patients were too poor to pay. He proposed to go back employed as a company physician. He specified an *annual* salary, not a monthly or fee-for-service payment. The sum that Virgil supposedly asked for, $600, was close to the $620 in gold that he had taken with him to Liberia in April 1848 and drawn on since. The salary would replenish his inheritance.

Virgil had burned bridges with his condemnation of all things Liberian—health, land, poverty, mission. Yet McLain made no mention of pleading or an apology. Was Virgil unmoored, at loose ends, desperate about where to turn next? Or did he soberly respond to narrowed options? The law and Paul Cameron had barred a return to North Carolina. Liberia constituted the last place for Virgil to be a physician, *if* paid by the American Colonization

Society rather than by impoverished patients. If he tried to practice medicine in Baltimore or Philadelphia or any other northern city, he would be up against white doctors and expectations that he be professionally trained and credentialed. In Liberia, he could be a doctor who had proved himself in the field. Surely aware that he would again endure the African fever, Virgil nonetheless proposed to sail once more to the African nation: at his risk but on his terms. If McLain had accepted the offer, one can conjecture that Virgil might have settled his family in Baltimore, mailed them money, and decided later whether to stay, send for them, or come back.

William McLain did not bother in his letter to John Newlin to declare that he rejected the proposal out of hand. He did not bother to say that he had already decided to up the pay of society doctors to a salary of $45 a month, amounting to an annual payment of $540, just short of the $600 that Virgil Bennehan had sought. Nor did he disclose that he did intend to employ a permanent physician in the Bassa area when migrations there resumed, because "lives must be saved!"[21] William McLain simply dismissed the "NC doctor's" proposal as further evidence that this man of color had gotten well above himself.[22]

Virgil Bennehan's vision of remaining a doctor—at home in North Carolina or back in Liberia—was finished.

What now?

———————————————

"I found here a very *short* letter from Virgil," Paul Cameron wrote his father on March 4, 1849.

Paul Cameron had been on his way to the inauguration of Zachary Taylor as president when a train mishap derailed his plans. The army general, a Louisiana planter and slaveholder, had come out of the recent war with Mexico as one of its military heroes. The Whig Party, desperate for victory against a fractured Democratic Party, chose him as its presidential candidate, though he'd never before entered politics and little was known about his convictions. For Paul Cameron, it was time to celebrate. A seemingly reliable southerner had carried the Whig Party to its second victory since coalescing against the presidency of Andrew Jackson. Paul Cameron's last-minute decision to go to the capital put him on the train that broke down. It was when he returned home from the aborted trip that he found Virgil's message.

"I found here a very *short* letter from Virgil, written in Baltimore, where he says he has settled his family & that he was soon to embark for the gold region of California, to be about two years."[23]

Paul Cameron didn't underline *California*, or *Baltimore*, or *two years*. He highlighted only that it was a "*short* letter." Virgil Bennehan gave no detailed assessment of his chances for making a living, as he once had in his letter of May 1848 from Liberia. He conveyed no suggestion that he was still weighing options, or that uncertainties lingered, or that he sought advice. Tersely, he simply stated his plan: California; Baltimore for his family; two years away. Virgil added no final farewells to neighbors, friends, and family members on the plantation—no deferential "how-dos" to Paul Cameron, his father, his sisters, or to his wife, Miss Anne. Virgil was done with asking or explaining, greeting or confiding.

Had Virgil felt he could communicate with Paul Cameron with the candor his friend had once encouraged, there was more to say. He could have reported that before he decided on California, he had retraced his journey to Baltimore, had met with William McLain, and without apologies had proposed to return to Africa on his own terms. Virgil made no mention of the overture or the rejection. Faithful, just, and honest as he had always been—Paul Cameron's own words—he could have conveyed astonishment at being seen as untrustworthy on his return to North Carolina. Even though he knew the obstacles to taking him back, how could he not resent the friend who sealed his final exile from home? Nevertheless, in his *short* note and in the endless silence that followed, Virgil Bennehan chose restraint. What could be gained by recrimination? Better not to burn more bridges, as he had done with his denunciation of Liberia.

And best not to burn Paul Cameron's letter, a testimonial of attachment once heartfelt. By the medium of his note and his commitment to California, Virgil Bennehan had declared his self-dependence. If fortune did not smile, he knew that his family might again need the Camerons' goodwill. Virgil entrusted the letter to his wife, Phoebe. If ever in dire need, the letter might help her rekindle the sentiment, and gain the assistance, of the man who once wrote her husband, "You have no friend this side of the grave who will be more interested in hearing that you are happy and comfortable."[24]

"A very *short* letter." The brevity, the firmness, and above all the destination constituted Virgil Bennehan's declaration of independence. For the first time in his life, he would take his destiny into his own hands.

9

The Certainty of Uncertainty

Paul Cameron didn't seem startled by Virgil Bennehan's decision to embark for California. The planter had unquestionably read about the discovery of gold in 1848 and the rush of thousands of men to the goldfields starting late that year. When Virgil declared in March 1849 that he planned to join the venture, Cameron made no comment. Cameron was himself scouting for better fortune—for virgin land and bonanza profits in the Deep South—after what he viewed as the dismal failure of his cotton plantation in Alabama. Prospective sellers understood exactly what the North Carolina buyer was looking for: "a making bank," a means to "perfect independence."[1] The planter may have fathomed all too well the emergence of Virgil's similar desire, a route to independence. Perhaps recognizing his own role in foreclosing his friend's wish to stay a medic, Cameron could appreciate Virgil's impulse to go for broke in California.

But *did* Virgil make his way west? And if he made it, how did he fare?

Two pieces of evidence raise doubts. On July 31, 1850, a census-taker came through the Fells Point neighborhood of Baltimore. Fells Point was just blocks from the city's Inner Harbor, teeming with laborers who made a living on the docks or at the skilled work required for shipbuilding. The census-taker's assignment was to record the names, ages, race, and occupation of each of its residents for the US Census of that year. Census-taker M. M. Mearis—operator of a furniture store in his everyday job—recorded that there were four "mulatto" residents in the dwelling of Virgil Bennehan. With flawed spelling, the census-taker reported that Virgil Bunohan and his family—his wife, Foebe, niece Margaret, and nephew William—resided at an alley dwelling in Fells Point, on the last day of July 1850, seventeen months after Virgil's note of March 1849 declared his intention to go to California.[2] The second detail raised a different and more ominous question mark. It came as a brief aside in a letter written by Paul Cameron on February 14, 1856. This letter, to Cameron's sister Margaret, mentioned the death of the enslaved woman "Dicey" and identified Dicey as the older sister of "Toast"—the nickname given to William Bennehan—who "went off with poor Virgil."[3] *Poor Virgil* signaled an unhappy outcome to Virgil's life, and perhaps his death, by 1856. What happened to Virgil between 1849 and 1856 was a mystery.

There was a clue in the Census of 1850: the occupation the census-taker recorded for Virgil Bennehan on July 31. The occupation given was "speculator." Virgil may well have been a "speculator" in Baltimore through the middle of 1850. He most certainly did not have the means to speculate in land but could have trafficked in goods bought and sold around the harbor of Baltimore, at the tip of the Fells Point ward where he lived. He had money. When he left for Liberia in April 1848, he possessed $620 in gold. In Liberia, he could have kept almost all of that money, say $550. He had to pay $160 for the return passage of his family back to Baltimore at the end of 1848 and perhaps another $100 for them to travel to North Carolina and back in early 1849. That would leave him $90 to pay for a year's lodging for his family in Baltimore and $200 to speculate with. All that said, as a man of color, Virgil Bennehan did not fit the profile of a speculator in Baltimore. The free Black neighbors of the Bennehans in their Argyle Alley neighborhood had jobs more typically held by persons of color: caulker, whip sawyer, mariner, laborer. The six other Baltimore men who listed their occupations as speculators in the 1850 Census were white. Two of them had far greater means than Virgil, an immigrant from Holland who gave his worth as $20,000 and a Maryland-born grocer who lived nearby.[4]

It nonetheless may be that with his funds, literacy, and experience in keeping accounts, and with his skill in dealing with white and Black people, Virgil made a go of it as a speculator in Baltimore. If so, he apparently had the acumen enough to find buyers and sellers whose word he could trust. There is no written record of deeds, contracts, or lawsuits involving his dealings.[5] It's possible that Virgil had a grander goal—namely, to cultivate shippers and ship captains in the nearby harbor of Baltimore, three blocks from his residence, and to win their assent for him to go to San Francisco, meet them or their wares on the dock, and supply information about buyers ready to offer the best price for their cargo of tobacco, flour, oysters, boots, and shoes. He could start as a speculator in Baltimore and transition to the role of middleman in California.[6]

The hypothetical scenarios leave open the question of whether Virgil ever *left* Baltimore. A different survey in 1850 provides an answer. Richard J. Matchett was the publisher of the city directory of Baltimore. Starting early in 1850, Matchett's employees fanned out over the city and went block by block and dwelling by dwelling to gather information for the directory to be published in January 1851. Their instructions were precise. At each household, the surveyor was to record the exact street address, the name of the head of the household in residence at that address, and the occupation if any of that person. The survey for 1850 concluded on August 16, 1850, to give publisher Matchett five full months to check and collate all information. The published listing for 51 Argyle Alley—the Bennehan residence in the Fells Point ward of the city—gave *Phoebe* Bennehan as the head of the household. By mid-August 1850, her husband, Virgil, was no longer in residence.[7]

Had Virgil Bennehan left Baltimore—and finally boarded a ship for California—in the exact interval of two weeks between the end of July 1850 and the middle of August? Or did he go before—long before—as far back as the "*short* letter" of March 1849? The city directory listing established only that Virgil was gone by the time the survey ended in August. But Matchett's recorder could have come by earlier in 1850 and found Phoebe in residence as the head of the household. It is entirely possible that Virgil was gone from the dwelling at 51 Argyle Alley before *either* recorder arrived in the summer of 1850. To the census-taker on July 31, Phoebe Bennehan could have named her husband as the family head, even though he was absent. There was no rule that all residents had to be present for their information to be recorded. If Virgil was across the continent in California, Phoebe may nonetheless have viewed and identified him as the head of the family, away for work but committed to return. The two surveys don't unequivocally settle *when* Virgil left Baltimore.[8]

Then there is the matter of the occupation recorded by the census-taker: *speculator*. Phoebe Bennehan could have given "speculator" as Virgil's occupation in California, rather than Baltimore. In the first year and a half of the gold rush that began in 1848, the word "speculator" was an encompassing term. Along with "adventurer," the label embraced all who hastened to find wealth in California. "Speculator" included those who sped west to find gold, whether in streams to pan or surfaces to dig with pick and shovel. As a "speculator" in 1849, Virgil could have gone to the goldfields. By 1850, more specific labels replaced the generic term "speculator." Newspapers called the gold seekers "prospectors" and census-takers recorded them as "miners." In 1849 and thereafter, "speculator" covered other ways of pursuing wealth. Both in the mining districts and in the cities of San Francisco and Sacramento, speculators bought land or goods at one price and sought to sell at a higher price. Goods included everything marketable—pots and pans, boots and shoes, potatoes and tobacco, lumber and bricks, even ice from Alaska, and on scale ranging from hundreds to thousands of dollars. In the California Census of 1850, dozens of men gave trader or speculator as their occupation.[9]

Whether Virgil Bennehan stayed with a plan to mine in the gold region or switched to a city to buy and sell, he had to know that there were high risks as well as fabled rewards. Word of mouth, and weekly accounts in the *Baltimore Sun*, reported on the riches and perils found by those who went west. By the time that Virgil returned from Liberia in early 1849, he'd have learned that outgoing president James K. Polk declared in a message to Congress that "there must be a vast and inexhaustible deposit of gold in the mountains of the Sierra Nevada" that "thousands of years would not exhaust." A week after Virgil's arrival back in Baltimore on January 18, 1849, the *Sun* relayed the assessment of the head of the engineer corps in California. Captain Henry Halleck pronounced that "no tale in the Arabian Nights was so romantic or golden as these mines," a "swath of gold three hundred miles long and fifty miles wide." No wonder, reported the Baltimore newspaper, that "thousands of speculators" were "now on foot" for California.[10]

But glowing reports were almost always paired with grim warnings. "It does not follow that every one who may go into the gold mining business . . . will make a fortune by it," cautioned the *Baltimore Sun*. Mining "is and must be precarious and expensive." Illness felled many, some en route and others on site. If forty-year-old Virgil chose to mine, he'd find that those who panned for gold were obliged to "stand in water over their knees, with an intense sun over their heads." Fully "one half of the people will have fever and ague," and many had already died.[11] Though 3,000 miles from the plantation and 8,000 miles from Liberia, Virgil would find in California that another toxic terrain awaited him. If Virgil resolved to steer clear of the mines, he'd learn from the papers that in mushrooming California cities, too, there was a "dark side of things." A Baltimore emigrant to San Francisco wrote back to report: "I am here alive, and that's all. . . . To my countrymen and friends say that they will never know disappointment until they reach here. Let everyone remain at home that is at home, for out of one hundred, ninety-nine are either sick, broken down in spirits or lose their all in gambling. Never leave a happy home for the delusive snare set by a few dreaming ones." An emigrant from Boston reiterated that San Francisco was no haven. Sixty to seventy died each week, and at least half a dozen had "no friends to care for them while sick, or to bury them when dead." The city was a place of "suffering, misery, and death."[12]

Virgil could have had no illusions about California. Dangers abounded. Yet Virgil Bennehan had already decided the issue of risk. In February 1849, he'd offered to go back to Liberia as a physician if employed and paid $600 by the American Colonization Society. He knew that Liberia was a deathtrap that had claimed two-thirds of the passengers he'd arrived with and that it could still claim him. Virgil was nonetheless ready to gamble health for a guaranteed salary. Rejected for a return to both the plantation and Liberia, why not dare California for its promise of self-emancipation—and for the long shot of a gold-enabled "perfect independence"?

Despite the clues suggesting that Virgil left Baltimore and struck out for speculation in California, the clues only pointed to a *possibility*. What seemed like the last best hope for settling the matter was a return to the American Colonization Society records—and to the ongoing correspondence of the two major leaders of the society. Writing to each other almost every day were head agent William McLain who resided in Washington, and agent Dr. James Hall, who worked at the ACS room in the US Post Office building of Baltimore. James Hall had taken an instant dislike to Virgil, not so much on his own account but because his patron Duncan Cameron had strong-armed William McLain into taking Virgil's family on board what was then the overcrowded *Liberia Packet* for its voyage of April 1848 to Africa. Though not happy to comply, William McLain had accepted that it was politic to do so. McLain's own reservations about Virgil, held back in 1848, became explicit after "the NC doctor's" return in January 1849, when Virgil denounced Liberia. Virgil's searing indictment provoked McLain to release his resentment. Virgil was a well-heeled, well-garbed, overendowed, unenthusiastic emigrant—a man "petted" in bondage and "above himself" in freedom, who was too "rich and stuck up" to appreciate liberty in Liberia. After what McLain regarded as Virgil's hypocritical offer to go back to Liberia as a doctor if sufficiently paid, McLain and Hall ceased writing about Virgil. Nonetheless, given their lingering animosity and the persistence of Virgil's family in Baltimore, they might pay attention to his destiny out of spite, especially if the highflier fell.

The answer to Virgil's fate came in a postscript at the bottom of James Hall's letter to his fellow agent William McLain, dated January 15, 1851. The postscript was cryptic: "Is this your Bennehan?" Taped beneath the query to McLain was a clipping from the *Baltimore Sun*. It was news from California, an article originally published in the San Francisco newspaper *Alta California* and republished in the *Sun* after the ship bearing the newspaper arrived in Baltimore on January 15. The clipping reported the "DEATH OF MARYLANDERS" in California for the week ending on December 1. Among the three who died was "Virgil Bennehan, of Baltimore, of congestive fever, aged 41."[13]

"*Is this your Bennehan?*" James Hall didn't need to write anything more. Hall knew that William McLain would feel just as he did about the notice. The highflier had fallen.

Virgil had died in San Francisco the last week of November 1850. Alas, all other questions remained open. How did he make his way west? When did he arrive? While he lived, had Virgil's experience in California come close to realizing the hopes—and escaping the constraints—that brought him there?

There is no record of how Virgil Bennehan got to California or of his response to his first sight of San Francisco when he arrived. Baltimore ships that departed for California were laden with cargo and carried only a handful of passengers. The cost for those passengers was high, and the trip around the tip of South America took 160 days or more. More likely is that Virgil left on a passenger ship that departed from Philadelphia. Its more expeditious route took passengers south to and around the tip of Florida, west to the isthmus that crossed Panama. Landed there, migrants had to travel a hazardous weeklong trek by mule or foot across Panama and, after a tedious wait, finally to board another crowded vessel that took them up the Pacific Coast of Mexico to San Francisco. By 1850, the entire trip could be made between 35 and 45 days. Even then, a regular berth was expensive, $500 or more. Steerage cost $200 for a filthy bunk and inedible food. Regular-paying passengers had their names recorded in a registry when they docked in San Francisco. Steerage passengers were simply disembarked. There was no registration of Virgil Bennehan's arrival.[14]

Nor is there a record of Virgil Bennehan's response to his first sighting of the harbor of San Francisco. By the accounts of others, the scene was stunning. An Australian recorded his astonishment on his arrival. "About five hundred sail of shipping came into view, presenting a complete forest of masts—a sight well calculated to inspire us with hope, and remove the feelings of doubt'" that arose over an interminable voyage. A photograph taken in 1850 showed those masts towering over the height of the one- and two-story buildings in the mushroom city and higher still than the tents that dotted the hills that rose from the shore. Not only did the number of ships startle. The flags on the masts revealed the breathtaking array of countries that the ships, sailors, and cargo came from. New Hanover, Prussia, Holland, England, New South Wales, France, Ecuador, and dozens of American vessels all flew their colors as they anchored in San Francisco and waited to unload cargo and passengers. Virgil had seen his share of ships and ports by 1850—in Monrovia and along the coast of Liberia and in Baltimore near where he'd left his family just three blocks from the city's harbor. He glimpsed even greater variety at the Philadelphia port from which he likely departed for California. But Virgil would have been at one with seasoned sailors and spellbound immigrants who invariably confessed that they'd never seen anything like the spectacle of vessels in the San Francisco harbor. For a man who had spent almost forty years on a plantation and endured six months in Liberia, San Francisco had to seem like a new world.[15]

The contrasts with the plantation and with the patron state of Liberia were palpable. On the plantation Virgil was a servant—the most favored and faithful of servants, to be sure—but nonetheless an unfree man. In Liberia, as he learned, unless a man had a patron—or came with money—he was also a man beholden to authorities, to leaders salaried and largely still governed by the American Colonization Society or to missionary society sponsors back in the United States. Without patronage and support, whether it be a society salary or trade goods from a former owner, Virgil learned that he would be as vulnerable as the meanest soul to debt and, if indebted, to beggary and drift. San Francisco, for better and worse, was a place of extremes of wealth and poverty. Tall tales, not all apocryphal, captured the allure of a topsy-turvy world. In December 1848, a story found its way back East of a man of color, his $100 sack of gold in hand, spurning the request to carry trunks for a white man. In January 1849, a New York paper reprinted

San Francisco in 1850. Virgil Bennehan encountered a city that contrasted dramatically with the plantation in North Carolina and the settlements in Liberia. The hundreds of vessels in San Francisco's harbor came from all countries of the world. Many sailors abandoned their ships for the same reason that Virgil and others left their homes—to seek wealth to lift them above the lives they had left. *San Francisco Maritime National Historical Park Research Center, San Francisco.*

a letter from an army officer that asserted, "'The merest Negro could make more than our present governor.'"[16]

Money was the most dramatic contrast. On the plantation, Virgil and his family had provisions and privileges but not payments. His grandfather Phillip Meaks had earned small amounts of credit at the plantation store and purchased goods for himself or traded with other enslaved people. Household servants in Raleigh used small-scale pilfering of greenhouse plants, the thefts winked at by indulgent owners, to barter for whiskey from local grogshops. For extraordinary service, one enslaved man received a five-dollar gold piece. In Liberia, money was more accessible yet still scarce. Indeed, during Virgil's six months in Liberia, the entire country's trade was virtually paralyzed.

By comparison, in the goldfields and in San Francisco, money abounded. Gold dust and other forms of money were ubiquitous—in saloons, stores, and gambling tables. Wages dazzled. Workmen made $9 a day if Black, $10 a day if white; cooks and stewards made hundreds of dollars each month. Of course, over against the huge rewards when fortune smiled were the extreme costs of everything: food, raiment, boots, shelter. The most basic lodging, a tent on rented land or a cot in a boardinghouse, cost $100 to $200 a month.

Chapter 9

Whether incoming or outgoing, money flowed as in no other place that Virgil Bennehan had ever been.[17]

Whether Virgil landed in San Francisco and headed immediately to the goldfields or chose to stay and make his way in the city, he'd have needed two things to succeed: good luck and providential timing.

In the mining region, luck was indispensable. Virgil's experience might have mirrored that of an adventurer from Boston who, with two companions, arrived at the mines in mid-1849. The three immediately went "off nearly all the time [in] what is called here 'prospecting': i.e. looking for diggings." The gold seeker's letter home recounted the hardships of their first year—"dysentery, fever, scurvy, and other diseases," autumn rains that forced an early exit from the diggings, roads grown "soft and miry," "cattle and mules sunk almost to their bellies," wagon wheels "up to the hubs in the mud," and "enormous prices" charged for everything. Why did men persist in the face of rampant "privations and dangers"? They held out hope for a lucky strike. The writer had seen "prudent, industrious men" not make enough to pay their way and at exactly the same time—"within twenty or thirty feet of [them]—men who were taking [gold] out in abundance." "It is a *grand lottery*, as chance wills it." Virgil most certainly would have observed in the goldfields that for many if not most, luck determined destiny. Even if lucky, Virgil would have needed allies, white and Black, to protect him from vigilantes, slavecatchers, and hostile white miners who preyed on free men of color in the goldfields.[18]

Timing, too, determined destiny. Especially in San Francisco, the year 1849 was the heyday for speculators. The demand for all manner of produce and merchandise was close to inexhaustible. Miners needed equipment; city dwellers needed foodstuffs. Clothing, blankets, tobacco, flour, lumber— every item unloaded at the docks—sold at multiples of their cost back East. Virgil would have been, by comparison with others, the smallest of speculators. In 1849, he nonetheless could have parlayed his small start into respectable winnings and earned enough to make something to send back to the family in Baltimore, where Phoebe Bennehan listed no occupation for herself until 1853. He'd have to make enough to offset the extortionate cost of living in San Francisco—then as now the most expensive city in the nation because of inflated costs of everything. He'd have needed gumption enough to recover when a competitor undercut him—and to have money in reserve to make up the lost deal on the next day's, or the next hour's, shipment. But if Virgil *did* disembark at San Francisco in 1849 and decided to forego the goldfields, he'd have arrived at the optimal moment to make the most of speculation in goods.[19]

The destiny of all California speculators darkened in 1850. The year 1849 had been the best of times; the year 1850 became the worst of times. Shippers from all over the country and the world, calculating that the demand for goods in California was insatiable, flooded the seaport with merchandise, only to find in 1850 that the market was sated with everything. With goods oversupplied, prices plummeted. Even at cost, produce and supplies couldn't be sold. Speculators failed. Goods went at auction for whatever they could bring or were simply abandoned. Surplus tobacco got dumped and used to fill holes in the roads. Laborers who the year before commanded eight to ten dollars a day, cooks who got hundreds a month, now found themselves out of work for eight to ten weeks at a time. If Virgil had come to the goldfields or to San Francisco in 1849, he'd have come in the best of times. Starting in 1850 he'd have been caught in the downturn. If he didn't arrive until the fall of that year, he'd have encountered disaster from the get-go.[20]

As much as luck, timing determined when or whether Virgil might have realized the possibility that had brought him to California—the hope that a man, even a man of color, could change the course of his life.

———————————————

The person who captured in a phrase the reason why men rushed to California, even as he cast doubt on their hopes, was a man that Virgil never met: Frederick Douglass. If Virgil ever heard of Frederick Douglass, it was perhaps from the two free men of color who were Virgil's shipmates on the *Liberia Packet*. They both knew that Douglass was a fierce Black abolitionist and an indomitable speaker who, even as they sailed, was about to crisscross the Midwest with white abolitionists to crusade against slavery. But Samuel Ball and Moses Walker may have muted any talk about him. They knew that Frederick Douglass was an unrelenting adversary of colonization. He excoriated both white and Black people who proposed Liberia as a refuge from American racism. To Douglass, all colonizationists played into the hands of those who wanted every free Black expelled from the North and all but a handful of the enslaved kept captive in the South.[21]

Frederick Douglass proved equally skeptical about the prospects of Black people—and indeed of white people as well—to find nirvana in gold rush California. He was especially doubtful about the good it would do for Black people. Black emigrants to California hoped to escape the constraints that confined free persons of color. For Black and for white people alike,

Frederick Douglass thought the risks of California more real than the rewards, the sacrifices more likely than the payoff. California adventurers left sweethearts and wives, jobs and communities, to exchange a "certainty for an uncertainty."[22]

A certainty for an uncertainty. When Virgil Bennehan wrote Paul Cameron in early 1849 that he intended to go to California, the certainties of his life were self-evident. There was no going back to the plantation or to Liberia, the two worlds he had known. He could choose to remain in Baltimore, but what future did he have there? He might have sought to practice medicine; there was at least one physician of color listed in the city directory who practiced Thomsonian medicine, with minimally invasive treatments for ailments. There was a white medical practitioner less than a block from Argyle Alley, where Virgil settled his family. John Wentz, a German immigrant, resided at 199 S. Ann, a regular street rather than an alley. Wentz called himself a "bleeder and cupper" and offered the traditional medical remedies of his day, including bleeding by hot cups to remove blood thought to contain ill humors. Other practitioners used leeches rather than cups to draw out the bad blood. Virgil could quickly surmise that for him, a new and uncredentialed "doctor" in Baltimore, medical practice was a long shot. Lesser occupations were open to Baltimore's free Black persons. But Virgil lacked the know-how of skilled Black workers, the caulkers and sawyers who lived where he settled his family in Fells Point. Common labor was always a possibility, though not even that was a sure thing. Quickly he'd have heard tell of the rivalry between Black and white people on the docks, the way that native white and immigrant workers used muscle and mayhem to keep those jobs for themselves. The one role that Virgil might transfer from the plantation to the city was that of house servant. Yet he'd have competition there, too, with enslaved men, unpaid, summoned to that position.[23]

A certainty for an uncertainty. More than almost anyone else, Frederick Douglass had a comprehensive understanding of the "certainties" that persons of color faced in the free North in the 1840s. Free Blacks were a scorned people. When the laws didn't keep them down, the frowns of white people did. Nor did white persons alone subordinate free persons of color. To Douglass, too many Black people kept themselves down by the hope that, at some distant day, evils would go away, in the meantime avoiding "anything that will make a stir." The overriding certainty was that people of color were "an outraged people—weighted down under greater oppression than any other people. Everywhere we are treated as a degraded people." "Wherever we move, we are confronted by an almost invincible and overwhelming prejudice."[24]

Frederick Douglass went on to insist that struggle—and only struggle—was the way to confront those certainties and to overcome them. Everything else—passive hope for the best, acceptance of one's place, prayer—would keep things as they were. Escape? He understood that such places beckoned. *Canada*. For those with a price on their head or hounds on their trail, Canada was a legitimate refuge. *Liberia*. An illegitimate refuge in every way: a faux nation, nominally run by Black persons after its declaration of independence, but still a tool of white people who wanted all Black people out of America, save the masses enslaved in the South. *California*? California was no remedy for those in bondage or for most Black or white individuals in the North. But at least Frederick Douglass fathomed the fantasy behind desertion of hearth and home for the goldfields. Given the certainties that held men of color down, why not gamble on the uncertainty of California?[25]

Virgil Bennehan's death in San Francisco at the age of forty-one seemed to confirm the initial conviction of Frederick Douglass and fellow doubters that fortune-seeking in California was not only delusory but dangerous. Yet one could argue that congestive fever was a fate that could have overtaken Virgil in any of the toxic places he had dwelled in his life, an arbitrary finale that could have happened anywhere. Or was failure or death the foredoomed end to his high-risk hope to remain an exception in freedom as he'd been in bondage?

It seemed best to start with more mundane questions. Where in San Francisco had Virgil lived? Exactly what day in November 1850 had he died? The city's *Alta California* newspaper was digitized, and on inquiry, Virgil Bennehan's name came right up. His death notice was provided by one William Newell, the sexton and undertaker for the Little Chile district of the city. Just half a block in 1850 from the Yerba Buena Cove of San Francisco Bay, Little Chile was four square blocks bounded by Stockton and Kearny Streets going from east to west and by Washington to Pacific Streets going from south to north. Subsequently the close-by tidal marsh of the cove was filled in; the bay and the embarcadero of wharves now lie six blocks to the east. By the century's end, later immigration transformed the Little Chile district into the upper part of San Francisco's Chinatown, which it remains today.

Newell's duty was to report weekly the deaths in Little Chile, so named because emigrants from Chile were the first to cluster there in 1849 when San Francisco mushroomed as a gold rush town. By the fall of 1850, Little Chile was a district of mostly ramshackle wooden dwellings that housed

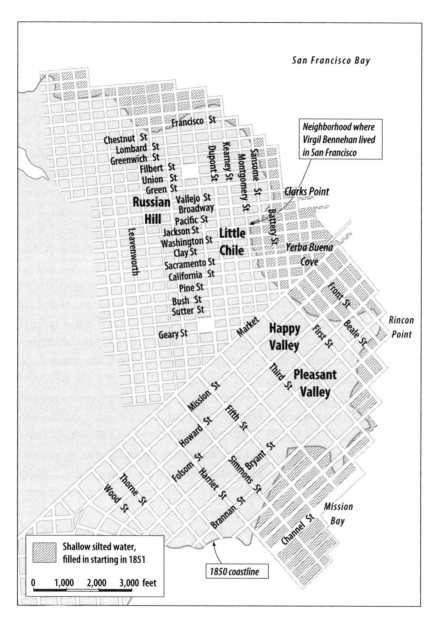

San Francisco Bay

Francisco St

Chestnut St
Lombard St
Greenwich St
Filbert St
Union St
Green St

Kearney St
Dupont St
Sansome St
Montgomery St

Russian Vallejo St
Broadway
Hill Pacific St
Jackson St
Washington St **Little**
Clay St **Chile**
Sacramento St
California St
Pine St
Bush St
Sutter St

Leavenworth

Battery St

Clarks Point

Yerba Buena
Cove

Neighborhood where
Virgil Bennehan lived
in San Francisco

Geary St

Market

**Happy
Valley**

First St

Beale St

Front St

Rincon
Point

**Pleasant
Valley**

Third St

Mission St

Fifth St

Howard St

Folsom St

Harriet St

Simmons St

Bryant St

Thorne St

Wood St

Brannan St

Channel St

**Mission
Bay**

Shallow silted water,
filled in starting in 1851

0   1,000   2,000   3,000 feet

1850 coastline

Virgil Bennehan's San Francisco, 1850

poorer emigrants from across the globe. William Newell had delayed his November report for over a week. The *Alta California* had chastised him for his tardiness, then apologized when it learned that Newell's reason was the illness and death of his two-year-old daughter Florence. The sexton was playing catch-up with his report, so it wasn't certain what exact day Virgil and ten others from the Little Chile area died during the week of November 23 to November 29.[26]

What William Newell's list did reveal was the range of persons, places of origin, and fatal illnesses of the eleven persons who lived and died that week in Little Chile. Among them were two women, one from Scotland and one from New Zealand; two men from Italy and one from Prussia; three men from New York State and two from Boston; and Virgil Bennehan from Baltimore. All but one were younger than Virgil; seven died of cholera, one from dysentery, two from fever. Virgil had escaped the more chronic and widespread killers in gold rush San Francisco. He was the sole victim to perish from what was later reported as "congestive fever."[27] It seemed likely malaria had felled Virgil. It could not have been the deadly strain of malaria found in Liberia—that parasite did not travel or remain in the bodies of passengers who returned to America. More probable is that it was the malaria parasite pervasive in the South and found as well in California, wherever water pooled and stagnated. That variant of "ague" usually produced temporary chills and intermittent fevers. But when unrelieved it could worsen into "brain congestion" and death.[28] Whether doctors in San Francisco, overwhelmed by cases of cholera and dysentery, had the time or knowledge or medicines to counter Virgil's "congestive fever" remains uncertain. Equally uncertain is whether Virgil could have advised them, if his congestive fever brought on delirium, as in the worst cases it did.

William Newell's list of the dead did not divulge where Virgil or others were buried. For burials, the best record was kept by the leading coroner and undertaker of San Francisco, N. B. Gray. The N. B. Gray & Company Funeral records gave the names of all those Gray interred at the newly opened Yerba Buena cemetery, the public cemetery of San Francisco. Of the eleven persons on William Newell's death list, most were buried at Yerba Buena, under the auspices of coroner N. B. Gray. Friends or relatives had possessed the wherewithal to pay twenty-five dollars for a wooden plank coffin and the ten-dollar fee to transport the body to the cemetery, as well as the price that Gray charged for the burial. At least four on the list were not buried at Yerba Buena: Italians Guisti and Grappa, a Mrs. Ward from Scotland, and Virgil Bennehan. William Newell was an undertaker as well as a sexton and received payments from the city for burial of indigents in an unspecified pauper's grave. Virgil Bennehan was most likely among the indigents.[29]

Virgil Bennehan had died a pauper in San Francisco. What an unwelcome end for a man who had traveled from bondage to manumission, from America to Africa and back, and finally from Baltimore to San Francisco, to seek better fortune in California. He'd been alert enough to give his name, age, and city of origin to the attending physician but perished without means or friends to pay for a coffin and burial in the public cemetery. Had he lost everything in "speculation" and then gotten sick? Had sickness come first and depleted his means? Paul Cameron's cryptic aside in 1856—"poor Virgil"—offered no answer.

There was another omission in William Newell's listing: *color*. It was customary for the sexton turning in the names, for the newspaper publishing the names and homeplaces of the dead, and for the undertaker listing those interred in the public cemetery to write "col" or "colored" if the deceased was a person of color. There was no "col" or "colored" after Virgil's name. That could have been an error, either by the physician who reported Virgil's death to William Newell or by the sexton in his haste to assemble the list that was late.

But the omission may have signified something else. Perhaps in the spectrum of persons and complexions in Little Chile, where there were Chileans, Mexicans, and Italians, as well as New Zealanders, Scots, and Americans, Virgil did not stand out as a "mulatto" man, as he would have in Maryland and North Carolina. There was yet another possibility—namely, that Virgil had chosen to exploit his light complexion as a man of mixed white and African American parentage to lighten the liabilities that went with a man of color in San Francisco. Virgil certainly would have learned that, in California as elsewhere, persons of color were at risk. Before Virgil arrived, and recurrently thereafter, there were white individuals who advocated banning Black people altogether from California, starting with the first territorial governor of the state. Exclusion failed, but other laws of the state were arrayed against emigrants of color, including the prohibition of Black testimony against a white person. It would be understandable had Virgil taken a loophole of lightness—and silence—to protect what means he had, or gains he might make, at least for the time he planned to stay in the West. Color would not have prevented his burial in the Yerba Buena cemetery; numbers of men of color were interred there. Poverty would have, and apparently did.[30]

When Virgil Bennehan died a pauper in the last week of November 1850, he was far from the only speculator to lose out or the only adventurer whom

Chilean sailor daguerreotype. The Chilean sailor who deserted ship in San Francisco likely settled in the Little Chile district of the city, where Virgil also dwelled. Others from South America and Mexico gravitated there, as did emigrants from Italy. If Virgil Bennehan decided to leave open the question of his "color," he could have blended in with those of many hues who lived in Little Chile. *Photograph by William Shew, 1850, courtesy of Stanley B. Burns, MD, and the Burns Archive, New York.*

illness stalked and felled. For many, 1850 had become the year that fortunes became failures, banks closed, the rich turned to bankruptcy, and the poor resorted to beggary. When seasonal rains started, those in Little Chile and elsewhere had to shelter in makeshift lodgings surrounded by contaminated water and mired in filth. When rains became incessant in November, conditions worsened still.[31] As illness afflicted so many around him, memories of Bassa Cove must have haunted Virgil, who thought he had left monsoons, poverty, and rampant death behind in Liberia, only to find himself at their mercy in California.

If William McLain and James Hall knew the story of Virgil Bennehan's travails in California, they might be forgiven for seeing grim irony in Virgil's fate. The critic who had damned Liberia as a place of poor people and poor land and starvation had become a pauper in gold rush California. The man who had survived lethal fever in Africa had perished of congestive fever in San Francisco. James Hall, who read the *Baltimore Sun* every day in his downtown office, would have seen Virgil as a victim who ignored the abundant warnings the city's newspaper had published. A man who thought too much of himself and overreached one time too many met the fate that hubris always brings—such might be the smug moral drawn by the colonizationist.

Yet one could look at Virgil's end, not as the inevitable destiny of an unmoored man, but as the will of chance. To return to the words of a fellow gold rush speculator, might a different outcome have validated his gamble on the "grand lottery" of California to transcend the confining certainties of his life in 1849?

It is easy for the historian to read about persons of color in either San Francisco or Baltimore and to conclude that there would be no escape from their burdens in either place. In the 1850s, Black people who survived in San Francisco and elsewhere in California settled into roles prescribed for men of color. At best, they became cooks and stewards. Others served as washermen in the mining areas, day laborers in the cities, or bootblacks at the lowest rung of occupations. An exception was Mifflin Gibbs of Buffalo, New York, who came as a carpenter, faced exclusion from the building trade by white people, and then found success in moving up from bootblack to partnership with a Black associate in the boot and shoe business. Gibbs believed that a man of enterprise, even if Black, could find a niche. That niche proved vulnerable to the law that barred persons of color from testifying against white people, which in Gibbs's case meant that when he was robbed and his partner beaten, they were helpless to prosecute the culprit. That experience, coupled with ongoing denial of civil and political rights and recurrent efforts in the legislature to ban more Black persons from entering California, ultimately led Gibbs and hundreds of others to exit the state for better chances—and citizenship—in gold rush Vancouver, Canada. Those who didn't leave with Gibbs in 1858 remained to cope with ongoing hostility.[32]

Similar forces were at work in Baltimore. In the 1850s, additional thousands of emigrants from Germany and Ireland poured into the city. They intensified their pressure to exclude Black workers from all the trades pursued by the neighbors of the Bennehans in Fells Point. As in California, a law forbidding Black testimony against white people was on the books in Maryland, though a handful of intrepid Black people found ways to get agreements enforced and minimal "rights" recognized. Proposals in the Maryland House of Delegates to further restrict Black people and to deport free Black people out of the state led some persons of color to despair about their future. They met in Baltimore in 1852, where minister Darius Stokes, a drayman in Baltimore and for a short time a minister in Sacramento, made the case for exodus to Liberia. Vociferously challenging him were free Black people who insisted that America was home, that they were born with the birthright of Americans, that they were due the rights of citizens. Opponents threatened the colonization supporters, shut down the meeting, and forced a remnant to reconvene elsewhere and to back off advocacy of Liberia.[33]

The accounts of Black people in San Francisco and Baltimore in the 1850s suggest that even had Virgil lived, his hope to escape the fate of a man of color and to change his destiny through good fortune and good earnings was doomed.

But all that is to downplay the plan that Virgil laid out in his short letter to Paul Cameron—namely, to settle his family in Baltimore, journey to California, and be there for two years. In Virgil's mind, and indeed in the mind of most who joined the adventurers, California was not a final destination but a way station—a way station where they hoped to do well enough, to make money enough, to alter the life course and trajectory they were on. Some did so, and perhaps they are the models of what Virgil hoped to achieve. In February 1850, the leading abolitionist newspaper of Boston, the *Liberator*, published a letter from California announcing the formation of a mutual relief society of free Black people in San Francisco. The letter was from a friend of a printer employed by the *Liberator*'s editor, William Lloyd Garrison. The society gave the names of thirty-seven men who had joined. Virgil's name was not among them. For at least two of those men, gold rush California did change their lives. Robert Forman was listed as a hackman in a Boston city directory when he left for California. Back in Boston, his occupation changed from hackman to owner of a livery business. Washington Rideout gave his occupation as laborer in the Pittsburgh city directory at the end of the 1840s. After his return from California, his occupations fluctuated from the mundane to the exotic, but the value of his real estate property soared to $20,000. The two easterners appeared to have hit paydirt in California and returned home different men, elevated above their previous and preordained place and station.[34]

Exceptions? Of course. Virgil was an exception at birth, an exception on the plantation, an exception in Liberia. Can one fault him for hoping that he could use two years in California—if of good fortune—to reclaim in a new form the elevation he had known? This time, on his own?

———————————————————————

As word got back to Baltimore, and then to North Carolina, of Virgil's death in California, there were doubtless regrets and second thoughts all around.

His demise left his wife, Phoebe, a widow living in the Fells Point ward of Baltimore, with enough means to continue without work for another year but obliged to labor as a laundress for the next dozen years. As did many persons of color, she left the waterfront area of Fells Point, moving in 1852 to a different part of the city where her employment chances improved. She fell ill but had her niece and nephew and friends to support her, felt sustained by prayer, and found a capable physician to see her back to health. The return of health did not bring a return of equanimity. Her deepest affection was for the still-enslaved Anna, who lived in Raleigh and had become the servant of Duncan Cameron's invalid daughter, Mildred. Having reared her young niece until leaving for Liberia, Phoebe regarded Anna as her adopted daughter, wrote her letters from Baltimore in the 1850s, and signed those letters as "Your Mother." Compounding widowhood and its consequences was the heartbreak of getting no replies from Anna, possibly because the Camerons intercepted the letters or prohibited the correspondence. Silence left Phoebe, abandoned by the departure and then the death of Virgil, feeling as if her daughter, too, had forsaken her.[35] Only with Emancipation were Phoebe and Anna—now called Annie—able to resume contact and, with contact and with Annie's marriage, to arrange for Phoebe to return to North Carolina. There, from the 1870s until her death in 1900, she lived out her life. United in Raleigh with her beloved Anna and other nieces and nephews, she was buried in the city's Mount Hope Cemetery for persons of color, with a handsomely engraved tombstone that her family inscribed:

OUR AUNT

PHOEBE BENNEHAN

BORN

May 10, 1808

DIED

Apr. 22, 1900[36]

Paul Cameron likely got word through Phoebe Bennehan's letters to Anna that Virgil had died in San Francisco. In person surely, but never in a letter, did he elaborate on the regret he felt at the death of his "old friend Virgil." The closest he came was as an aside in the letter of February 1856 about the death of the sister of William Bennehan, who went off with "poor Virgil."

Frederick Douglass, had he learned of Virgil's story, likely would have been of two minds about his gamble, as he was about the decision of other free Black people who ventured to California. Yes, Virgil had chosen to leave his wife and family, to leave certainty for uncertainty, for the dubious prospect of winning wealth in the gold rush. In 1849, Douglass thought little of that choice. But Frederick Douglass also came to understand the longing of those who hoped that money could surmount color. Those who succeeded would offer at least one boon for all persons of color. Success would showcase Black people who transcended constraints, who could and did become better off than the many of talent confined to menial tasks or, at best, to be barbers of brilliance, obliged to work with white patrons whose fad for growing beards was curbing what business they did have. By 1852, a more open-minded Douglass, though continuing to see the speculators as choosing "the certainty of uncertainty," more accurately grasped the transcendence that persons such as Virgil Bennehan sought in California.

Might luck and better timing, what one adventurer referred to as the "will of chance" in California's "grand lottery," have altered Virgil Bennehan's fate? Perhaps. Yet no amount of luck, good or bad, should be allowed to obscure the larger reality of Virgil's life story—that, enslaved or freed, a fettered destiny bound most persons of color in antebellum America.

EPILOGUE

Outcasts

Virgil Bennehan's life was cut short at the age of forty-one. What might he have encountered had he lived longer?

If he had continued in California for another year and a half, he might well have been asked to join the 293 persons of color who signed a petition in March 1852 to protest—"in the name of republicanism and humanity"—the state law that barred their testimony against white persons, allowing the "vicious and unprincipled" to "prey upon their rights with impunity" and denying them protection of life, liberty, and property. If he had persisted in California for another decade, he would have had to decide whether to ally himself with 242 persons of color who on January 16, 1862, asked Congress to provide "means for their colonization to some country in which their color will not be a badge of degradation." Would he reluctantly have agreed with them—and with President Abraham Lincoln seven months later—that Haiti, Central or South America, and even Liberia were preferable to the United States, where they were "marked out by law and public sentiment as an inferior and degraded caste"?[1]

Had he lived, Virgil could have sought out what happened to the two midwestern men of color who had come on his voyage in April 1848 to scout the prospects for achieving authentic freedom in Liberia. He would

Fleetwood Walker and baseball team. Moses Fleetwood Walker (*center, top row*) was the son of Moses W. Walker, who went to Liberia in 1848 and returned to encourage others to go there. Despite a plan to migrate with his family, at the last minute he stayed. In 1884, his son, Fleet Walker, became the first African American to play a season of Major League Baseball. His team was the Toledo Blue Stockings. *Courtesy of Matteo Omied / Alamy Stock Photo.*

have learned that Samuel Ball of Illinois, who came home in August 1848 to declare Liberia the worst country for a poor man, nonetheless took up the banner of emigration and Liberia immediately after the Fugitive Slave Law of 1850 placed persons of color everywhere at the mercy of kidnappers and reenslavement.[2] Had he lived still longer, what might Virgil Bennehan have thought about the legacy of his other free Black shipmate, Moses Walker of Ohio, the zealous convert in 1848 from abolitionism to colonization? Likely Virgil would have recognized a familiar trajectory in the fate of Moses Walker's son, an arc which mirrored that of the father, and which echoed Virgil's own life course from exception to outcast.

In 1884, Moses Walker's son—twenty-six-year-old Oberlin alumnus Moses Fleetwood Walker—became the first African American to play a full season of Major League Baseball, a breakthrough not duplicated for another sixty-three years.

After a stint as a catcher for the Toledo Blue Stockings, and then as a player for other teams, Fleet Walker was harassed and finally ostracized out of the major leagues and out of baseball altogether by managers and players who refused to take the field with a man of color. A checkered career

Epilogue

Our Home Colony

A Treatise on The Past, Present and Future of the Negro Race in America

"Ergo Agite, et, Divum ducunt qua jussa, sequamur"--Virgil

By M. F. Walker

THE HERALD PRINTING CO.
Steubenville, O.

Our Home Colony. Ostracism, discrimination, lynchings, and what he saw as betrayal by fair-weather white allies brought Fleet Walker and his brother William Wilberforce "Weldy" Walker to the same conclusion that their father had reached in 1848. Black people in white America, despite nominal freedom, were forever doomed to be subjects and "scullions." In 1908, he wrote and published a forty-eight-page pamphlet calling for Black emigration to the only country in the world where Black people governed and where persons of color could be truly free. Liberia and only Liberia was *Our Home Colony.* *Library of Congress, Washington, DC.*

afterward, and the rise of lynching and exclusion in Ohio, led Fleet Walker to take up the cause of protest against the racist tide resurgent in the state, to no avail. Exasperation with politics and protest—the abolitionism of his day— brought Fleet Walker to the same conclusion that his father had reached in 1848 and that the California petitioners reiterated in 1862. In America, persons of color were and would always be a subjugated "class of aliens." In 1908, a hundred years after Virgil's birth, Moses Fleetwood Walker became an outspoken advocate of emigration. Liberia, and Liberia alone, was *Our Home Colony*. He prefaced his forty-seven-page call for a Black Exodus with a Latin quotation: "Ergo Agite, et, Divum ducunt qua jussa, sequamur" (Come now, let us follow where the Gods command).[3]

The summons was from Virgil's *Aeneid*.

Without at all agreeing with the California petitioners of 1862 or with Fleet Walker in 1908 that Liberia was a panacea—"magic," to use parent Moses Walker's term—Virgil Bennehan surely would have understood the certainties that drove them and others to seek a genuinely open territory for persons of color, whatever the uncertainties ahead.

———————————————

Among the thousands given special roles in bondage, Virgil Bennehan rose to unusual heights and attainments, only to learn the fragility of privilege. Manumitted in return for his service and fidelity, he encountered what one historian has called the "tragic nature of Black freedom in the era of slavery"—the fleeting promise, the steep price, and the harsh limits of liberation. Virgil Bennehan's odyssey illustrates extremes of what was possible and finally not possible for an enslaved and then freed man of color in the antebellum South—and for generations to follow.

ACKNOWLEDGMENTS

It is a pleasure to thank many persons who helped bring this book to fruition.

For almost forty years, I have benefited from the foundational work of Jean Bradley Anderson, whose book *Piedmont Plantation* (1985) remains the most careful, detailed, and balanced study of the white and Black people of the Bennehan-Cameron plantation of North Carolina. Time and again, it has proved a source of insight and information that keeps on giving. For even longer, I have repeatedly turned for inspiration to Herbert Gutman's book *The Black Family in Slavery and Freedom* to draw on the ingenuity and passion with which he ferreted out the story of Black families from hitherto underused lists and letters, in the Cameron archives and others. For almost a half century, I have returned to the Southern Historical Collection at the University of North Carolina at Chapel Hill to anchor my work in the 30,000 letters and documents of the Bennehan-Cameron papers. Archivists Carolyn Wallace, Richard Shrader, Tim West, Matt Turi, and their associates proved unfailingly helpful and unendingly patient with my reams of requests over those years.

Sheer tenacity fueled me to persist through years of research and writing that concluded with the first two books that came out of my projects on African Americans on the Cameron place. When I faltered, the model and support of John Blassingame, Peter Wood, Bill Chafe, Raymond Gavins, Bill Price, George McDaniel, and Ira Berlin helped me keep the faith. Cherished friends and Duke colleagues Peter Wood and Bill Chafe played a special generative role for me, as they have for generations of graduate students at Duke who have gone on to do landmark work in African American, Native American, and civil rights history. All helped me to stay the course.

For Virgil Bennehan's story, it took the guidance of others to stay *on* course. Partly the challenge was one of sources. Of the 30,000 letters in the Cameron Family Papers—which felt like 90,000 letters since I'd been through the collection so many times—only 3 were composed by Virgil, and, of those, 2 were medical reports. Drift into untethered netherworlds of guesses and possibilities led to zigzags of direction and multiple flights of interpretation. The greater challenge was temperament: mine. As my Duke colleague Larry Goodwyn once pointed out to me, I gravitated to stories that ended in triumph—escaped bondwoman Mary Walker recovered two of the children she left behind, as recounted in my book *To Free a Family*; forced migrant Paul Hargress wound up owning Alabama land he bought from his former enslaver, told in *A Mind to Stay*. As Goodwyn viewed history, many if not most stories ended more tragically. Could I allow myself to see and tell Virgil's story with tragic limitation as an undercurrent and perhaps as its ultimate outcome?

The help I needed for this book—to stay the course and to stay *on* course—I received from colleagues and friends, old and new. From Bill Chafe, my Duke comrade of fifty years, I received a one-sentence assessment. Wasn't Virgil's story "the exception that proved the rule"? I made that a central question, to test against the evidence. From longtime friend and fellow historian Steve Channing, who had initial doubts about my pursuing the project, I received belated encouragement. Virgil's was an account of slavery's complexity, worth telling. From historian Leo Spitzer, I drew on his empathetic account of two other men of color whose *Lives in Between* shifted from enslavement to flawed emancipation to unsettling denouements. Richard Dunn forcefully countered my centrifugal impulse to expand the story to embrace others on the margins of Virgil's life: keep the focus on *Virgil*. When I finished a draft, I turned to a gifted younger scholar for his candid opinion, Damian Pargas of Leiden University. Author of *Freedom Seekers* and editor of *Studies in Global Slavery*, it was Pargas who discerned "the red thread" of "this story as a tragedy"—expectations built high in bondage that proved fragile, liberation that ended in exile and immiseration.

This book builds on research carried out over decades, but in what was lightning speed for me, the writing of this one took a mere six years. Uncertain bearings marked much of that time, and with uncertainty came bouts of doubt. Dear friends steadied me. It's been a blessing to have Harold and Susan Skramstad as soulmates here in Denver, who radiate joy with their presence and offered wise reassurance when needed. Deedee Decker has ever been a generous friend; before Peter Decker died, he never failed to ask me what I was reading and always feigned tolerance when I replied I was still and exclusively *writing*. My former Duke student and longtime University of Colorado professor John Stevenson has always lifted my spirit at our lunches in Boulder with his wit, brilliance, and undiminished effervescence. Dennis Grogan, Tina Proctor, and the Conscious Aging group of friends whom they convene monthly have modeled the richness there is to life besides a Project. Wendell and Janine Pryor inspire with their boundless generosity and their unselfish engagement on behalf of others. Mary Wolff and Linda Cowan, whose family archive opened the Mary Walker story, have remained fonts of grace and good cheer for thirty years. For each of my books, I've been fortunate to find a therapist to help see me through. For this book, David Chernikoff consummately stepped up to that role, with paradoxical good advice: I needed to *complete* this book; I needed to envision life *beyond work*. Two cousins stepped into the breach at timely moments. Tom Spiro gave three cheers for literary speculation and urged fearlessness over timidity. Ben Nathans, himself a historian, responded with appreciation whenever I talked about the project.

I tried to honor the good advice that I received by following it whenever I could. The book's flaws of understanding or interpretation are mine alone.

I thought the best match for the Virgil Bennehan story would be the University of North Carolina Press, and editor Debbie Gershenowitz agreed. She sent the manuscript to two excellent anonymous readers, who offered enthusiastic responses and made welcome suggestions for improvement. At the press, JessieAnne D'Amico fielded my ceaseless questions with grace and good counsel, exhibiting patience beyond measure for the techno-troglodyte that I am. Vera Cecelski, site manager of Historic Stagville, received fewer queries but provided crucial answers. I have watched with great admiration her extraordinary widening of Stagville's outreach to its descendant families and to the community. My guides at Mike's Camera in Denver—Duane, Isaac, and Rebecca—skillfully provided the technical assistance needed to produce the fine images that enhance the book. For maps, I once again turned to Philip Schwartzberg, who had created maps for my two previous books. Once again, he did beautiful work. I'm grateful to author Lisa Lindsay, her mapmaker Meghan Cohorst, and to publisher Scott Sipe, whose books provided guidance for Phil's rendition of Liberian settlements in 1848, and to Stephen Cruse, whose adaptation in 1985 of a map of Paul Cameron's landholdings from 1890 offered the framework for Phil's rendering of the Bennehan-Cameron lands in 1845. I was fortunate to have Laura Dooley as the manuscript's exceptionally skillful and meticulous copyeditor and Valerie Burton as the project editor to guide the manuscript smoothly to publication.

It takes a family to nurture an author and, in my case, sometimes simply to endure a writer as self-absorbed as I have been. My children, Heather Nathans and Steve Nathans-Kelly, were under ten when I began work on what turned out to be a trilogy of tales. Then and for decades since, their good humor and generosity have buoyed me always and blessed their families and friends far and wide. Gifted writers, capacious in the fields they command, Heather and Steve have made their own contributions to understanding our history. I am grateful for the joy they've brought to me and for the creativity they share with all.

Judith White has been with me for thirty-five years and through the creation of three books. Early on, a friend alerted her that with historians, "where there is life, there is research." Undaunted, Judith has always been there for me and graciously shared our lives with numerous persons reanimated from the past and, by good fortune, with some of their wonderful descendants in the present. For this book as for all, Judith read every word that I kept and with her counsel, many more that I mercifully discarded. Her love has sustained me, and the bounty of her spirit has enriched our lives and elevates the lives of all who know her. When Judith and I wed, a wise family member said to me, "You're a lucky boy." So I have been, and so I am.

NOTES

ABBREVIATIONS

ACS   American Colonization Society Records, 1792–1964, microfilm,
        Manuscript Division, Library of Congress, Washington, DC
CFP   Cameron Family Papers, 1757–1978, Southern Historical
        Collection, Wilson Library Special Collections,
        University of North Carolina at Chapel Hill

CHAPTER 1

1. Anderson, *Piedmont Plantation*, 5.

2. "Bennehan-Cameron Slave Families and Generations, Orange County, North Carolina, 1777–1842," table 24 in Gutman, *Black Family*, 172–74. Mary had two more sons, Albert, born 1812, and Solomon, born 1815. Solomon was also named after a brother, who died earlier in 1815. Gutman, *Black Family*, 173–75.

3. Jones, *Fathers of Conscience*. Numerous biographies and books chronicle the special treatment or manumission of the children of slave owners. Among them are Drew Faust's biography of *James Henry Hammond*, Henry Wienceck's book on *The Hairstons*, and Annette Gordon-Reed's account of *The Hemingses of Monticello*.

4. Nathans, *To Free a Family*, 12–13.

5. Thomas Gale Amis to Thomas D. Bennehan, February 9, 1797, February 22, 1807, CFP.

6. On Amis's abrupt departure from the Bennehan household, see Anderson, *Piedmont Plantation*, 14–15. T. G. Amis to Thomas Bennehan, January 4, April 8, 1803 (Guadeloupe), September 12, 22, 1805, CFP. Thomas G. Amis letters from the Caribbean can also be found under "Amis" in the Undated Correspondences of the Cameron Family Papers. For the French decree of 1803 reestablishing slavery in Guadeloupe, the rebel resistance by fire, and

the "murderous" French military repression and reprisal, see Scott and Hébrard, "Rosalie of the Poulard Nation," 255–57.

7. Scott, *Common Wind*, 83. In 1786, a British abolitionist reported that mounting opposition to slavery and the slave trade had divided families in Liverpool, a city with numerous merchants enriched by the trade. The "struggle between interest and humanity has made great havoc in the happiness of many families."

8. Rebecca Bennehan Cameron to Duncan Cameron, April 26, 1815, and Duncan Cameron to Rebecca Cameron, April 27, 1815, CFP. To his wife, Cameron responded that he deplored "the continuing disease among our negroes. I participate in your sympathy for the distress of your Brother on the occasion. Knowing the particular frame of his mind, I can readily conjecture what his own sufferings are, amid so much sickness."

9. Anderson, *Piedmont Plantation*, 15. For Thomas Bennehan's self-assessment of his "constitutional coldness," see Bennehan to Mary Ann Cameron, February 5, 1821, CFP. Bennehan's wary view of marriage came to the fore in response to a "wedding" invitation from Shadrach, one of his enslaved men. He agreed to attend the ceremony, but in a sardonic note wrote, "Tomorrow is to make Shadrach (as he supposes) one of the happiest of men. To give him a good relish for matrimony, I shall heat him over the [hog] scalding tub until near 12 o'clock," the time appointed for the wedding and feast. Thomas Bennehan to Duncan Cameron, December 14, 1808, CFP.

10. H. V. Pride to Thomas Bennehan, May 15, June 26, [no year], Undated Papers, folder 1890, CFP.

11. My calculations are based on the land acquisitions made by Richard and Thomas Bennehan between 1776 and 1825. The acquisitions and acreage of each are itemized in Anderson, *Piedmont Plantation*, 146–49, appendix A, "Lands of Richard and Thomas D. Bennehan." Most lands purchased were identified in deeds as located on the sides of rivers and creeks—namely, the Flat River, Eno River, and Little River, and Reeds and Panther Creek. The first mill, purchased in 1806, was situated on the Eno River.

12. For the origin of the term "malaria" and a description of its symptoms, see Webb, *Humanity's Burden*, 1–6, 90–95. For the description of extreme symptoms, see Paul Cameron to Duncan Cameron, July 17, 1848, CFP.

13. Thomas Bennehan to Richard Bennehan, [n.d.], 1803, and Thomas Bennehan to Duncan Cameron, December 14, 1808, CFP.

14. Rebecca Bennehan Cameron to Thomas Bennehan, March 4, 1809, and Richard Bennehan to Thomas Bennehan, July 28, 1809, CFP.

15. Richard Bennehan to Thomas Bennehan, August 11, 1814, and Rebecca Cameron to Duncan Cameron, May 3, 1815, CFP. Joseph Skinner to Thomas Bennehan, November 16, 1825, and Dr. Thomas N. Cameron to Duncan Cameron, February 15, 1826, CFP, cited in Anderson, *Piedmont Plantation*, 106–7. To the assessment of Bennehan's contemporaries, Jean Anderson adds an observation made decades later by Paul Cameron to his son Bennehan Cameron, acknowledging the harm done by the damming of water required to operate the mill dams. Writing in 1889, he urged the son to make no repairs on damaged mill dams. Paul Cameron was "'fairly convinced it would [be] a hard sum to work to say to what extent the Mill pond water poisoned the land & shortened the product & destroyed the health of the neighborhood. The Harris Hill and Little River Grave yard [slave graveyards] can make the

best response.'" Paul Cameron to Bennehan Cameron, August 22, 1889, cited in Anderson, *Piedmont Plantation*, 107.

16. Rebecca Cameron to Duncan Cameron, April 26, May 3, 1815, CFP.

17. Humphreys, *Malaria*, 6, 9–11, 24–29, 36, 39. Both James Webb and Margaret Humphreys note the role of swamps, wetlands, deforestation, vegetable debris on shorelines, and stagnant water in breeding mosquitoes. Webb, *Humanity's Burden*, 86–87; Humphreys, *Malaria*, 10, 23.

18. Nathans, *Mind to Stay*, 31.

19. Duncan Cameron to Rebecca Cameron, April 27, May 3, 1815, CFP.

20. Thomas Ruffin to Duncan Cameron, September 4, 1830, CFP.

21. The Pork List for Stagville, Little River, Mill, Fish Dam, Peaksville, with the quantities enumerated and added up, was made out by Virgil and in his handwriting. Bennehan Quarters Pork List, January 1, 1831, CFP. For the compliment on Virgil's "propriety" as a house servant, see Anderson, *Piedmont Plantation*, 103. The letter is from [Joseph Skinner] to Thomas Bennehan, October 5, 1841, CFP.

22. For Virgil as a courier between the plantations, Hillsborough, and Raleigh, see [Samuel?] Kollock to Duncan Cameron, November 5, 1828, and Duncan Cameron to Paul Cameron, June 5, 1831, CFP.

23. In a note to his father in April 1848, Paul Cameron summed up Virgil's first request for remembrance. "I had a letter from Virgil, by the mail of last Friday. . . . [Virgil] desired me to tender [an] affectionate 'farewell to all his friends,' naming you and my sisters especially." Paul Cameron to Duncan Cameron, April 19, 1848, CFP. A month later, Virgil requested a wish for remembrance to fourteen specific friends and asked for greetings to "a hundred more I could name." Virgil Bennehan to Paul Cameron, May 29, 1848, CFP. See chapter 5.

24. Mary's year of death is given in Gutman, *Black Family*, table 24, 173. To determine Phillip Meaks's age when his daughter Mary died, I worked backward from the information on his grave marker in the Little River Cemetery, where the tombstone listed his full name as Phillip Meaks, specified his date of death as June 22, 1837, and gave his age at death as seventy-four. Inventory of grave markers at the Little River Cemetery (for enslaved persons) compiled by Jean Anderson, *Piedmont Planation*, appendix D, 175.

25. See the signature on the original manuscript of the letter from Virgil P. M. Bennehan to Paul Cameron, May 29, 1848. CFP. Difficulty in deciphering Virgil's handwriting led to an error in the transcription of the signature in the published version of this letter in Wiley, *Slaves No More*, 261. Editor Bell I. Wiley transcribed the signature as "Virgil P. McPharrhan [Bennehan?']." The Cameron papers contain two earlier letters written by Virgil, both written while he was still enslaved, and both signed with his first name only.

26. About to go off to fight in Cumberland County near Moore's Creek, Richard Bennehan wrote to the clerk at his store that "'it is said that negroes have some thoughts of Freedom. Pray make Scrub sleep in the house every night & that the overseer keep in Tom.'" Richard Bennehan to James Martin, February 15, 1776, CFP. The "notions of freedom" detected by Richard Bennehan in 1776 were also discerned that same year by planters in Jamaica, as France and England contested for control of islands in the Caribbean. See Scott, *Common Wind*, 80–81. Reported a white Jamaican in 1776: "'Dear Liberty has run in the heart of every House-bred slave, in one form or other, for these ten years past.'" They "'went no farther than

their private reflections upon us and it; but as soon as we came to blows, we find them fast on our heels. Such has been the seeds sown in the mind of our Domestics by our Wise-Acre Patriots.'"

27. Two reward notices for "Scrub" are included in an invaluable book of reprinted runaway advertisements compiled by historian Freddie L. Parker in *Running for Freedom*. I found and accessed one of Richard Bennehan's two advertisements for "Scrub" in the Digital Library on American Slavery, North Carolina Runaway Slave Notices, 1765–1865. I quote from the notice in the New Bern *North-Carolina Gazette*, September 2, 1784. Scrub ran away on May 15, 1784. Owner "Richard Benneham [*sic*]" stated that he believed that "Scrub" would go by his full name, which Bennehan gave as Charles Thomas or Charles Fry, and would attempt to get to Norfolk, Virginia, where he was raised. He gave Scrub's age as twenty-five. Bennehan added that "as he has great notions of freedom," he very probably "will try to make his escape by sea." A subsequent tip that Scrub was in Norfolk led Thomas Amis, an in-law of Richard Bennehan, to travel to Norfolk and Petersburg in search of him, with no results. Thomas Amis to Richard Bennehan, December 20, 1784, March 12, 1785, CFP. Amis reported in March that he "made every possible inquiry after Scrub, but could not get the least intelligence of him."

28. The runaway advertisement for "Scrub" noted that, among many roles, he had groomed Bennehan's horses. For Phil as a caretaker of horses and riding equipment, see Thomas Bennehan to Duncan Cameron, April 28, 1806, and Anne Ruffin Cameron to Duncan Cameron, May 7, 1835, CFP. For Phil's expertise as a person who produced "blacking" to keep leather supple and polished, I consulted a ledger that Richard Bennehan kept for purchases, payments, and credit exchanges at his mercantile store at Stagville. Between 1807 and 1812, he opened the store for purchases by enslaved persons belonging to Bennehan and Cameron, as well as to a handful of outside bondmen. Most of those purchases were made by men working overtime to clear land for the construction of Duncan Cameron's new plantation dwelling. The men paid in cords of wood (a cord of wood was eight feet long, four feet wide, and four feet deep) and received credit to buy whiskey, calico cloth, Dutch ovens, and hats. Nathans, *To Free a Family*, 16. Between June 1808 and July 1812, Phillip Meaks got credit for blacking that he "sold" to the store and traded his credits for whiskey, chocolates, needles, and shoes for his daughter Mary. He also traded with others in the enslaved community. See the entries for "Phill" in the Bennehan Store Ledger, vol. 73, CFP.

29. Richard Bennehan to Thomas Bennehan, July 30, 1796, CFP.

30. Nathans, *To Free a Family*, 13.

31. Thomas Bennehan paid down the accumulated debt of Phillip Meaks (L.0.10.0) on January 7, 1809. Bennehan Store Ledger, vol. 73, p. 31, CFP.

32. Joseph B. Skinner to Thomas Bennehan, November 16, 1825. Joseph Skinner, a close friend of Thomas Bennehan who lived in Edenton, North Carolina, had received "melancholy tidings" of the death of "Phillip," likely from someone else. The Phillip who died in 1825 was actually Phillip Meaks's twenty-four-year-old son. Gutman, *Black Family*, table 24, 173.

33. Phil and Esther had seven children. All but Jamima died between 1796 and 1825. Virgil (1791–96), Mary (1793–1816), John (1794–1823), Solomon (1796–1815), Nathan (1799–1826), and Phillip (1801–25). While she lived, daughter Mary gave birth to Virgil, Albert, and Solomon. While her father, Phillip, was alive, Jamima (b. 1801) gave birth to Mary, John, Anna,

Mariah, and Rebecca; she bore Jane and Margaret after Phillip's death. Gutman, *Black Family*, table 24, 173–75.

34. Hunter, *Bound in Wedlock*, 4, 50–51, 71. Examining the records of the Rose Hall plantation in Jamaica, with its plethora of children designated as "mulatto" and "quadroon," historian Celia Naylor demonstrates that at Rose Hall "the sexual violation of enslaved girls and women was one of the deeply embedded tenets of chattel slavery." She cites seventeen additional books to argue that the same prerogative held "throughout Jamaica and the Americas." Naylor, *Unsilencing Slavery*, 67–69, 201n118, 201n121. At the same time, she notes that the archives of Rose Hill and almost all other plantations are entirely silent on the intimate lives of enslaved women and their responses to coerced sex. Following scholars Saidiya Hartman and Marisa Fuentes, she endeavors to overcome pervasive archival silence by seeking to "'imagine what cannot be verified.'" Naylor, *Unsilencing Slavery*, 12–14. Envisioning ways in which nineteenth-century enslaved women coped with the "entrapment of White power" and the "inevitability of men's conquests," religious studies professor Alexis Wells-Oghoghomeh proposes that some defaulted to an "ethics of acquiescence," hoping to survive themselves and perhaps to gain a better life for their children. Wells-Oghoghomeh, *Souls of Womenfolk*, 84–89. She suggests that, for their part, men "endured the sense of powerlessness that accompanied the sexual assault of their daughters, partners, sisters," and others by "disremembering." They pursued silence and "'calculated erasure'" to "weather the assaults on their psychological and social stability." Wells-Oghoghomeh, *Souls of Womenfolk*, 113. Historian Jennifer Morgan found more painful options for seventeenth- and eighteenth-century enslaved women. First captives and rape victims on slave ships and then sold into brutal bondage on Caribbean sugar plantations, some chose abortion, infanticide, or suicide; some experienced madness; some undertook sabotage. Morgan, *Reckoning with Slavery*, 15, 110–11, 162, 220–28, 245–46, 253–54.

35. Anderson, *Piedmont Plantation*, appendix D. On p. 172, Jean Anderson provides the inscription for Richard Bennehan's tombstone at the Stagville Cemetery. On p. 175, she records the inscriptions on the grave marker for Letty and on the tombstone for Phillip Meaks, both at the Little River Cemetery. Kenneth McFarland, site manager at Stagville in the late 1970s and early 1980s, took a photograph of the Phillip Meaks tombstone, which Jean Anderson reproduced on p. vi of the insert of photographs in *Piedmont Plantation*.

CHAPTER 2

1. For an example of Paul Cameron's use of "we" to describe the medical care that he and Virgil provided, see Paul Cameron to Duncan Cameron, November 8, 1847, CFP.

2. Thomas Bennehan to Paul Cameron, August 27, 1845, CFP.

3. For Duncan Cameron's marriage and the building of Fairntosh, see Anderson, *Piedmont Plantation*, 27–29; for Duncan Cameron's cycles of breakdown and recovery until he relinquished plantation management, see Nathans, *To Free a Family*, 18–20; and Anderson, *Kirklands of Ayr Mount*, 122–24.

4. William Haywood to Duncan Cameron, March 19, 1821, CFP.

5. William Haywood to Duncan Cameron, April 20, 1821, CFP.

6. Anderson, *Piedmont Plantation*, 44–46.

7. William Anderson to Duncan Cameron, December 20, 1825, CFP. Duncan Cameron fully endorsed disciplining Paul for the breach of Partridge Military Academy regulations and for helping to curb "the impetuosity of his ill-governed passions." Reassuring Captain Alden Partridge, Cameron wrote, "I have always practiced discipline and enforced it." Correcting Paul's faults would make him a "respectable and useful member of society." You are "a Benefactor of my son." Duncan Cameron to Alden Partridge, November 16, 1825, Alden Partridge Papers, Norwich University Archives and Special Collections, Northfield, VT.

8. Paul Cameron to Mary Ann Cameron, January 5, April 11, 1826, and Alden Partridge to Duncan Cameron, May 14, 1826, CFP.

9. See, for example, the episode involving the man named Jim, who defied and got beaten by an overseer. Paul blamed the overseer for the brutal beating but conceded that Jim was an "ungovernable slave." Nathans, *Mind to Stay*, 29.

10. Nathans, *To Free a Family*, 81.

11. In 1846, Cameron lamented the death of "our faithful old friend Aunt Easter," the elderly enslaved woman who for ten years had looked after Fairntosh when the Camerons were away. On their return they never found the first article out of place. With little direction from the Camerons, "she has acted well the part." Paul Cameron to Duncan Cameron, October 28, 1846, CFP.

12. Paul Cameron to Anne Ruffin, February 17, 1832, CFP.

13. Nathans, *Mind to Stay*, 26–27.

14. Thomas Bennehan to Duncan Cameron, August 23, 1830, and Rebecca Cameron to Duncan Cameron, January 12, 1831, CFP.

15. Thomas Bennehan, Deed of Person County Land to Paul Cameron, January 1, 1831, CFP.

16. See Anderson, *Piedmont Plantation*, appendix B, "Slaves Acquired by Purchase or Gift," 165. Her name was given as Ferrabee (Phoebe) in the list of those acquired. Her sisters Nelly and Dicey and her niece Margaret and nephew William were included in the group of fourteen acquired for $3,150.

17. Phoebe and her sister Nelly were among the enslaved persons purchased by Thomas Bennehan from Dr. John Umstead. After the purchase, Nelly became the mate of David Bell, who was owned by Duncan Cameron. Nelly gave birth to their child in 1834. They named her Anna; Cameron records listed her as Annie. Annie married William H. Davis after emancipation. After Annie Belle Davis died in Raleigh on June 25, 1918, the North Carolina Death Certificate gave her father's name as David Bell and her mother's unmarried name as Nelly Meeks. I accessed the death certificate on Ancestry.com.

18. Anna was born in 1834, the child of Nelly and David. See the list of Children Born at Stagville [1834–42]. In the death certificate for Annie Belle Davis, her date of birth is given as October 1836. The date is in error. Her mother, Nelly, was reported as mortally ill in mid-May 1836 and died on June 28, 1836. Anne Cameron to Paul Cameron, May 14, 1836, and Paul Cameron to Thomas Bennehan, June 28, 1836, CFP. The hand-inscribed stone marker for Nelly at the Little River Cemetery is marked "d. 1836." But the age given for her—sixty-nine years—is incorrect. For the grave marker for Nelly, see Anderson, *Piedmont Plantation*, appendix D, "Little River Cemetery," 175.

19. Phoebe Bennehan to Anna Bell, March 16, 1852, CFP. Phoebe Bennehan addressed the letter to Anna Bell, care of Judge Cameron in Raleigh, NC. On slave lists and in letters written before 1865, the Camerons referred to the niece as Anne or Annie; after emancipation, in US Censuses and in property documents, Phoebe's niece gave her name as Annie. Paul Cameron to Virgil Bennehan, August 8, 1848, CFP.

20. Nathans, *Mind to Stay*, 28.

21. Paul Cameron to Thomas Bennehan, January 27, March 23, 1836, and Paul Cameron to Duncan Cameron, January 25, 1836, CFP.

22. Thomas Bennehan to Paul Cameron, April 5, 1836, CFP. The uncle noted that three of his elderly workers were doing poorly and needed his attention: Old Man Phillip, old man Lewis, and Ephraim.

23. Anderson, *Piedmont Plantation*, 50; Nathans, *Mind to Stay*, 32.

24. Virgil to Thomas Bennehan, September 3, 1839; Thomas Bennehan to Paul Cameron, January 14, 1841, CFP.

25. Paul Cameron to Mary Anne Cameron, January 5, 1825, CFP.

26. Paul Cameron to Duncan Cameron, May 6, August 19, August 21, November 9, 1847, CFP.

27. For Virgil's role as the main administrator of blistering, see Paul Cameron to Duncan Cameron, October 16, 1845, March 25, April 1, 1847, CFP.

28. Near the end of 1848, two Fairntosh overseers—Samuel Harris and William Harris—declared their intention to leave because of pervasive illness that sickened them and their families. Paul Cameron to Duncan Cameron, November 9, 1848, CFP.

CHAPTER 3

1. Nathans, *To Free a Family*, 21–22.

2. Thomas Bennehan was healthy and in Raleigh in mid-January 1841. Thomas Bennehan to Paul Cameron, January 14, 1841, CFP. The bequest to his sister is in the Will of Thomas D. Bennehan, February 10, 1841, CFP.

3. Will of Thomas D. Bennehan, February 10, 1841, CFP.

4. Virgil to My Dear Master, September 3, 1839, June 7, 1845, CFP.

5. Thomas Amis Jr.'s *Will*, dated October 7, 1796, left all his property real and personal to his niece, Rebecca Bennehan, and made no mention of Gracie and Harry. On November 12, 1797, thirteen months later, he wrote a *Codicil* to the will in which he left Gracie and Harry in the custody of his "friend and partner" in business, Jesse Rhymes, "requesting that he will on his part embrace the first opportunity to obtain their liberation whenever the same shall be allowed by Law." Amis provided that Gracie should receive $100 when liberated. The will of 1796 can be found in folder 2175 of the Cameron Family Papers. I accessed the will and the codicil in the digitized wills of Halifax County, NC. Thomas Amis Jr. died in December 1799. Ebenezer Stott to Rebecca Bennehan, December 7, 1799, CFP. For the context and discreet language of other slave owners who bequeathed freedom and an inheritance to their enslaved offspring, see Jones, *Fathers of Conscience*.

6. Paul Cameron to Duncan Cameron, June 21, 1848, CFP.

7. Nathans, *Mind to Stay*, 55–60.

8. Anderson, *Piedmont Plantation*, appendix B, "Slaves Acquired by Purchase or Gift," 163. While living, John Umstead sold twenty-seven persons to Thomas Bennehan in 1822. He arranged for sale of the rest in his will; executors sold them to Bennehan after the doctor's death late in 1828. Fourteen were sold in 1829, eight in 1831. Anderson, *Piedmont Plantation*, appendix B, 163.

9. Will of John Umstead, [1828], probated January 23, 1829. I found the Umstead will in the digitized wills of Orange County, NC.

10. Franklin, *Free Negro*, 27n60, 66–72; Milteer, *North Carolina's Free People of Color*, chap. 3.

11. Petition of Thomas D. Bennehan and Catlett Campbell to the Orange County Superior Court, September 19, 1829.

12. Will of John Umstead, probated January 23, 1829. The two executors put up the required 100-pound bond on November 30, 1831, and received the court's license to free Dicey and her future increase forever from slavery. Orange County Superior Court Decree, December 1, 1831. Freedom was granted with the proviso that "she and they [would conduct] themselves in all respects as becomes people of color, & observing & complying with the laws of this State and demeaning themselves as peaceable citizens thereof."

13. Thomas Bennehan's will of 1841 bequeathed to Duncan Cameron his one half of the slaves given to him by the late Dr. John Umstead "to have [them] emancipated & freed, which I have not been able to effect. . . . He fully understands all my wishes to carry the desire of Dr. Umstead into full effect." In Catlett Campbell's will of January 11, 1845, he confirmed that Dicey's children could not be liberated at the time of Umstead's death. Perhaps "under the present laws of the state upon that subject, it may be done; and I do most earnestly entreat Mr. Bennehan (if in his power) to perform the trust thus confided in us by our mutual friend." Campbell gave his executors full power to release "any interest I have in such negroes or their increase present and future" to Bennehan, "to enable him to accomplish this purpose." If that provision failed, he requested that they sell or convey the women and their children to any other person or persons for a nominal price, for the purpose of effecting their freedom. I infer that Campbell thought that if Thomas Bennehan could not free them, his executors could find a Quaker who would accomplish their liberation. Campbell's will was probated on May 11, 1845. In her book on the legal standing of parental bequests of freedom and inheritances to their mixed-race offspring, legal historian Bernie D. Jones argues that neither the Umstead will of 1829 nor the Campbell will of 1845 had legal standing recognized by the courts in North Carolina. My reading is that the John Umstead liberation of Dicey *was* recognized in 1831 but that, by 1845, the changed law and the extensive claims of creditors cast doubt on this provision in Catlett Campbell's will. See Jones, *Fathers of Conscience*, 44–46.

14. Thomas Bennehan's will of April 28, 1845. Land that Bennehan owned in adjacent Wake and Granville Counties he left to his surviving nieces, Margaret and Mildred Cameron. After Bennehan's death, although the nieces owned the land, Paul Cameron and overseers managed it, and Virgil and Paul continued to provide medical care to those who worked it. The will of 1845 stipulated that the enslaved persons that Bennehan bequeathed were "to be equally divided . . . between my nephew and my nieces," with "the slaves [allocated] as near as can be in families."

15. Virgil Bennehan to Paul Cameron, May 29, 1848, CFP. For examples of free Black Virginians whose family bonds led them to choose reenslavement over expulsion and exile, see Maris-Wolf, *Family Bonds*.

16. Paul Cameron's recurrent times of depression are noted in numerous letters. Anne Ruffin Cameron to Paul Cameron, April 1, 1833; Thomas Ruffin to Paul Cameron, December 11, 1839; Paul Cameron to Duncan Cameron, January 23, 1840; Thomas Bennehan to Duncan Cameron, February 13, 1840; Rebecca Cameron to Duncan Cameron, October 28, 1840; and Duncan Cameron to Paul Cameron, March 12, 1841, CFP. For the conduct of father and son when thwarted, see the "Narrative of James Curry," cited in Blassingame, *Slave Testimony*, 135, 139. Enslaved man James Curry claimed that Duncan Cameron carried a large cane and that if he "met a negro on the road, and he did not raise his hat and bow to him, he would beat him with his cane." James Curry also reported hearsay about the volatility of Paul Cameron. For the testimony of Anne Ruffin Cameron on Paul Cameron's irascibility when depressed, see Anne Cameron to Paul Cameron, [May 10, 1850], CFP.

17. Nathans, *Mind to Stay*, 44.

18. Nathans, *Mind to Stay*, 21, 39–40. The statement came in an interview with descendants of Cameron's enslaved workers, conducted in the 1990s by Alice Eley Jones, and on deposit at the Stagville State Historic Site in Durham, NC. Interview cited in Nathans, *Mind to Stay*, 250n11.

19. The testimony came from Mary Walker, who escaped from the Camerons' possession in 1848. Nathans, *To Free a Family*, 28, 269n40.

20. Paul Cameron to Duncan Cameron, March 25, April 1, 1847, CFP.

21. Thomas Bennehan to Paul Cameron, May 15, 1847, CFP.

22. Paul Cameron to Duncan Cameron, July 25, 1847, CFP.

23. Paul Cameron to Duncan Cameron, July 25, 1847, CFP.

24. For Paul Cameron's conviction that he'd been duped by his Ruffin relative in Alabama, see Nathans, *Mind to Stay*, 45–46. For his glumness and refusal to visit Ruffin family members on his return to North Carolina, see Patty Ruffin to Catherine Ruffin Roulhac, March 22, May 1, 1845, Ruffin, Roulhac, and Hamilton Family Papers, 1784–1951, Southern Historical Collection, Wilson Library Special Collections, University of North Carolina at Chapel Hill.

25. Nathans, *Mind to Stay*, 42, 50–51. The four angry letters from Paul Cameron and the two reprimands from his father began on November 18, 1845, and continued through December 30, 1845. At the prompting from Duncan Cameron, Thomas Bennehan wrote a letter to calm his nephew and "reconcile" him to his Alabama purchase. The uncle assured him that despite disappointing cotton crops in Alabama, his workers were more productive there than in North Carolina. The uncle reported his attempt at reassurance in Thomas Bennehan to Duncan Cameron, December 4, 1845, CFP.

26. Duncan Cameron to Paul Cameron, December 13, 1845, CFP.

27. Paul Cameron to Duncan Cameron, December 13, 30, 1845, CFP; Nathans, *Mind to Stay*, 51.

28. Paul Cameron to Virgil Bennehan, August 8, 1848, typed transcript in CFP.

29. For Paul Cameron's plan to seek new land and send more people to labor in the southwest, see Nathans, *Mind to Stay*, 55–56. In Virgil Bennehan's letter of 1848 to Paul Cameron, he revealed that Cameron had confided the plan to him. Thinking that Paul Cameron had followed through on his plan to purchase new land and send more persons west, Virgil asked

Cameron "to write me who you have sent to the South." Virgil Bennehan to Paul Cameron, May 29, 1848, CFP. Virgil apparently knew about Cameron's intention long before the son proposed the plan to his father on November 2, 1848. Nathans, *Mind to Stay*, 58–60.

30. Virgil addressed his letter of May 1848 to "My dear young Master and friend," and Paul addressed his letter of August 1848 to "My old friend Virgil." Virgil Bennehan to Paul Cameron, May 29, 1848, and Paul Cameron to Virgil Bennehan, August 8, 1848, CFP. It was in Cameron's August letter that he urged Virgil to tell what he felt and suffered.

31. Several historians have pioneered in demonstrating that large numbers of *fugitive slaves* sought to remain undercover in the South as "illegals" who risked recapture to be near family members and communities they were attached to, rather than flee to the North or, if in the Southwest, to Mexico. See Pargas, *Fugitive Slaves*; Pargas, *Freedom Seekers*; and Muller, *Escape to the City*. In his equally revealing book, historian Ted Maris-Wolf shows that the same desires led numbers of Black Virginians who were *freed or promised freedom* to choose to remain in or return to bondage. "For some free blacks, the freedom to live in one's home community and to have a meaningful family life could be more significant than legal freedom, if the latter . . . required their removal from the state. Liberty was something that was defined personally, according to one's particular circumstances." That some freed Black people were prepared to "resort to enslavement to remain in the state among family and community illustrates vividly one of the central tragedies of southern and American history." Maris-Wolf, *Family Bonds*, 208–9.

CHAPTER 4

1. Paul Cameron to Duncan Cameron, August 5, 1847, CFP.

2. Paul Cameron to Duncan Cameron, July 25, August 8, 14, September 2, 28, 1847, CFP.

3. Duncan Cameron to Paul Cameron, July 7, August 31, September 12, 1847, CFP. The father returned to Raleigh in October. Margaret Cameron to Duncan Cameron, October 6, 1847, CFP.

4. For the illness of Mildred Cameron that brought them to Philadelphia for her treatment, see Nathans, *To Free a Family*, 21, 25–26; and Nathans, *Mind to Stay*, 56.

5. A large number of the medical students at the Jefferson School of Medicine were from the South and likely to be inhospitable to a student, teacher, or physician of color. That animus existed farther north as well. In the fall of 1850, a majority of the Harvard Medical School faculty voted to admit three male students of color. Two admissions came at the request of sponsors from the Massachusetts Colonization Society, who sought the pair's training at Harvard as preparation for service in Liberia. The third student admitted was Martin Delany, an outspoken abolitionist advocate (and opponent of colonization). A group of white medical students protested the admissions as disruptive to their education; their protest led the faculty to terminate the admissions at the term's end in December 1850. Wilkinson, "1850 Harvard Medical School Dispute."

6. For the origins of the American Colonization Society in December 1816, see Burin, *Slavery and the Peculiar Solution*, 13–16. Over the years, views have diverged over the legitimacy of land cessions by African leaders to Americans who pieced the accessions together to form Liberia. The most balanced view of the ongoing debate is Burin, "Cape Mesurado

Contract." Challenging the view that land treaties were coerced, misunderstood, or fraudulent is C. Patrick Burrowes, emeritus Penn State history professor, who searched for and finally found a Liberia purchase contract in the Justice Bushrod Washington Papers at the Chicago History Museum. He believes that his discovery should "help put to rest the claim, long advanced by historians and others, that no legitimate contract ever existed." He contends that the Africans who signed the contract understood that it "implicitly" obliged them to give up the slave trade, the most lucrative source of their wealth. Crawford, "How One Historian Located Liberia's Elusive Founding Document."

7. Mitchell and Mitchell, "Philanthropic Bequests of John Rex: Part I," 260, 267, 276–79; and Mitchell and Mitchell, "Philanthropic Bequests of John Rex: Part II," 353–55. At John Rex's request, Duncan Cameron and his associate at the State Bank of North Carolina, George Mordecai, agreed to be executors of the Rex estate. In November 1839, the head of the ACS, Samuel Wilkeson, asked Cameron to hasten money to the manumitted Rex slaves, already in Liberia but destitute there. Samuel Wilkeson to Duncan Cameron, November 25, 1839, quoted in Anderson, *Piedmont Plantation*, 102, 206n70.

8. Malinda Rex to Duncan Cameron, November 3, 1839, in the Pattie Mordecai Collection, State Archives of North Carolina, transcribed and quoted in Wiley, *Slaves No More*, 252–53. I have used the published letter (Document 229).

9. Malinda Rex to Duncan Cameron, November 3, 1839, in Wiley, *Slaves No More*, 252–53.

10. The Camerons boarded at 19 Sansom Street in Philadelphia. Elliot Cresson was a seventh-generation Quaker who lived nearby on Samson Street. Paul Cameron to Duncan Cameron, July 18, 1847, CFP. The Camerons' boardinghouse was owned and run by Quaker women, who surely knew Elliot Cresson, their prominent Quaker neighbor. For the Camerons' Philadelphia address, see Paul Cameron to Duncan Cameron, August 6, 1848, CFP. Duncan Cameron returned to Raleigh in early October. For Cresson's background and his residence on Sansom, see Tomek, *Colonization and Its Discontents*, 96–97.

11. Levitt, *Evolution of Deadly Conflict*, 40; Saha, *Culture in Liberia*, 49.

12. Clegg, *Price of Liberty*, 110–11. For the founders' expectation that King Joe Harris would welcome their settlement and schooling for his people, see Murray, *Atlantic Passages*, 153–57.

13. Levitt, *Evolution of Deadly Conflict*, 27, 62–63; Tyler-McGraw, *African Republic*, 138, 163. Robert Murray believes that land disputes and Quaker self-disarmament more than jeopardy to the slave trade brought on the attack. Murray, *Atlantic Passages*, 157.

14. Tomek, *Colonization and Its Discontent*, 96, 129, 158–71. The manumitted emigrants who arrived in Bassa in 1834 and experienced the disaster six months later came from Virginia. Tyler-McGraw, *African Republic*, 137–38. For the best analysis of the "Bassa-Settler War of 1835" and its background, see Levitt, *Evolution of Deadly Conflict*, 44, 49, 62–70; and Clegg, *Price of Liberty*, 145.

15. Clegg, *Price of Liberty*, 145–46, 239; Levitt, *Evolution of Deadly Conflict*, 92.

16. Cresson won the assent of the ACS in October 1846. William McLain, the secretary and chief administrative officer of the ACS, officially notified Cresson in January 1847. William McLain to Elliott Cresson, Philadelphia Board of Pennsylvania Colonization Society, January 4, 1847, ACS. By the 1840s, Bassa consisted of several small villages; Bassa was on the Atlantic Coast, and the village of Bexley was eight miles inland. "Your resolution of sending a company to Bassa or Bexley was duly considered by the Executive Committee of the ACS

on Oct 5, [1846]." The committee resolved to send a company there as soon as possible. McLain added that almost all emigrants currently offered to the ACS were from the South and had friends at other settlements; they preferred being near their friends. But the ACS head did instruct the colony's governor Joseph J. Roberts to locate at Bexley the emigrants just sent out on the *Liberia Packet*.

17. Duncan Cameron came back to Raleigh in October and left his daughters behind in Philadelphia. He returned to Philadelphia to get them and bring them home in November 1847. By then the will of Thomas Bennehan was probated and Virgil's manumission made official. Virgil and his family were "on the clock" to depart the state soon. It is likely on his return visit that Cameron spoke to Elliot Cresson about Virgil. Two November letters from Paul Cameron were addressed to his father in Philadelphia. Paul Cameron to Duncan Cameron, November 6, 8, 1847, CFP.

18. Elliot Cresson to William McLain, November 6, 1847, ACS. I found this letter in digitized form in a collection of selected ACS letters. The digitized source was "Fold 3," pp. 739–40. I came across this letter after working through the reels of microfilmed ACS papers, hence the citation to a different source, without reel numbers.

19. Elliot Cresson to William McLain, November 6, 1847, ACS, "Fold 3," 739–40.

20. Elliot Cresson to William McLain, November 29, 1847, ACS, "Fold 3," 940, digitized letter. McLain was all too aware of the frustrating delay in getting the Rex money, as well as of Duncan Cameron's role as the Rex estate executor. Mitchells, "Rex Bequests, Part II," 354n71; William McLain to Duncan Cameron, July 12, 1844, CFP; William McLain to J. J. Roberts, January 27, 1848, ACS, reel 238. The never-ending obstruction was "a burning shame."

21. John N. Lewis to William McLain, January 4, 1848, ACS, reel 238; William McLain to [Henry] Comingo, March 4, 1848, ACS, reel 188. Duncan Cameron read the notice of the *Liberia Packet*'s arrival—and of its April 11 date for a return trip, in the Washington *National Intelligencer*. Duncan Cameron to William McLain, March 27, 1848, ACS, no reel number.

22. Duncan Cameron to Paul Cameron, April 2, 1848, CFP.

23. Duncan Cameron to William McLain, March 27, 1848, CFP. Nothing in the *National Intelligencer* announcement indicated that *Bassa* was the target for the *Packet*'s next shipload of emigrants. Hence my inference that it was the connection with Cresson—and his Bassa project—that led Cameron to underscore Virgil's destination.

24. In the 1840s, Joseph Gales Jr. was the publisher of the *National Intelligencer*. Cameron knew both publisher Gales and his late father, Joseph Gales Sr., who had founded and edited the *Raleigh Register* before the father's death in 1841. Cameron wrote McLain he wished to fulfill Thomas Bennehan's will "as soon as practicable."

25. William McLain to Duncan Cameron, March [30], 1848, ACS, reel 188.

26. By 1846, the ranks of passengers to Liberia had thinned dramatically. The next year, the ACS sent only 51 emigrants to Liberia—the second lowest total in its history. Thanks to McLain's recruiting efforts, the number in 1848 climbed to 441, and it increased exponentially thereafter. Between 1848 and 1854, the total sent was 4,019, in contrast to 4,829 for the first thirty years of the ACS's existence. Power-Greene, *Against Wind and Tide*, 98. The ACS budgeted sixty dollars each for 310 emigrants in 1848 and hence came up thousands of dollars short when it committed to take another hundred. By the end of 1848, 95 were waiting in Baltimore and 472 in New Orleans for their passage and provisions.

27. William McLain to Joseph Tracy, April 20, 1847, ACS, reel 188. The ACS agent in Boston, Joseph Tracy, had asked McLain why interest in emancipating and sending people to Liberia had dropped so drastically in 1846 and early 1847. McLain offered guesses but assured Tracy that "we are making a strong effort to get colored people to go to Liberia" and are focusing for the moment on recruiting more free persons of color. As to enslaved persons, a "good many persons have made their wills & left their slaves to us [but] how can I tell who of them [the emancipators] are going to die soon?" McLain intended to go South and sway more owners. Of course, he had no intention "to [talk] up slaves" directly; southern whites "would soon *lock him* up."

28. William McLain to Samuel Ball, March 25, 1848, ACS, reel 188.

29. "*And still they come!*": James Hall to McLain, January 15, 1848, ACS, reel 54 (italics added). To his agent in Savannah, McLain stated his plan for the *Packet* plan to board 134 passengers in Baltimore and pick up 80 in Savannah. William McLain to Rev. Thomas Benning, March 4, 1848, ACS, reel 188. For James Hall's background and lifelong work for colonization, see Campbell, *Maryland in Africa*, 54–55, 81–86, 192–83.

30. Cameron telegram to Hon. A. H. Venable, April 1, 1848, ACS, reel 55, part 2. Cameron reported that he'd written "a Mr. McLean [*sic*]" requesting passage on the *Liberia Packet* for Mr. Bennehan's Virgil and family. "No answer yet. See him immediately Inform me whether they can have passage and on what terms." Congressman Venable telegrammed McLain and asked for an immediate answer. A. H. Venable to [William McLain], April 1, 1848, ACS, reel 55, part 2.

31. William McLain telegram to Duncan Cameron, April 1, 1848, ACS, reel 188. It may be that by the time McLain capitulated to place Virgil's family on the overcrowded ship, he had learned that threat of a smallpox outbreak in Savannah frightened away emigrants scheduled to leave from that port and led to the cancellation of that stop. William McLain to J. P. Russell, March 28, 1848, ACS, reel 188. Cameron replied that his son Paul would arrive with the emigrants in Baltimore by April 7.

32. William McLain to Joseph Tracy, April 20, 1847, ACS, reel 188.

33. William McLain to J. J. Roberts, December 17, 1847, ACS, reel 238.

34. Power-Greene, *Against Wind and Tide*, 6–7, 59, 93, 97–98. David W. Blight, *Frederick Douglass*, 374–77.

35. Burlingame, *Abraham Lincoln*, 103–4, 365; Kaplan, *Lincoln and the Abolitionists*, 180–83. Samuel C. Conkling to William McLain, March 13, 1848, ACS, reel 53. To white colonizationist Conkling, the Illinois vote made clear that "a large majority of our people are in favor of excluding free negroes from our State. The people do not want them here and the question naturally follows, 'What place so suitable for them as Liberia?'"

36. J. B. Crist to William McLain, November 24, December 17, 1847, ACS, reel 53. "Mr. Ball is a remarkably sensible colored man; a tolerable scholar and an elder of the Colored Baptists Association of Illinois; he is a very interesting preacher and a man of most excellent character. He was selected at a convention of seven or eight hundred of his colored brethren held last August in Madison County of this state to visit Liberia and report to them the prospects in that country. I hope great good will result from this enterprise . . . raised funds for trip and family." The Illinois Colonization Society raised $200 for Ball's journey and $100 to care for his family in his absence. Samuel Conkling to William McLain, December 18, 1847, ACS, reel 54.

37. Ball married Amanda Fry, who was six years younger. The US Census reported that in 1850, their household included two older (fourteen and sixteen) and three younger children (ages two, four, and six).

38. Entry for Moses Walker, Warren Township, Jefferson County, Ohio, Seventh Census of the United States, 1850, microfilm roll 432_600, p. 200A, image 706, accessed through Ancestry.com. For a fuller story of Moses Walker's background and family, see the epilogue.

39. Henry Comingo to Rev. McCaine [sic], [December 1, 1847], ACS, reel 53; Henry Comingo to William McLain, January 19, 1848, ACS, reel 54. McLain accepted Walker's proposal and wrote Comingo to have Walker report to Baltimore as soon as the *Packet* arrived back from Liberia. Before he left Steubenville, Walker spoke at a meeting there to raise money for his trip. The fundraiser came up short, and his mission met strenuous opposition from other free Blacks in the community. J. B. Pinney, the ACS agent in western Pennsylvania (soon to become the ACS agent in New York), paid for Walker's passage to Liberia. Henry Comingo to [William McLain], March 21, 1848, ACS, reel 55; J. B. Pinney to William McLain, April 7, 1848, ACS, reel 55, part 2.

40. William McLain to President J. J. Roberts, April 10, 1848, McLain to John Lewis, April 10, 1848, and McLain to Dr. J. W. Lugenbeel, April 10, 1848, ACS, reel 238.

41. Paul Cameron to Duncan Cameron, April 7, 1848, CFP.

42. Back at Fairntosh on April 19, Paul Cameron reported to his father that he got a brief letter from Virgil written on board the *Packet* on the morning of its April 11 departure. In that note, Virgil stated that "all [was] well—said his 'heart [w]as too full to write.'" Paul Cameron to Duncan Cameron, April 19, 1848, CFP.

43. Discontent on the part of manumitted people over their forced deportation to Liberia was expressed by the *Liberia Packet*'s Virginia emigrants and relayed to William McLain. John Chambliss to William McLain, November 4, 1847, ACS, found in a digitized letter in "Fold 3," 825. John Chambliss was the executor for the will of a deceased neighbor, Mrs. Nancy Cain. When he explained to her former enslaved persons that their freedom was contingent on mandatory removal to Liberia, he found some resistant. The difficulty of the dissenters "arises from the very natural and laudable feeling, of regret at separation from their families." Chambliss added that the oldest of the Cain people, whom he called "the old African woman," probably will not go. In fact, she did emigrate, and her departure attracted public notice. William McLain to Joseph Tracy, August 8, 1848, ACS, no reel number.

44. Undated correspondence of Thomas Bennehan, CFP. In the 1870s, Paul Cameron declared that Virgil received $1,000 in gold. See chapter 8. Thomas Bennehan's will bequeathed $500 to Virgil. It is my conjecture that Duncan Cameron doubled the amount to avoid a repeat of the poverty that befell Malinda Rex a decade before.

45. The repressed resentment of both William McLain and James Hall became clear later. In letters written on April 10 to the Liberian president and to two top ACS employees in Liberia, McLain instructed them that no emigrants be allowed to disembark from the *Packet*. I found no such *written* instructions to the ship captain. I concluded that McLain gave him orders in person. It is my conjecture that the oral orders included a last-minute instruction to invite Virgil to join the two midwesterners for their Monrovia tour and to keep all others on the *Packet*.

1. Virgil Bennehan to Paul Cameron, May 29, 1848. The original letter is in the Cameron Family Papers at the Southern Historical Collection. The letter was transcribed and published in Wiley, *Slaves No More*, 260–61. The Wiley transcription is true to the content of the original but has occasional errors because of difficulties in reading Virgil's handwriting. As noted earlier, for Bell Wiley the biggest problem came in reading Virgil's signature. Virgil P. M. Bennehan was transcribed as "Virgil P. McPharran [Bannehan?]." For purposes of easy reference to the document, I cite and use the published version. Virgil's spelling was phonetic. In quoting Virgil, I have chosen to correct his spelling.

2. Philadelphia emigrant John Lewis described Hilary Teage's Monrovia dwelling in a letter of 1848 published in the *African Repository* (Washington, DC), November 14, 1848. A white visitor described President J. J. Roberts's parlor. Tyler-McGraw, *African Republic*, 158.

3. Virgil Bennehan to Paul Cameron, May 29, 1848, in Wiley, *Slaves No More*, 260.

4. John N. Lewis to John Day, May 19, 1848, John Day Correspondence, 1846–59, Southern Baptist Historical Library and Archives, Nashville, TN. I've concluded that it was the meeting with John Lewis that induced Virgil to change his location from Bassa to Bexley. Before the visit to Monrovia and while still on the *Packet*, Virgil had dashed off a quick letter to Paul Cameron and stated that he was eager to get to *Bassa*, "his future home." Paul Cameron to Duncan Cameron, July 12, 1848, CFP. Only after the meeting with Lewis did Virgil change his plan to *Bexley*. In the next chapter I suggest the unstated reasons behind Lewis's recommendation. I'm indebted to Janie Leigh Carter, who many years ago generously shared this crucial letter and other reproduced archival materials while she was writing her master's thesis on John Day. Her splendid final project is on deposit at the Wake Forest University Library. See Carter, "John Day."

5. Abraham Blackford to Mary B. Blackford, September 9, 1844, in Wiley, *Slaves No More*, 21–22. Blackford reported his conversation with society physician J. W. Lugenbeel, a "white gentleman" whom he met in his office. Blackford called him "Dr." and the doctor replied to "Mr. Blackford. It is much better than to be in the state" where they "call you boy." See also Jacob Harris to N. M. Gordon, July 4, 1848, in Wiley, *Slaves No More*, 261. "Tell my friends that 'we have grown to the full stature of men—an experience [they are] unacquainted with . . . in America.'"

6. Virgil P. M. Bennehan to Paul Cameron, May 29, 1848, CFP.

7. Virgil Bennehan to Paul Cameron, May 29, 1848, in Wiley, *Slaves No More*, 260–61.

8. Levitt, *Evolution of Deadly Conflict*, 82–86; Clegg, *Price of Liberty*, 163–64; Lindsay, *Atlantic Bonds*, 91.

9. Virgil Bennehan to Paul Cameron, May 29, 1848, in Wiley, *Slaves No More*, 260–61.

10. Virgil Bennehan to Paul Cameron, May 29, 1848, in Wiley, *Slaves No More*, 261. For the backgrounds of those Virgil listed by name, I consulted the invaluable database of information on enslaved persons created by researcher Chris Hughes. The compilation is held at the visitor center of the Stagville State Historic Site in Durham, NC. Working through thousands of letters and slave registers held in the Cameron Family Papers at the Southern Historical Collection, and drawing books by Jean Anderson and Herbert Gutman, Chris Hughes compiled the "Database of Slaves on the Bennehan-Cameron Plantation, Stagville,

North Carolina." He completed the project on HyperCard in 1988. The data were reformatted into Microsoft Word in 2003. The compilation is a database of all entries, with names and data given in alphabetical order. All researchers are deeply indebted to Chris Hughes for his work. I am further obliged to former site manager Jennifer Farley for making the "Database" available to me.

11. The Rev. William Mercer Green was the Episcopal bishop who preached intermittently at the small Salem chapel that Duncan Cameron had built at Fairntosh in 1826; Fendall Southerland was the senior overseer at Stagville from 1824 to 1845. See Anderson, *Piedmont Plantation*, 32 (Green) and 80 (Southerland). It was the custom of Cameron workers to use the phrase "how day" or "howdy" as a greeting, rather than "hello," a greeting used by whites.

12. Stephen Benson to William McLain, July 24, 1848, published in the *African Repository* (Washington, DC) 24, no. 12.

13. The agent for the ACS in the Lexington, Virginia, area was William H. Ruffner. At first hopeful in November 1847 that he could engage a good many free persons of color to consider Liberia, agent Ruffner reported in May 1848 that a negative letter that came earlier that year from Lexington émigré Samuel Harris had dissuaded most of his friends—and Ruffner's potential recruits—with its hostile report from Bexley. Ruffner to "My Dear Sir" (William McLain), May 20, 1848, reel 56, cited in Tyler-McGraw, *African Republic*, 58–59, 76, 198n62, 202n44.

14. Samuel Harris reported a change of heart about Liberia in a subsequent letter, written to William McLain, and intended for publication in the *African Repository*. Samuel D. Harris and Polly D. Harris to William McLain, May 3, 1849, in Wiley, *Slaves No More*, 225–26. I speculate that Harris could have shifted in his views soon after posting his negative first report much earlier in 1848. Letters sent from Liberia took two months or more to arrive at rural destinations in the South. See, for example, Paul Cameron's report on Virgil's hasty note confirming his arrival in Monrovia. Written and sent on May 17, it did not reach Cameron until July 12, 1848. Paul Cameron to Duncan Cameron, July 12, 1848, CFP.

15. Gatewood, "'To Be Truly Free,'" 154–58. For Sheridan's report of desertion by hired local workers, see Louis Sheridan to [Samuel Wilkeson], September 25, 184[3], ACS, reel 171.

CHAPTER 6

1. William McLain to Elliot Cresson and the Board of the Pennsylvania Colonial Society, January 4, 1847, ACS, reel 188; A. P. Davis to McLain, January 3, 1846, ACS, reel 171; Stephen Benson to McLain, April 7, 1846, ACS, reel 171; William McLain to Dr. J. W. Lugenbeel, February 2, 1848, ACS, reel 238.

2. On mortality, see McDaniel [now Zuberi Tukufu], *Swing Low, Sweet Chariot*, 104; Burin, *Slavery and the Peculiar Solution*, 86, 146–48; and Tomek, *Colonization and Its Discontents*, 233–35.

3. Tomek, *Colonization and Its Discontents*, 234–35; Burin, "Rethinking Northern White Support," 200. Eric Burin concluded that the ideological rigidity of ACS officials and advocates "left them impervious to evidence that conflicted with their preconceived views."

4. William McLain to Rev. A. B. McCorkle, December 8, 1847, and McLain to Anne Rice, December 13, 1847, ACS, reel 188.

5. J. W. Lugenbeel to William McLain, March 15, 1848, ACS, reel 238.

6. Claude Clegg notes that in 1838, Louis Sheridan was appalled that the only housing provided for his fellow arriving passengers consisted of "huts" and "pens of thatch and bamboo." Newcomers to Bassa in 1851 found its provision for new emigrants the same: rickety thatched houses and inadequate medical care. Clegg, *Price of Liberty*, 155–56, 208–9.

7. J. W. Lugenbeel to William McLain, March 15, 1848, ACS, reel 238.

8. John Lewis to William McLain, May 12, 1848, ACS, reel 238.

9. McLain had written to his colleague James Hall of his concern that if they allowed the *Packet* to stop at Monrovia and the emigrants went ashore, "that would be the end of them." They would refuse to go to Bassa. Both ACS officials worried that Liberian president Joseph J. Roberts would again capitulate and allow the newcomers to remain in the capital or go to another settlement, as he had once before. William McLain to James Hall, March 15, 1848, ACS, reel 188. Hall wrote back emphatically that the emigrants MUST go to Bassa and that McLain must preempt any attempt by the Liberian president to send them elsewhere. James Hall to McLain, March 17, 1848, ACS, reel 55. Hence McLain's instruction to Roberts, Lewis, and Lugenbeel that the "*Masters*" had irrevocably "designated" McLain to send all the emigrants to Bassa and to nowhere else. William McLain to J. W. Lugenbeel, April 10, 1848, and McLain to John Lewis, April 10, 1848, ACS, reel 238. "*None* of these people are to be [unboarded] at *Monrovia*. My orders are *precise* on this point. Their *Masters* directed me to pursue this course." McLain made the same claim to Liberian president Joseph J. Roberts. "They have all been designated to Bexley & Bassa. The instructions which I have received from those who have had them in their charge, are positive & unconditional, to send them to Bexley & Bassa." McLain to J. J. Roberts, April 10, 1848, ACS, reel 238. In fact, only Duncan Cameron wrote that he expected Virgil and his family to go to Bassa. John Chambliss, who was in charge of the largest group of emigrants, all from Virginia, gave him no such instruction. McLain told widow Anne Rice that the Virginia settlement up the St. Paul River was the destination for the family of Anderson Brown, whom she had emancipated and designated for Liberia. William McLain to Anne Rice, December 13, 1847, ACS, reel 188. Only after the fact did Anne Rice receive from McLain his "reasons for sending him to Bassa" instead of the St. Paul settlement. Anne Rice to McLain, August 23, 1848, ACS, reel 56.

10. William McLain to J. W. Lugenbeel, April 10, 1848, ACS, reel 238.

11. John Lewis to Willian McLain, May 17, 1848, ACS, reel 238.

12. J. W. Lugenbeel to William McLain, June 16, 1848, ACS, reel 238. Lugenbeel reiterated the next month that while he "advised" Roberts to go to Bassa, as McLain "requested," Lugenbeel did "not positively order or direct him to do so," since Roberts also was needed to attend to immigrants elsewhere. Lugenbeel to McLain, July 19, 1848, ACS, reel 238.

13. Both Lewis and Lugenbeel believed that the farther from the shore and the "pestiferous mangrove swamps in the vicinity of the ocean," the safer the emigrants would be from attacks of fever. J. W. Lugenbeel to William McLain, January 4, 1848, ACS, reel 238. In his letter to McLain, Lewis noted that "the bag of medicines in the Packet will be landed here at the request of Dr. Roberts. I don't know if you sent any to Mr. Benson." If none were sent to him, "I shall direct Dr. R. to make up an assortment" and send it down. John Lewis to William McLain, May 17, 1848, ACS, reel 238. Benson of Bassa soon reported that the medicines he received were insufficient and discreetly noted that the president's brother "took out some medicines from the box meant for Bassa." Benson added that Roberts "did not write me what

he took out," nor did Benson receive a list of what was sent from Baltimore. Stephen Benson to William McLain, [illegible date] June 1848, ACS, reel 238.

14. W. W. Davis to William McLain, June 22, 1848, ACS, reel 238. Benson reported that though he threatened to stop supplies to those who wouldn't go to Bexley, "they obstinately refuse saying they had money and . . . would buy enough for their own food." Only "some families went to Bexley," which as Benson later reported, were those who had decided to "follow Dr. Bennehan." Benson to McLain, [illegible date] June 1848, ACS, reel 238. Benson noted that all of those who went to Bexley, to be under Virgil's care, survived. Stephen Benson to William McLain, May 8, 1849, ACS, no reel number.

15. Stephen Benson to William McLain, [illegible date] June 1848, ACS, reel 238; J. W. Lugenbeel to McLain, June 16, 1848, ACS, reel 238; W. W. Davis to McLain, June 27, 1848, ACS, reel 238. New York Colonial Society agent J. B. Pinney claimed that while he was an official in Liberia, "we discharged [Davis] some years ago for drunkenness & knavery." "Who appointed him Physician?" J. B. Pinney to McLain, January 24, 1849, ACS, reel 58.

16. W. W. Davis to McLain, June 22, 27, 1848, ACS, reel 238; Lewis to McLain, July 1, 1848, ACS, reel 238. For Benson's declaration that the "worst is over," see Benson to McLain, [illegible date] June 1848, ACS, reel 238; Benson to McLain, July 24, 1848, letter published in the *African Repository* (Washington, DC) 24, no. 12, 357.

17. For the minimal temperature of 66 degrees Fahrenheit required for the African malarial parasite to reproduce, see Humphreys, *Malaria*, 11; and Webb, *Humanity's Burden*, 5–7, 44. Webb also noted that because mosquitoes fed in the early evening and after midnight, sleeping indoors or outdoors "near a smoking fire" deterred mosquitoes from biting. Emigrant Anderson Brown reported the sustained cold weather and warming nighttime fires of June and July to Anne Rice, his Virginia benefactor. She passed on the report to William McLain. Anne Rice to William McLain, August 12, 1848, ACS, reel 56. On the heavy rains, see Lewis to McLain, July 1, 1848, ACS, reel 238; and *Liberia Herald* (Monrovia, Liberia), June 30, 1848.

18. Stephen Benson to William McLain, May 9, 1849, ACS, no reel number.

19. Stephen Benson to William McLain, May 9, 1849, ACS, no reel number.

20. In his letter of May 29, 1848, to Paul Cameron, Virgil stated that while temporarily in Bassa, he resided at the home of the Rev. A. P. Davis. I infer that Davis conveyed to Virgil the same assurance that he relayed to William McLain in 1846—that the "difficulties" encountered earlier at Bassa were now in the past and that the settlement was now "on the highway to prosperity and independence." A. P. Davis to McLain, January 3, 1846, ACS, reel 171.

21. Walter P. Jayne, *Liberian Journal, 1839–1841* (transcribed from the original), United Methodist Church Archives and History, Drew University, Madison, NJ. During the summer of 1840, Jayne received intermittent reports of the surging death toll among emigrants who had come to Bassa aboard the ship *Salada*. He detailed those reports in his *Journal* entries of July 8, August 9, August 13, and September 2, 1840, transcribed on pp. 209–13 of his *Journal*. For the description of the malaria symptoms by other contemporaries, which match Walter Jayne's account, see Carlson, *African Fever*, 26, 38, and the appendix.

22. Louis Sheridan to [Ralph Gurley], September 25, 1843, ACS, reel 171.

23. Tomek, *Colonization and Its Discontents*, 234; Tyler-McGraw, *African Republic*, 73.

24. Moses Jackson to Elliot West, March 22, 1846, in Wiley, *Slaves No More*, 256. Illinois free Black "delegate" Samuel Ball also mentioned the overgrowth—which he characterized as "verdure"—in a *Report* he would give and publish in August 1848. Historian Ibrahim

Sundiata explained that in Liberia, "as in much of Africa, vegetational 'tropical exuberance' belies a sad fact: the soils are laterite and easily leached out of their nutrients" by the 180 inches of rain that falls along the coast in the rainy season from April to October. "Only 2 percent of the country's soil is ideal for agriculture." Sundiata, *Brothers and Strangers*, 50. As historian Lisa Lindsay reports, a North Carolina family that arrived in Liberia in March 1849 found that "during the rainy season" it "was nearly impossible to start" planting; in addition, summer downpours were so heavy that it took "months to wait before a crop could be harvested." The recurrent daily downpours and dense vegetation barred the growing of food crops until September. Lindsay, *Atlantic Bonds*, 68, 95. Dennis Carlson observes in his book on West Africa that in the nearby British colony of Sierra Leone, the supposedly fertile soil of the region likewise produced poor crops. Heavy rainfall washed away most of the organic and mineral substances needed for good agriculture. Carlson, *African Fever*, 3.

25. Stephen Benson to William McLain, November 1, 1848, ACS, [reel 238?]. John Day to James B. Taylor, April 3, 1849, John Day Correspondence, 1846–49, Southern Baptist Historical Library and Archives, Nashville, TN. Writing from Bexley, John Day reported that the natives "would not strike us, but killed those under our protection." The war that followed is described by Solomon Page to Charles Andrews, April 29, 1849, in Wiley, *Slaves No More*, 107.

26. Stephen Benson to William McLain, [date illegible] November 1848, no reel number.

27. J. W. Lugenbeel to McLain, November 25, 1848, and John Lewis to McLain, December 7, 1848, ACS, reel 238. Benson himself reported that 67 of the 138 emigrants had died in Bassa. Stephen Benson to William McLain, December 2, 1848, ACS, reel 238.

CHAPTER 7

1. William McLain to James Hall, April 4, 1848, ACS, reel 56; McLain to J. B. Pinney, February 26, 1848, and McLain to Samuel Ball, March 25, 1848, ACS, reel 188. In his letter to Samuel Ball, McLain added that the ACS had made firm commitments to send another 400 emigrants to Liberia at a cost of $20,000. Two years later, McLain reported that the ACS was $26,000 in debt. McLain to David Christy, March 26, 1850, ACS, reel 190.

2. James Hall telegram to William McLain, August 4, 1848, ACS, reel 56.

3. Rev. C. Soule to William McLain, August 3, 1848, ACS, reel 56.

4. William McLain to Rev. C. Soule, August 8, 1848, ACS, reel 188.

5. *National Intelligencer* (Washington, DC), August 7, 1848. "The emigrants who went in the Packet to Liberia are all doing well." Stephen Benson to William McLain, [illegible date] June 1848, ACS, reel 238; Benson to McLain, July 24, 1848, *African Repository* (Washington, DC) 24, no. 12. If the women with venereal disease were also pregnant, they would have had greatly lowered resistance to the impact of malaria. As medical historian Margaret Humphreys observes, during the reduced immune state of pregnancy, malaria may flare, potentially killing the fetus, the mother, or both. Humphreys, *Malaria*, 9.

6. William McLain to John Lewis, September 2, 1848, ACS, reel 238. To physician Henry Roberts, McLain described the damage done to ACS recruitment by the eighteen deaths reported at Bassa. Most of the victims were women manumitted by a Miss Early and her late brother. The sister had planned to send more. Now how could they convince her that the people should go to Liberia? McLain felt that he could not reveal to Miss Early, a single lady

from Virginia, that venereal disease was involved in the deaths of all the women. McLain to H. J. Roberts, September 1, 1848, and McLain to Benson, September 4, 1848, ACS, reel 238.

7. John Lewis to William McLain, July 1, 1848, ACS, reel 238; Beverly Yates to McLain, July 6, 1848, ACS, [reel 238]. In Monrovia, on the eve of the departure of the ship back to the United States, Yates spoke with "the commissioners" from Ohio and Illinois and declared, "They seem highly pleased and their report will be favorable to Liberia." In 1848, Beverley Page Yates was a colonel of the First Regiment of the Liberian Volunteers and a leading merchant in Monrovia.

8. *African Repository* (Washington, DC) 24, no. 9, 261–63.

9. The response to Ball's return on August 25 was reported in the *Springfield Journal*, August 1848, quoted in Richard Hart, "Honest Abe and the African Americans," *Illinois Times* (Springfield), February 12, 1998, 10–11. For the vote on the referendum, see Burlingame, *Abraham Lincoln*, 103–4; and Kaplan, *Lincoln and the Abolitionists*, 180–83.

10. Ball, *Liberia*, 5–8. Ball admitted that his account of the land's productivity was provided by Liberian advocate Hilary Teage; he deemed it "essentially correct" though "rather highly drawn." He noted there were no horses, oxen, or mules at work in the country. "Let the truth be told." Ball, *Liberia*, 8 (italics added).

11. Ball, *Liberia*, 8–11. South Carolina freedman James Churchill Vaughn arrived in Liberia in 1853, five years after Samuel Ball; he left it soon afterward, in part because of the colonists' treatment of indigenous people. Churchill Vaughn found that the Black plantocracy that ruled Liberia was as oppressive to Africans as was the white plantocracy to Native American and enslaved people in South Carolina. American settlers in Liberia had "displaced natives and were coming close to enslaving indigenous Africans" and to "creating an American-style ethnic caste system." Lindsay, *Atlantic Bonds*, 101. For the early and ongoing domination of Liberia by the country's "coastal mercantile elite," see Mills, *World Colonization Made*, 140, 227n34. Joshua Levitt, writing in 2005, would undoubtedly have concurred with every point of Samuel Ball's critique of the ACS and the successor Black elites who controlled Liberia from the outset; their legacy became "deadly" in the nineteenth century and into the twenty-first. He distills his thesis—and encompasses Ball's astute observations—into a single composite word: "paternaltarianism." The ACS and post-ACS regimes created an "extremely paternalistic and authoritarian social political order instituted to dominate and subjugate the original Black settlers," an order that was and remained "ethnically exclusive." Levitt, *Evolution of Deadly Conflict*, 3–5, 8.

12. Ball, *Liberia*, 14. For the background of the legal case of the wife of Anthony Bryant, in which Abraham Lincoln was involved as an attorney for the slaveholder suing to keep her in bondage, see McKirdy, *Lincoln Apostate*.

13. Ball, *Liberia*, 12–14.

14. Might Samuel Ball's alternative vision—of an ethnically inclusive and democratic colony in Liberia—have stood a chance of success? Ball implicitly envisioned that his separate Illinois colony would have free Black leaders and settlers from the Midwest rather than Black leaders from the South, who took the planter aristocracy as their political and social model. That said, it's worth noting that Ball's fellow midwesterner, Ohioan Moses Walker, never acknowledged subjugation or mistreatment of Africans. If they civilized and converted to Christianity, he asserted, they could readily become citizens. In fact, with their own culture and society, few indigenous people wished to be *either* "citizens" or subjects of American

rulers. Historian Claude Clegg found that as of 1858, of the several thousand Africans resident in Bassa County, *fifteen* had received citizenship. Clegg, *Price of Liberty*, 242.

15. Ball, *Liberia*, 14–15. The Rev. Ebenezer Rodgers, a British immigrant and white Baptist minister who lived in Upper Alton, Illinois, had encouraged the formation of the Illinois Black Baptist Association. Rodgers attended the Baptist convention in 1847 that authorized Ball to scout Liberia and was appointed treasurer to receive funds collected to pay for Ball's journey and to cover his family's expenses while he was gone. Rogers was present at the Alton conference in 1848 when Ball denounced Liberia as an aristocracy. After Ball's critical report on the colonists' treatment of indigenous Africans, the Rev. Rodgers wrote McLain that Ball simply didn't understand the customary privileges of class. The Englishman believed that Ball was affronted by the way the Liberian elite treated their servants and naively feared that free Black émigrés to Liberia would be treated as slaves were in the United States. Rev. Ebenezer Rodgers to William McLain, February 1, 1850, ACS, no reel number. Seven years later, manumitted Kentuckian Alfred Russell reached the same conclusion about the toxic dominance of Liberia's Black aristocracy. Freed and sent to Liberia in 1833, young Alfred Russell thought he had left "masters and lords behind." Writing in 1855, he regretfully reported that he found that a few large families held all the offices and the "avenues to every emolument"—and that they had ever since he'd arrived. "Kissing the 'big toe,' this very 'big negro' business, has been the greatest 'night maire' that ever crippled the energy of Liberia and does to this day." The "battle of Liberty is still to be won." Kazanjian, *Brink of Freedom*, 86.

16. See the two articles on "Liberia" in Frederick Douglass's antislavery paper, which approvingly reprinted the critical assessment of Liberia from Ball's *Report* ("one of the worst countries" a poor man "can go to") but dismissed Ball's material arguments for Liberia as "undeserving of our confidence." *North Star* (Rochester, NY), April 13, 20, 1849. For McLain's repudiation of the "delegate system," see William McLain to David Christy, April 19, 1849, ACS, reel 189; and McLain to David Christy, March 26, 1850, ACS, reel 190. The best immigrant, McLain concluded, was one who was willing to sacrifice comfort, gain, and self-advantage for a higher good. McLain to Christy, March 20, June 27, 1853, ACS, no reel number.

17. Virgil Bennehan reported that Walker was with him for their dinner with Hilary Teage. Virgil Bennehan to Paul Cameron, May 29, 1848, in Wiley, *Slaves No More*, 260. Moses W. Walker's white sponsor, the Rev. Henry Comingo, had earlier given Walker "some 20 numbers of [ACS] publications," including issues of the *Liberia Herald*. In the same letter, Comingo noted that Walker was a well-regarded lay minister. Rev. Henry Comingo to Rev. McCaine [*sic*], [December 1, 1847], ACS, reel 53. A correspondent for the Presbyterian *New York Observer* published a later story about Walker and his advocacy in an article entitled "A Picture of Liberia." The article of November 20, 1849, was reprinted in the *National Intelligencer* (Washington, DC), December 11, 1849, 3. The correspondent wrote that after Walker's recovery from illness, he took up speaking and "defending the colony as the only hope of the colored man, both here and in Africa." The writer remarked on his "zeal and earnestness that cannot fail to be impressive. He has for a long time enjoyed the name of freedom, but never felt the true import of the term till he placed his foot on the soil where all the political and social barriers by which he had been restrained and oppressed at home, were as by magic removed." Walker spoke to two evening meetings in Steubenville and then addressed the Presbyterian Synod of Wheeling, Virginia—a large body of ministers and laymen. To a member of the audience who denounced the colonists' treatment of Africans, Walker

dismissed the criticism, alleging without evidence that one in seventeen had the right of suffrage and that their children were apprenticed and not enslaved to colonists. The report was widely reprinted by other newspapers, including the *Louisville Daily Journal*, December 17, 1849, and the *Green County Torch-Light* of Xenia, OH, December 27, 1849. Moses W. Walker's advocacy for Liberia had enough of an impact on Black Ohioans for a songwriting critic of colonization to make Walker a target of rebuke. As a young free Black, orphaned Joshua McCarter Simpson was a servant in the household of white families in Xenia, Ohio, 200 miles west of Walker's home outside of Steubenville. The adult Simpson became a full-fledged abolitionist and wrote songs opposed to slavery and to colonization. In "Old Liberia Is Not the Place for Me," Simpson took special aim at Moses Walker (published in Simpson, *Emancipation Car*, 69–70).

> Although (as Moses Walker says,)
>   There, children never cry:
> And he who can well act the hog,
>   For food will never die;
> For there the yams and cocoa-nuts,
>   And oranges are free—
>   Yet Old Liberia
>   Is not the place for me.
>   . . .
> I deem this as my native land,
>   And here I'm bound to stay.
> *I have a mind to be a man*
>   *Among white men and free;*
>   *And* OLD LIBERIA!
>   *Is not the place for me!!*

18. David Christy to William McLain, September 30, 1848, ACS, [reel 58]. After Moses Walker received twenty past copies of the *Liberia Herald* before he left for Liberia, he met its editor, Hilary Teage, in person in May 1848. Teage had called for the ACS colony to become a self-governing nation in 1846. "Rise Fellow Citizens! . . . 'give the answer, whether the African race is doomed to interminable degradation.'" In 1847, Teage wrote the Liberian Declaration of Independence, which denounced the United States for its exclusion of African Americans from all rights and privileges of whites. Mills, *World Colonization Made*, 138, 140–41. I infer that "in manner and message," Moses Walker's speech echoed Hilary Teage. The ACS agent in Ohio who found Walker's talk and tone objectionable was white geologist and prolific pamphleteer David Christy. After the talk, Christy pledged to work with Moses Walker, to urge him to get well before he spoke again, and to subordinate his denunciation of white mistreatment of Blacks and instead to highlight the virtues of nation-building for emigrants to Liberia. Walker obliged. His health restored, by March 1849, Walker was eager to canvass Ohio on behalf of Liberia and colonization. *African Repository* (Washington, DC), March 1849, 71. His speeches in Steubenville, Ohio, and in Wheeling, Virginia, in 1849 were more tempered. Moses Walker's zeal in 1848 reflected the influence of and personal encounter with Hilary Teage. McLain, Christy, and other ACS agents sought to downplay Teage's indictment of white racism and instead to present Liberia as a transplantation to Africa of

American ideals and form of government—the "'principles of liberty in the United States.'" Mills, "'The United States of Africa,'" 88, 90–93.

In the fall of 1849, Moses Walker's patron and advocate in Steubenville, Henry Comingo, wrote to McLain that Walker had decided to emigrate to Liberia with his wife and three children, one of whom was an infant. Walker proposed to be a missionary. On Walker's behalf, Comingo inquired if McLain might communicate with the Southern Baptist Board about employing Walker as a minister in Liberia. Henry Comingo to McLain, October 8, 1849, ACS, no reel number. McLain did write the head of the Southern Baptist Board, James B. Taylor. McLain to Rev. James B. Taylor, October 15, 1849, ACS, reel 189. McLain wrote Taylor that Walker "is now making arrangements with his wife and 3 children to go to Liberia. I doubt not he will make a useful man there. He is a good preacher and was much admired in Liberia while he was there." In response, Taylor was encouraging, asking McLain to procure testimonials about Walker's church standing, character, and education. James B. Taylor to William McLain, October 31, 1849, ACS, no reel number. Walker appeared to be ready to depart in December 1849. However, Robert T. Brown's comprehensive enumeration in *Immigrants to Liberia* lists no Moses W. Walker. I have not been able to determine if Walker went as a *missionary* and therefore might have been unlisted as an *emigrant*. I have concluded that for reasons never detailed—quite possibly his wife's refusal to go, having seen how ill Walker was on his return in 1848—Moses Walker failed to leave. Because of Walker's decision to stay, his additional sons, Moses Fleetwood Walker and Wendy Wilberforce Walker, were born in the United States and not in Liberia.

19. Historian Eric Burin, using a database that he complied of 10,939 African Americans known to have moved to Liberia in the antebellum period, calculated that between 1820 and 1843, 22 *percent* of all emigrants who survived acclimation quit Liberia. However, only one in five of those who left made it back to the United States—113 in all. Others were deterred by insufficient funds to pay forty dollars or more for return passage or by southern state laws banning their reentry; most moved elsewhere in Africa. Almost all of those who did return to the United States "had found Liberia disappointing, and they broadcast their discontent widely." Burin, *Slavery and the Peculiar Solution*, 66–67, 184n26, 184n28. Burin describes his ACS Database on 175–76, 176n5.

20. James Hall telegram to William McLain, January 18, 1849, ACS, [reel 59].

21. James Hall to William McLain, February 1, 1849, ACS, reel 59. All historians of Liberia report far greater mortality than the average of 5 percent of emigrants claimed by McLain, but none of their calculations approach Virgil Bennehan's count or percentage of fatalities of Virginia emigrants at Bassa. The deaths of 85 of his 134 fellow passengers constituted 63 *percent* of all who came. Historian Lisa Lindsay notes, in her biography of South Carolina emigrant Churchill Vaughn, that 21 of his 149 shipmates perished after his arrival in 1853. He viewed the loss of 14 percent of the emigrants as an "appalling mortality." Lindsay, *Atlantic Bonds*, 84. Claude Clegg reports that the death rate of the 649 emigrants who came to Liberia between 1832 and 1833 was 21 percent; of those who settled in Bassa in 1835, 30 percent died. Of the North Carolina passengers who arrived at Bassa with Louis Sheridan in 1838, 22 percent died. The overall census taken of all emigrants from 1820 to 1843 indicated that 20 percent died of the fever in their first year. Clegg, *Price of Liberty*, 139, 145, 155, 160. In his book on Liberia, Eric Burin calls the colony a "death trap" during the first decade of emigration—when 29 percent of all emigrants died. Drawing on the work of Thomas Schick and

demographer Antonio McDaniel, he agrees with demographer McDaniel that the overall death rate up to 1843 may have reached 50 percent: "'the highest rate of mortality ever reliably recorded.'" Burin, *Slavery and the Peculiar Institution*, 16, 146–48, citing McDaniel [now Zuberi Tukufu], *Swing Low, Sweet Chariot*, 104. Those mortality rates—ranging from 20 to 50 percent—led historian Beverly Tomek to conclude that the supporters of colonization "refused to let themselves see the extent of the mortality at the colony" and handled the issue with a "tragic sense of stubborn righteousness." Tomek, *Colonization and Its Discontents*, 233–35. The mortality rate of almost *two-thirds* of the Bassa arrivals in 1848 makes clear why Virgil felt compelled to sound the alarm—and why ACS leaders McLain and Hall hastened to discredit the messenger and discount his numbers—before McLain finally returned to asserting that Liberia mortality was 5 percent or less.

22. James Hall to William McLain, [January 26, 1849], ACS, [reel 59].

23. William McLain to John Chambliss, January 30, 1849, ACS, reel 189. McLain to Stephen Benson, February 14, 1849, ACS, reel 238.

24. John B. Pinney to William McLain, January 24, 1849, ACS, reel 58. Pinney was in Liberia during earlier "terrible disasters" at Bassa in 1834 and 1835, where many died for "want of medical advice" and when W. W. Davis served as the colonial physician until he was dismissed. Cooperating as ever with McLain and the ACS, the *National Intelligencer* kept silent about the loss of life at Bassa. Reporting on the return of the *Liberia Packet* after a later voyage and its visits to "various settlements," the newspaper reported that among the emigrants who went out in September 1848, "nearly all had an attack of the acclimating fever" but "none of them had died . . . and they all seemed well satisfied." *National Intelligencer* (Washington, DC), January 24, 1849. McLain commissioned physician J. W. Lugenbeel to write a positive medical account for the *African Repository*. William McLain to J. W. Lugenbeel, February 15, 1849, ACS, reel 238.

25. William McLain to Stephen Benson, February 14, 1849, and McLain to J. W. Lugenbeel, February 14, 1849, ACS, reel 238. Mark, Clairborne, and Eppes Collier—the three Virginia emigrants in 1848 who returned from Liberia with Virgil in January 1849—appealed to the Sussex County Court to return to bondage in 1850. They professed to prefer American slavery to Liberian freedom. West, *Family or Freedom*, 101. In 1858, two other Virginians returned from Liberia to seek reenslavement. Not devastating mortality, but what they denounced as deceit, fraud, and the collusion of Liberian officials in the slave trade, led to their exit. The complex story of James Booker and William Watson is recounted, along with the reasons that others returned or resisted deportation in the first place, in Maris-Wolf, *Family Bonds*, 138, 142–53, and throughout chapter 5, "To Liberia and Back." As in 1849, ACS head William McLain immediately sent out a stream of letters to refute the denunciations in 1858. He also solicited testimony from contented emigrants who remained in the country, all to counter the humiliating press coverage that pronounced "Liberia a Swindle."

26. William McLain to Stephen Benson, February 14, 1849, ACS, reel 238.

27. "The Narrative of Lunsford Lane" (1842) in Andrews and Davis, *North Carolina Slave Narratives*.

28. William McLain to Henry Brown, February 6, 1849, ACS, reel 189. Despite what occurred at Bassa, McLain continued to regard it as the exception. Just a few months later, he returned to claim that the mortality in Liberia was no more than 5 percent of the emigrants who went there. Most had died in the early years. He assured a Kentucky correspondent

in June that "there never has been a colony planted with as little sacrifice of life as Liberia." William McLain to W. P. Thomasson, June 13, 1849, ACS, reel 189.

29. Henry Brown to William McLain, February [13], 1849, ACS, reel 58.

30. "Victory seemed close for Newlin and people ... and provisional arrangements." Since the manumissions were authorized by a confidential verbal trust in Newlin rather than by a written provision in the will of his Quaker friend Sarah Freeman, her heirs claimed that the liberation had no standing. It took three court rulings to confirm the validity of the oral trust. Mitchell, "Out of Africa," 271–73. For the ambiguities of the "trust," which led Justice Richmond Pearson to dissent from the court's ruling, see Burin, *Slavery and the Peculiar Institution*, 53.

31. John Newlin to William McLain, [February] 21, 1849, ACS, reel 171. A more detailed indictment, purportedly written to "reform" rather than simply condemn Liberia, came from Augustus Washington, a freedman from New England who moved to Liberia in early 1854. His letter, "Liberia as It Is, 1854," written after six months in the country, was first published in *Frederick Douglass' Paper*. His harrowing warning amplified both the critique of Samuel Ball in 1848 and the alarm of Virgil Bennehan in 1849. Washington wrote of the unmitigated "sufferings of Southern emigrants after their arrival here," the "shameful" inadequacy of medical care, the "fearful mortality," the "conniving at these faults" by Liberia's men of wealth and influence—and the complicity of "Agents of the American Colonization Society." He was especially incensed that the settlers' "letters of complaint have been [intercepted] and kept from public" and the country's "wrongs never ... redressed." Only if persons come to Liberia with means, as he had, could they fare well. For the mass of poor emigrants, "where one succeeds with nothing, twenty suffer and die, leaving no mark of their existence." Washington's letter is published in Moses, *Liberian Dreams*, 208–12.

32. Longtime residents and newcomers at Bassa and Bexley confirmed the abject poverty of the villagers who lived there. John Day to James B. Taylor, February 12, 1847, John Day Correspondence, 1846–59, Southern Baptist Historical Library and Archives, Nashville, TN. Virginia emigrant Anderson Brown, who came on the *Liberia Packet*, reported that he found the people at Bassa "poor and [fearful]." Anne Rice to McLain, August 12, 1848, ACS, [reel 56]. Money was short throughout Liberia in 1848. R. C. Murray to William McLain, June 17, 1848, ACS, [reel 238]; Stephen Benson to McLain, November 1, 1848, ACS, no reel number. On the preference of newcomers for trade, see McLain to Rev. C. Soule, August 8, 1848, ACS, reel 188; on the surrounding Bassa's pullback from trade, see Benson to McLain, November 1, 1848, ACS, no reel number.

33. In England, free Black Alexander Crummell, who would become an advocate for Liberia and colonization in the 1850s, was in 1849 a bitter opponent of both. Crummell repeated the claim that Liberian leaders had engaged in the slave trade. Samuel Miller to William McLain, March 20, 1849, ACS, no reel number. Samuel Miller's son James Miller reported from Britain that Crummell opposed Liberia "with all his might." Crummell asserted that the colony was an abject failure where newcomers soon found themselves ragged and worthless.

34. William McLain to John Newlin, March 6, 1849, ACS, reel 189.

35. Newlin reported to McLain that after a delay of eleven years in which heirs had contested the will, he won his case and the authority to free and expatriate the people in his charge. He intended to send them to Liberia in August 1850—*if* they elected to go there. John Newlin to William McLain, May 29, 1850, no reel number. In response, McLain offered them

free passage to Liberia. McLain to John Newlin, June 4, 1850, ACS, reel 190. The freed people opted for Ohio instead. John Newlin to McLain, December 18, 1850, ACS, no reel number.

36. Clegg, *Price of Liberty*, 208–10 (italics added).

CHAPTER 8

1. Wheeler, *Reminiscences and Memoirs*, 356 (italics in the original).

2. For Paul Cameron's feeling of betrayal and ingratitude, see Nathans, *Mind to Stay*, 98–99. For the account of Jane Johnson's escape and later return to Philadelphia to deny in court Wheeler's claim that she'd been kidnapped against her will, see Diemer, *Vigilance*, 115–33.

3. The second enslaved woman escaped from John Wheeler's possession around 1857. Under the pseudonym of Hannah Crafts, she later wrote a loosely fictionalized account of her life while enslaved by Wheeler. That manuscript did not surface until late in the twentieth century. The unpublished manuscript was found and purchased by Harvard professor Henry Louis Gates Jr. and published as *The Bondwoman's Narrative* in 2002 by Hannah Crafts. It was hailed as the first novel written by an African American woman. In 2013, professor of English Gregg Hecimovich discovered her true identity. She was Hannah Bond. She wrote her account sometime between 1857 and 1869. See Julie Bosman, "Professor Says He Has Solved a Mystery over a Slave's Novel," *New York Times*, September 18, 2013. Gregg Hecimovich's full story of his discovery, and of Hannah Bond's life as an enslaved Wheeler servant, is now told in full in *The Life and Times of Hannah Crafts*.

4. For Cameron's memorandum of 1865 to the Union official, see Anderson, *Piedmont Plantation*, 96.

5. Wheeler, *Reminiscences*, 356. Wheeler reported that Cameron told him that "when freed at the close of the civil war, the [Cameron bondmen] parted from their master with kindly feeling, and the elder ones greet him yet, whenever they chance to meet him, with the same exhibition of attachment." For the insurgency that in fact followed emancipation on the Cameron place, see Nathans, *Mind to Stay*, 98–100.

6. Wheeler, *Reminiscences*, 356.

7. Samuel D. Harris to William McLain, May 3, 1849, in Wiley, *Slaves No More*, 226.

8. William McLain to Paul Cameron, August 12, 1848, ACS, reel 188. The lengthy voyage of the *Packet* was reported by John Lewis to William McLain, December 7, 1848, ACS, reel 238. Lewis reported that the *Liberia Packet*, which departed Baltimore on September 8, arrived in Monrovia on October 29, 1848. He added that it had come with McLain's letters of September 2 and 6. The *National Intelligencer* reported that the *Packet* sailed "under Captain Goodmanson." *National Intelligencer* (Washington, DC), September 11, 1848. I conclude that Virgil received the letter of August 8 from Cameron when he boarded the *Packet* in November for his return trip. Physician J. W. Lugenbeel had boarded the vessel in early November at Monrovia and sailed in it to the settlement at Greenville, 150 miles south of the capital. He reported to McLain on November 25 that "on our way" the *Packet* had "stopped at Grand Bassa," where Lugenbeel learned of the great mortality among the emigrants there. Lugenbeel noted that the *Packet* had brought him letters that McLain had written in August. I infer that when James Goodmanson picked up Virgil's family at Bassa, the captain delivered Cameron's August letter to Virgil, which McLain had pledged would

be sent on the *Packet*'s September voyage. J. W. Lugenbeel to William McLain, November 25, 1848, ACS, reel 238.

9. Paul Cameron to Virgil Bennehan, August 8, 1848, typescript copy, CFP.

10. In the Cameron Family Papers, there is no explanation for why the original is missing, who made the typed copy, or when that was done. See note 24, below, for my speculation. I am confident that the transcription of the letter of August 8 itself is authentic. Two days before, Cameron had written to his father in Philadelphia; his letter of August 6 began with almost the same words. "*Here alone* in the dear old Home." See Paul Cameron to Duncan Cameron, August 6, 1848, CFP.

11. Paul Cameron to "My old friend Virgil," August 8, 1848, CFP.

12. Lindsay, *Atlantic Bonds*, 102. In 1852, sixteen-year-old Emily Hooper left enslavement in North Carolina after her free Black father purchased her freedom; she emigrated to Liberia. Six years later, disenchanted with Liberia, she wrote of her grievances to her former mistress, Chapel Hill resident Sally Mallett. In response to the letter, her former owner assumed she was ready to come back and successfully appealed to the state legislature in 1858 to pass a bill for the "Relief of Emily Hooper of Liberia," allowing her "voluntarily to return into a state of slavery"—and to Mallett's repossession. Emily Hooper did return, but not until 1871—and as a free person.

13. Nathans, *To Free a Family*, 23–30.

14. Paul Cameron to Duncan Cameron, November 18, December 2, 13, 23, 30, 1845, CFP; Nathans, *Mind to Stay*, 50–51.

15. Paul Cameron to Duncan Cameron, n.d., [1849], Undated Letters, folder 1803, CFP. For the hardened feelings expressed in Paul Cameron's changed language about the "black family," see Nathans, *Mind to Stay*, 58–60.

16. Nathans, *To Free a Family*, 16–17; Nathans, *Mind to Stay*, 61–63. Duncan Cameron detailed his ongoing depression in letters to his son in February 1849. On February 1, he stated that he was more excitable "than I had [been] for some weeks past." On February 15, he tried arranging his private papers but "the labor was *too much* for me. I became worried and excited" and experienced a "severe paroxysm of nervous suffering." On February 23, he was still "nervous, debilitated, and depressed." Duncan Cameron to Paul Cameron, February 1, 15, 23, 1849, CFP. It was Justice Frederick Nash who reported that the "old commanding figure is gone." Frederick Nash to [Sally Nash], January 2, February 3, [1849], box 72.2, Francis Nash Manuscripts, Pattie Mordecai Collection, State Archives of North Carolina, Raleigh.

17. Paul Cameron to Duncan Cameron, undated letter, [February 1849], Undated Letters, folder 1806, CFP.

18. Phebe [*sic*] Bennehan to Anna Bell, care of Judge Cameron, March 18, 1852, CFP. My belief that Virgil and his wife, Phoebe, had learned about Mary Walker's escape comes from an oblique reference in a letter that Phoebe Bennehan wrote in 1852 to her niece, Anna Bell, who resided at the Cameron residence in Raleigh as the enslaved caregiver for Mildred Cameron. Phoebe Bennehan had reared Anna from age two after the niece's mother died; Phoebe regarded Anna as her adopted daughter. Written from Baltimore, the letter of 1852 expressed Phoebe's hope that she could travel to Raleigh to visit Anna but stated that first she intended to pay a visit to Philadelphia. "I hope I shall be able to see you before long. I want to go to Philadelphia first and then will come to see you [if] I can." Philadelphia was the city in which Mary Walker escaped in 1848 and where Phoebe and others believed she still resided in 1852.

In 1853, a Cameron manservant who accompanied the sisters on their return to Philadelphia attempted to find Mary Walker there; that same year, Mary Walker's son Frank also thought she still lived in the city. Nathans, *To Free a Family*, 94–95. I believe that Phoebe's stated plan to go "to Philadelphia first" was a signal that she intended to seek out Mary Walker there— and that she'd learned about the escape. Neither Phoebe Bennehan nor Frank Walker knew that in the wake of the Fugitive Slave Law, passed in September 1850, Mary Walker had fled to Massachusetts, where she found sanctuary with an antislavery couple.

19. Covering the ACS office in Washington for the absent William McLain was his associate Noah Fletcher. Starting on February 16, McLain was in Baltimore awaiting the imminent departure of the *Liberia Packet* and communicating in person with James Hall. William McLain to Noah Fletcher, February 16, 1849, and Fletcher to McLain, February 22, 23, 1849, ACS, reel 58. McLain returned to Washington and resumed his correspondence with Hall by March 2. James Hall to William McLain, March 2, 1849, ACS, reel 58.

20. William McLain to John Newlin, March 6, 1849, ACS, reel 189.

21. William McLain to Henry Roberts, September 1, 1848, February 19, 1849, ACS, reel 238.

22. William McLain to John Newlin, March 6, 1849, ACS, reel 189.

23. Paul Cameron to Duncan Cameron, March 4, [1849], CFP. The letter is misdated *in pencil* as 1854 and is erroneously placed in the folder for 1854. Cameron had attempted a train trip to witness the inauguration of Zachary Taylor, which was not 1854 but March 1849.

24. It is my surmise that Virgil Bennehan left the original of the letter dated August 8, 1848, from Paul Cameron in the care of his wife, Phoebe, rather than take it to California. The letter was a remnant and a reminder of Cameron's earlier pledge of friendship and enduring care—"you have no better friend this side of the grave." My guess is that Virgil decided that if he failed in California and Phoebe found herself in need, the letter might help Phoebe rekindle attachment and summon assistance from Paul Cameron or one of his sisters. How did the letter wind up in the Cameron Family Papers as a typed and transcribed copy? I further conjecture that after emancipation, Phoebe shared the original with her niece Anna Bell, who, following the war, continued to serve as a caretaker for Cameron's sister Mildred on the Cameron estate in Raleigh and was rewarded for faithful service with a bequest of an acre of Cameron land. I believe that Anna (who after marriage became Annie Belle Davis) at some point shared the original with a Cameron family member in Raleigh, who in turn transcribed, typed, and added it to the family's papers.

CHAPTER 9

1. Nathans, *Mind to Stay*, 66, 77.

2. See the Seventh Federal Census, 1850, for Baltimore County, Maryland, Free Inhabitants, City of Baltimore, Ward 1, Dwelling 667, Family 839, accessed through Ancestry.com. I also used Ancestry and the 1850 Census to determine the occupation of census-taker M. M. Mearis. For a brief but vivid description of Fells Point in the 1830s, see Blight, *Frederick Douglass*, 36–37.

3. Paul Cameron to Margaret Cameron Mordecai, February 14, 1856, CFP.

4. I found names of five men who gave their occupations as speculator, either in the Baltimore Census of 1850 or in the Baltimore city directory for 1851: William Wardenburg,

William Delcher, Nicholas Berteau, Isaac Wareham, and Levi Benjamin. Some subsequently gave different occupations for themselves, including astrologer and pawnbroker.

5. In the Baltimore property records at the Maryland State Archives, and in court records at the Baltimore City Archives, Virgil Bennehan was not named as party to any property transactions, written contracts, or lawsuits. Since by Maryland law, African Americans were not recognized as citizens or entitled to sue whites, it is not surprising that I found nothing that involved Virgil as a party, plaintiff, or defendant. Nonetheless, as historian Martha Jones has shown, such lawsuits did occur and on occasion brought victories and partial recognition of "rights" for the intrepid. Jones, *Birthright Citizens*.

6. Historian Peter Decker demonstrated that numbers of men, representing merchants and investors in the East, went to California to sell the goods that easterners shipped to San Francisco for "grand speculation" and profit. Most of the middlemen were younger sons or trusted relatives of the white merchants who sent the goods for their relatives to sell to the highest bidder. Decker, *Fortunes and Failures*, 9–16.

7. Matchett, *Matchett's Baltimore Directory*, 303. No occupation was given for Phoebe Bennehan. I used the digitized versions of *Matchett's Baltimore Directory*.

8. Ideally, I'd have been able to *compare* the Baltimore Census of 1850 with the San Francisco Census of 1850 to see if Virgil Bennehan or any others from Baltimore were listed in *both* censuses. There was a census taken for San Francisco in 1850. But at the turn of the twentieth century, a flood at a storage facility damaged the original manuscript of that part of the US Census. It was destroyed.

9. Unable to check occupations for persons enumerated in San Francisco, I looked for occupations in the US Census of 1850 for Sacramento. There I found the names of ten men who explicitly listed their occupations as speculator or trader: James Alexander, William Burditt, Walter Burton, J. T. Chatham, D. H. Haskell, Ross Hughes, Walter Jackson, Ben Nickerson, John Shields, and James Watson. See also Eifler, *Gold Rush Capitalists*.

10. *Baltimore Sun*, December 9, 1848, January 24, 1849.

11. *Baltimore Sun*, December 9, 1848, January 24, 1849.

12. *Baltimore Sun*, February 13, 1849, March 15, 1850.

13. James Hall to William McLain, January 15, 1851, ACS, [reel 191?]. The clipping that Hall enclosed was from the *Baltimore Sun* of January 15, 1851. The *Sun* published the first report of Virgil Bennehan's death a week earlier. Summarizing the news from California up to December 1, 1849, the *Sun* noted on January 7 only that "Virgil Benneham [*sic*], of Baltimore, died at San Francisco." The January 15 issue was more complete, giving Virgil's age and adding that "congestive fever" was the cause of death.

14. Rasmussen, *San Francisco Ship Passenger Lists*. These records begin in 1850 and do not include 1849. Cargo ships departing from Baltimore took between 155 and 197 days, with fewer than five full-paying registered passengers and a handful more in steerage, listed only as "unidentified." On passenger ships arriving from all ports to San Francisco, no steerage passengers were registered or listed by name. Neither Virgil Bennehan nor any other passengers from Baltimore were listed among those indexed in Louis Rasmussen's compilation of California wagon train lists. Rasmussen, *California Wagon Train Lists*. Without naming passengers, there was a notice, reprinted in Rasmussen, of a Baltimore and Frederick Mining Company wagon train en route to California, published in the *New York Daily Tribune*, May 16, 1849. Rasmussen, *California Wagon Train Lists*, 89.

15. The account of Edward Hargraves, who arrived on October 4, 1848, after an eighty-one-day voyage from Sydney, is quoted in Brands, *Age of Gold*, 61. The report of the dozens of flags flying from vessels in the harbor is in the *Baltimore Sun*, December 10, 1849. The iconic photograph of the harbor and city in 1850 is reproduced as the frontispiece in Rasmussen, *San Francisco Ship Passenger Lists*.

16. Lapp, *Blacks in Gold Rush California*, 13. See also Daniels, *Pioneer Urbanites*. "Afro Americans' faith that gold—or speculating, commerce, gambling, even honest toil—would change their status is remarkable." "Speculation's potential rewards gave it widespread appeal." Blacks "waxed eloquent about the chances for improving their social station." Daniels, *Pioneer Urbanites*, 28–29.

17. For the salaries of stewards, see Daniels, *Pioneer Urbanites*, 29. For the cost of lodging, see reports in the *Baltimore Sun*, April 7, 1849, and January 31, 1850.

18. "Letter from a Gold Seeker," December 15, 1849, published in the *Liberator* (Boston), February 15, 1850. For the dangers faced by free and illegally enslaved Blacks in the goldfields, see Pfaelzer, *California, a Slave State*, chaps. 5 and 6, and esp. 131–37.

19. Decker, *Fortunes and Failures*, 34. Soulé, Gihon, and Nisbet, *Annals of San Francisco*, 215–16. In the Matchett city directories, Phoebe Bennehan provided no occupation for herself in 1851 and 1852. She was listed as a "washer" or washerwoman in Baltimore city directories from 1853 onward and was listed as a laundress in the 1860 US Census. By 1852, Phoebe Bennehan had moved from Argyle Alley in Fells Point to a different address near the new Camden Yards of the Baltimore and Ohio Railroad. Most free Blacks in Fells Point moved away from the port area in the 1850s because of "occupational competition between Free Blacks and immigrants." They shifted to the city's interior, and from waterfront trades to service and transportation occupations. Near the railroad hub around Union Station, Phoebe Bennehan and other women found work as laundresses. May, "Residential Change," 2.

20. Decker, *Fortunes and Failures*, 35–43; Soulé, Gihon, and Nisbet, *Annals of San Francisco*, 289, 302–4, 366.

21. For Frederick Douglass's damning view of colonization and Liberia, see Blight, *Douglass*, 238–39.

22. The quotation comes from an editorial of 1852 in *Frederick Douglass' Paper*, quoted in Daniels, *Pioneer Urbanites*, 62. Wrote Douglass: "Colored easterners expressed a madness known as the 'California excitement' and began making preparations for departure.... Married men left their wives and families. Some left profitable pursuits and 'a certainty for an uncertainty.' Discretion and reasonable considerations seem to have been abandoned."

23. John Wentz listed his occupation in the Matchett city directory for 1851 and also in the US Censuses of 1850 and 1860. During the 1850s, he changed his address several times but remained on Ann Street. In the 1860 city directory, he was listed as a cupper and leecher. For the occupations of those who lived on Argyle Alley in 1850, see the Matchett city directory for 1851. I found the listings intermittently between pp. 302 and 342. For intensifying white workers' attacks on all Black workers at Fells Point in the 1850s, see Phillips, *Freedom's Port*, 19–20, 195–99, 202–3, 206, 224–25, 236.

24. Blassingame et al., *Frederick Douglass Papers*, 2:89–91 (August 5–6, 1847), 2:168 (May 7, 1849), 2:240 (May 7, 1850).

25. Historian Rudolph Lapp determined that although Douglass's paper printed unfavorable coverage of the Gold Rush for most of 1849, by December the paper started to run

positive comments about Blacks in California. Lapp concluded that Douglass understood that American Blacks had to seize any opportunity to reach the same economic starting point as the lowest white American. In 1852, Douglass judged that "'some have returned much better off and some worse.'" Lapp, *Blacks in Gold Rush California*, 16, 23.

26. The *Alta California* complained about the delay in William Newell's listing of deaths in Little Chile, then apologized when it learned that his daughter Florence Newell had been ill and died. San Francisco *Alta California* (San Francisco), November 15, 1850. When Newell belatedly provided the list, the *Alta* published it on December 1, 1850.

27. Weekly report of Interments by William Newell, Sexton and Undertaker, Pacific Street, near Kearney. Newell provided no dates of deaths. *Alta California* (San Francisco), December 1, 1850. For the added information that Virgil Bennehan died of "congestive fever," see the *Baltimore Sun*, January 15, 1851.

28. *Plasmodium falciparum*, the deadly variant of the malaria parasite prevalent in Africa—does not in itself last long or cause a relapse of symptoms. The victim must be bitten and reinfected by another *falciparum*-laden mosquito, rare outside of Africa. The *Plasmodium vivax* parasite was the variant carried by mosquitoes in the United States; the *vivax* parasite infected those on the Cameron plantation. *Vivax* could last and recur up to three years after the most recent infection and "could travel with the seasonal settler." Webb, *Humanity's Burden*, 1–9. Normally, the *vivax* fever did not reach the point of "congestion." But when untreated, the parasite could reach a high density in the body, clog arteries, lead to congestion of the heart, spleen, and kidneys—or bring on cerebral malaria—especially in persons long enervated by fever. Humphreys, *Malaria*, 9. An older account of malaria, based on the direct observations of an American physician in 1910, probably comes closest to describing what Virgil Bennehan endured in San Francisco in November 1850. For Dr. Finley Ellingwood, "congestive intermittent fever" and "congestive chill" were *synonyms* for malaria, which he defined as a "sudden, profound, general congestion accompanied with a violent chill and rapid, serious, often fatal prostration." Congestion was "apt to occur during the progress of severe, protracted fevers." Dr. Finley Englewood, "The Eclectic Practice of Medicine with Especial Reference to the Treatment of Disease, 1910," accessed on the digitized *Henriette's Herbal Homepage*. It seems probable that Anne Cameron experienced the symptoms of "congestive fever" when sustained fever led to excruciating headaches and delirium and turned her fingers purple.

29. I checked the digitized database of San Francisco Area Funeral Home Records, 1835–1979; the Funeral Home Records for San Francisco, 1850–1931, accessible on Ancestry.com; and the microfilmed N. B. Gray Funeral Records for the names of those buried at Yerba Buena cemetery. The *Alta California* for August 1, 1850, reported that coroner William Newell billed the city for pauper burials he arranged in July.

30. Lapp, *Blacks in Gold Rush California*, 192, 239–40; Brands, *Age of Gold*, 273–81. In listing persons of color who died in California in 1850, the *Alta California* specified "colored" in parentheses after their names. The N. B. Gray funeral listings for Yerba Buena also added "colored" for those buried there. See, for example, the death notice for "Henry Fowler (colored), 53, cholera," *Alta California* (San Francisco), November 23, 1850; and the Yerba Buena cemetery report for "Henry Fowler, died or buried November 27, 1850, aged 53 years; colored." With support but without success, legislative efforts to ban Black immigration into the state recurred through the 1850s.

31. In November 1850, San Francisco's rainy season set in. So noted the *Alta California*, as relayed by the report published in the *Baltimore Sun*, January 8, 1851. Once rains came, the city became a quagmire of mud in which animals and carts and people got stuck, with special risk to those who lived in flimsy dwellings or in tents to "save ground rent."

32. Gibbs, *Shadow and Light*, 42–47, 59–61. In 1858, 200 free Blacks left California for Victoria with Mifflin Gibbs. Lapp, *Blacks in Gold Rush California*, 239–41. For unsuccessful protests led by Gibbs and others, see Savage, *Blacks in the West*, 139–43; and Broussard, *Expectations of Equality*, 17–19. The best recent treatment of Mifflin Gibbs's experience, the civil rights protest, and the Black exodus to Vancouver in 1858 is Pfaelzer, *California, a Slave State*, 204–9, 231–34.

33. Phillips, *Freedom's Port*, 213–14, 224–25; Jones, *Birthright Citizens*, 38–39, 46–48, 94–96.

34. "Letter to the Liberator," December 30, 1849, published in the *Liberator* (Boston), February 15, 1850. The letter announced the formation of the Colored Association in San Francisco and declared that its members "are doing something for ourselves toward our future welfare" and are earning "from one to three hundred dollars per month."

35. Bennehan to Bell, March 18, 1852, CFP.

36. Mount Hope Cemetery, Raleigh, NC.

EPILOGUE

1. Petition to "To the Honorable the Legislature of the State of California," San Francisco, March 10, 1852, original in California State Archives, Sacramento; "Colonization of Free Blacks. Memorial of Leonard Dugged, George A. Bailey, and 240 other free colored persons of California . . . ," January 16, 1862, tabled and printed, 37th Cong., 2nd Sess., House of Representatives, Misc. Doc. No. 31, pp. 1–6; Blight, *Douglass*, 374–75.

2. Burlingame, *Black Man's President*, 8–9.

3. Moses W. Walker was the father of Moses Fleetwood Walker, who in 1884 became the first African American to play a full season for a Major League Baseball team. The son's story is skillfully told and boldly interpreted in Zang, *Fleet Walker's Divided Heart*. Fleet Walker and his young brother William Wilberforce "Weldy" Walker both played baseball in the 1880s. They became advocates of emigration to Liberia in 1907, and in 1908, Moses Fleetwood Walker published *Our Home Colony*. I did not become aware of parent Moses W. Walker's journey to Liberia until I read Zang's biography and recalled mention of a "Walker" in Virgil Bennehan's letter of 1848 from Liberia. ACS records provided the fuller story of father Moses Walker's conversion to colonization and his wholehearted endorsement of emigration after returning from Liberia. His sons surely knew of their father's zeal when they themselves turned to emigration as the best hope for African Americans, seen forever as outcasts and "scullions" in the United States. The Walkers never went beyond verbal advocacy. Others did. See Field, *Growing Up in the Country*. The English rendering of the Latin quotation is from the Robert Fitzgerald translation of Virgil's *Aeneid*.

BIBLIOGRAPHY

PRIMARY SOURCES

Manuscript and Archival Collections

Chapel Hill, NC
    Wilson Library Special Collections, University of North Carolina at Chapel Hill
        Southern Historical Collection
            Cameron Family Papers, 1757–1978
            Ruffin, Roulhac, and Hamilton Family Papers, 1784–1951
Madison, NJ
    United Methodist Church Archives and History, Drew University
        Walter P. Jayne, *Liberian Journal, 1839–1841*
Nashville, TN
    Southern Baptist Historical Library and Archives
        John Day Correspondence, 1846–59
Northfield, VT
    Norwich University Archives and Special Collections
        Alden Partridge Papers
Raleigh, NC
    Pattie Mordecai Collection, State Archives of North Carolina
        Francis Nash Manuscripts
Washington, DC
    Manuscript Division, Library of Congress
        American Colonization Society Records, 1792–1964 (microfilm)

Newspapers

African Repository (Washington, DC)
Alta California (San Francisco)
Baltimore Sun
Illinois Times (Springfield)
Liberator (Boston)

Liberia Herald (Monrovia, Liberia)
National Intelligencer (Washington, DC)
New York Times
North Star (Rochester, NY)

Directories, Pamphlets, and Passenger Lists

Ball, Samuel S. *Liberia: The Condition and Prospects of That Republic: Made from Actual Observation.* Alton, IL: Telegraph Office, 1848.

Matchett, Richard J. *Matchett's Baltimore Directory, for 1851.* Baltimore: Richard J. Matchett, 1851.

Rasmussen, Louis J., ed. *California Wagon Train Lists.* Vol. 1, *April 5, 1849 to October 20, 1852.* Colma, CA: San Francisco Historic Records, 1994.

———. *San Francisco Ship Passenger Lists.* 3 vols. Colma, CA: San Francisco Historic Records, 1965–67.

Walker, M. F. *Our Home Colony: A Treatise on the Past, Present, and Future of the Negro Race in America.* Steubenville, OH: Herald Printing Company, 1908.

SECONDARY SOURCES

Books and Book Chapters

Anderson, Jean Bradley. *The Kirklands of Ayr Mount.* Chapel Hill: University of North Carolina Press, 1991.

———. *Piedmont Plantation: The Bennehan-Cameron Family and Lands in North Carolina.* Durham, NC: Historic Preservation Society of Durham, 1985.

Andrews, William L., and David A. Davis, eds. *North Carolina Slave Narratives.* Chapel Hill: University of North Carolina Press, 2003.

Blassingame, John W., ed. *Slave Testimony: Two Centuries of Letters, Speeches, and Autobiographies.* Baton Rouge: Louisiana State University Press, 1977.

Blassingame, John W., John R. McKivigan, Peter P. Hinks, and Gerald Fulkerson, eds. *The Frederick Douglass Papers. Series One: Speeches, Debates, and Interviews.* Vol. 2, *1847–54.* New Haven, CT: Yale University Press, 1979–92.

Blight, David W. *Frederick Douglass: Prophet of Freedom.* New York: Simon and Schuster, 2018.

Brands, H. W. *The Age of Gold: The California Gold Rush and the New American Dream.* New York: Doubleday, 2002.

Broussard, Albert S. *Expectations of Equality: A History of Black Westerners.* Wheeling, IL: Harlan-Davidson, 2012.

Brown, Robert T. *Immigrants to Liberia, 1843–1865: An Alphabetical Listing*. Philadelphia: Institute for Liberian Studies, 1980.

Burin, Eric. "The Cape Mesurado Contract: A Reconsideration." In *New Directions in the Study of African American Colonization*, edited by Beverley C. Tomek and Matthew J. Hetrick, 229–48. Gainesville: University Press of Florida, 2017.

———. *Slavery and the Peculiar Solution: A History of the American Colonization Society*. Gainesville: University Press of Florida, 2005.

Burlingame, Michael. *Abraham Lincoln: A Life*. Vol. 1. Baltimore: Johns Hopkins University Press, 2008.

———. *The Black Man's President: Abraham Lincoln, African Americans, and the Pursuit of Racial Equality*. New York: Pegasus Books, 2021.

Campbell, Penelope. *Maryland in Africa: The Maryland State Colonization Society, 1831–1857*. Urbana: University of Illinois Press, 1971.

Carlson, Dennis G. *African Fever: A Study in British Science, Technology, and Politics in West Africa, 1787–1964*. Canton, MA: Science History Publications, Watson, 1984.

Clegg, Claude A., III. *The Price of Liberty: African Americans and the Making of Liberia*. Chapel Hill: University of North Carolina Press, 2004.

Daniels, Douglas Henry. *Pioneer Urbanites: A Social and Cultural History of Black San Francisco*. 1980. Reprint, Berkeley: University of California Press, 1990.

Decker, Peter R. *Fortunes and Failures*. Cambridge, MA: Harvard University Press, 1978.

Diemer, Andrew K. *Vigilance: The Life of William Still, Father of the Underground Railroad*. New York: Alfred A. Knopf, 2022.

Eifler, Mark. *Gold Rush Capitalists: Greed and Growth in Sacramento*. Albuquerque: University of New Mexico Press, 2002.

Faust, Drew Gilpin. *James Henry Hammond and the Old South: A Design for Mastery*. Baton Rouge: Louisiana State University Press, 1985.

Field, Kendra Taira. *Growing Up in the Country: Family, Race, and Nation after the Civil War*. New Haven, CT: Yale University Press, 2018.

Franklin, John Hope. *The Free Negro in North Carolina, 1790–1860*. 1943. Reprint, New York: Russell and Russell, 1969.

Gibbs, Mifflin Wistar. *Shadow and Light: An Autobiography*. 1902. Reprint, Arno Press, 1968.

Gordon-Reed, Annette. *The Hemingses of Monticello: An American Family*. New York: W. W. Norton, 2005.

Gutman, Herbert G. *The Black Family in Slavery and Freedom, 1750–1925*. New York: Pantheon, 1976.

Hecimovich, Gregg. *The Life and Times of Hannah Crafts: The True Story of The Bondwoman's Narrative*. New York: HarperCollins, 2023.

Humphreys, Margaret. *Malaria: Poverty, Race, and Public Health in the United States*. Baltimore: Johns Hopkins University Press, 2001.

Hunter, Tera W. *Bound in Wedlock: Slave and Free Black Marriage in the Nineteenth Century*. Cambridge, MA: Harvard University Press, 2017.

Jones, Bernie D. *Fathers of Conscience: Mixed-Race Inheritance in the Antebellum South*. Athens: University of Georgia Press, 2009.

Jones, Martha S. *Birthright Citizens: A History of Race and Rights in Antebellum America*. Cambridge: Cambridge University Press, 2018.

Kaplan, Fred. *Lincoln and the Abolitionists*. New York: HarperCollins, 2017.

Kazanjian, David. *The Brink of Freedom: Improvising Life in the Nineteenth-Century Atlantic World*. Durham, NC: Duke University Press, 2016.

Lapp, Rudolph M. *Blacks in Gold Rush California*. New Haven, CT: Yale University Press, 1977.

Levitt, Jeremy I. *The Evolution of Deadly Conflict in Liberia: From "Paternaltarianism" to State Collapse*. Durham, NC: Carolina Academic Press, 2005.

Lindsay, Lisa A. *Atlantic Bonds: A Nineteenth-Century Odyssey from America to Africa*. Chapel Hill: University of North Carolina Press, 2017.

Lindsay, Lisa A., and John Wood Sweet, eds. *Biography and the Black Atlantic*. Philadelphia: University of Pennsylvania Press, 2014.

Maris-Wolf, Ted. *Family Bonds: Free Blacks and Re-Enslavement Law in Antebellum Virginia*. Chapel Hill: University of North Carolina Press, 2015.

McDaniel, Antonio (now Tukufu Zuberi). *Swing Low, Sweet Chariot: The Mortality Cost of Colonizing Liberia in the Nineteenth Century*. Chicago: University of Chicago Press, 1995.

McKirdy, Charles R. *Lincoln Apostate: The Matson Slave Case*. Jackson: University Press of Mississippi, 2011.

Mills, Brandon. *The World Colonization Made: The Racial Geography of Early American Empire*. Philadelphia: University of Pennsylvania Press, 2020.

Milteer, Warren Eugene, Jr. *North Carolina's Free People of Color, 1717–1885*. Baton Rouge: Louisiana State University Press, 2020.

Morgan, Jennifer L. *Reckoning with Slavery: Gender, Kinship, and Capitalism in the Early Black Atlantic*. Durham, NC: Duke University Press, 2021.

Moses, Wilson Jeremiah, ed. *Liberian Dreams: Back to Africa Narratives from the 1850s*. University Park: Pennsylvania State University Press, 1998.

Muller, Viola Franziska. *Escape to the City: Fugitive Slaves in the Antebellum Urban South*. Chapel Hill: University of North Carolina Press, 2022.

Murray, Robert. *Atlantic Passages: Race, Mobility, and Liberian Colonization*. Gainesville: University Press of Florida, 2021.

Nathans, Sydney. *To Free a Family: The Journey of Mary Walker*. Cambridge, MA: Harvard University Press, 2012.

———. *A Mind to Stay: White Plantation, Black Homeland*. Cambridge, MA: Harvard University Press, 2017.

Naylor, Celia E. *Unsilencing Slavery: Telling Truths about Rose Hall Plantation, Jamaica*. Athens: University of Georgia Press, 2021.

Pargas, Damian Alan. *Freedom Seekers: Fugitive Slaves in North America*. New York: Cambridge University Press, 2022.

———, ed. *Fugitive Slaves and Spaces of Freedom in North America*. Gainesville: University Press of Florida, 2018.

Parker, Freddie L. *Running for Freedom: Slave Runaways in North Carolina, 1775–1840*. New York: Garland, 1993.

Pfaelzer, Jean. *California, a Slave State*. New Haven, CT: Yale University Press, 2022.

Phillips, Christopher. *Freedom's Port: The African American Community of Baltimore, 1790–1860*. Urbana: University of Illinois Press, 1997.

Power-Greene, Ousmane K. *Against Wind and Tide: The African American Struggle against the Colonization Movement.* New York: New York University Press, 2014.

Saha, Santosh C. *Culture in Liberia: An Afrocentric View of the Cultural Interaction between the Indigenous Liberians and the Americo-Liberians.* Lewiston, NY: Edward Mellen Press, 1998.

Savage, W. Sherman. *Blacks in the West.* Westport, CT: Greenwood, 1976.

Scott, Julius. *The Common Wind: Afro-American Currents in the Age of the Haitian Revolution.* London: Verso, 2018.

Scott, Rebecca J., and Jean-Michel Hébrard. "Rosalie of the Poulard Nation: Freedom, Law, and Dignity in the Era of the Haitian Revolution." In *Biography and the Black Atlantic*, edited by Lisa A. Lindsay and John Wood Sweet, 248–68. Philadelphia: University of Pennsylvania Press, 2014.

Simpson, Joshua McCarter. *The Emancipation Car: Being an Original Composition of Anti-Slavery Ballads; Composed Exclusively for the Underground Railroad.* Zanesville, OH: N.p., 1874.

Soulé, Frank, John H. Gihon, and James Nisbet. *The Annals of San Francisco.* New York: Appleton, 1855.

Sundiata, Ibrahim. *Brothers and Strangers: Black Zion, Black Slavery, 1914–1940.* Durham, NC: Duke University Press, 2003.

Tomek, Beverley C. *Colonization and Its Discontents: Emancipation, Emigration, and Anti-slavery in Antebellum Pennsylvania.* New York: New York University Press, 2011.

Tomek, Beverley C., and Matthew J. Hetrick, eds. *New Directions in the Study of African American Colonization.* Gainesville: University Press of Florida, 2017.

Tyler-McGraw, Marie. *An African Republic: Black and White Virginians in the Making of Liberia.* Chapel Hill: University of North Carolina Press, 2007.

Webb, James L. A., Jr. *Humanity's Burden: A Global History of Malaria.* New York: Cambridge University Press, 2009.

Wells-Oghoghomeh, Alexis. *The Souls of Womenfolk: The Religious Cultures of Enslaved Women in the Lower South.* Chapel Hill: University of North Carolina Press, 2021.

West, Emily. *Family or Freedom: People of Color in the Antebellum South.* Lexington: University Press of Kentucky, 2012.

Wheeler, John H. *Reminiscences and Memoirs of North Carolina and Eminent North Carolinians.* 1888. Reprint Baltimore: Genealogical Publishing, 1966.

Wiencek, Henry. *The Hairstons: An American Family in Black and White.* New York: St. Martin's Press, 1999.

Wiley, Bell I., ed. *Slaves No More: Letters from Liberia, 1833–1869.* Lexington: University Press of Kentucky, 1980.

Zang, David W. *Fleet Walker's Divided Heart: The Life of Baseball's First Black Major Leaguer.* Lincoln: University of Nebraska Press, 1995.

Journal Articles

Burin, Eric. "Rethinking Northern White Support for the African Colonization Movement: The Pennsylvania Colonization Society as an Agent of Emancipation." *Pennsylvania Magazine of History and Biography* 127, no. 2 (2003): 197–229.

Crawford, Amy. "How One Historian Located Liberia's Elusive Founding Document." *Smithsonian Magazine* 53, no. 3 (July–August 2022): 22–28.

Gatewood, Willard B., Jr. "'To Be Truly Free': Louis Sheridan and the Colonization of Liberia." *Civil War History* 29, no. 4 (December 1983): 332–48.

Mills, Brandon. "'The United States of Africa': Liberian Independence and the Contested Meaning of a Black Republic." *Journal of the Early Republic* 34, no. 1 (Spring 2014): 79–107.

Mitchell, Memory F. "Out of Africa—with Judicial Blessing." *North Carolina Historical Review* 53, no. 3 (July 1976): 265–87.

Mitchell, Memory F., and Thornton W. Mitchell. "The Philanthropic Bequests of John Rex of Raleigh: Part I: Bon Voyage and a Lawsuit." *North Carolina Historical Review* 49, no. 3 (July 1972): 254–79.

———. "The Philanthropic Bequests of John Rex of Raleigh: Part II: More Lawsuits and the Tortuous Road to Victory." *North Carolina Historical Review* 49, no. 4 (October 1972): 353–76.

Wilkinson, Doris Y. "The 1850 Harvard Medical Dispute and the Admission of African American Students." *Harvard Library Bulletin* 3, no. 3 (Fall 1992): 13–27.

Dissertations, Theses, and Databases

Carter, Janie Leigh. "John Day: A Founder of the Republic of Liberia and the Southern Baptist Liberian Missionary Movement of the Nineteenth Century." Master's thesis, Wake Forest University, 1998.

Hughes, Chris. "Database of Slaves on the Bennehan-Cameron Plantation, Stagville, North Carolina." 1998. Reformatted on Microsoft Word, 2003. Durham, NC: Historic Stagville.

Jones, Alice Eley. "Interviews with Stagville Descendants." Durham, NC: Historic Stagville.

May, Patrick Joseph. "The Residential Change of the Free Black Population of Baltimore, 1850–1860." PhD diss., University of Maryland, College Park, 1999.

INDEX

Page numbers in italics refer to illustrations.

Bennehan, Richard, xii, 2, 6, 7, 12–13, 15–16

Bennehan, Thomas: bachelorhood of, 5, 142n9; Paul Cameron, relationship with, 25; childhood of, 3; death of, 40; illness of, 7; Phillip Meaks, relationship with, 13–14; and measles outbreak at Cameron holdings, 26–27; and medical care of slaves, 7, 8–9; sojourns away from Stagville, 27–28, 35–36; treatment of enslaved persons by, 5, 32; and John Umstead's enslaved persons, 25–26, 34–35; and Virgil's possible paternity, 2, 33; as Virgil's protector, 10–11, 38; wills of, xiii–xiv, 31–34, 35–36, 38–39, 44

Bennehan, Virgil
—California plans of: 110–11, 113–15, 123
—childhood and youth of: birth, xiii, 1–2, 9; paternity speculation, 10, 12, 33, 127
—correspondence of, xv, 61, 62, 65, 95, 102–4, 110–11, 123, 130
—early career of: education and training, 2, 10; marriage, 25–26
—as enslaved person: manumission possibilities, 36–37, 38–39; manumission required, 32–33, 35, 36, 44; reenslavement request, 101–5; role conflict and divided loyalties, xiv, xv, 11–12, 38; and patrons, help from, 38, 51, 53, 58–59, 117; special treatment, 10, 35, 36
—family and friends, relations with: in Thomas Bennehan's will, 32–34; Paul Cameron, partnership with, 29, 42, 43; and Cameron temperaments, 37; and use of middle initials, 12, 64
—Liberia: 1848 arrival to, 43, 61, 74–75, 78; 1849 departure from, 79–80, 88–89; and 1849 North Carolina, return to, 90–92, 91, 101, 107–8; disappointment about, 64–65; purchase of land in, 67–70; possible return to, 109–10; reports on, 95–96; views on, 49–52, 57, 76, 92–93
—as medical professional: as assistant to Thomas Bennehan, 10–11; Baltimore, barriers to medical practice in, 110;

medical care provided in Liberia, 76–77; medical care provided in United States, 11, 27–28, 44; and 1836 measles outbreak, 26–27; treatment of Thomas Bennehan's final illness, 40
—final years of: death, 118, 124, 126–27; undocumented years (1849 to 1856), 114–17, 118

Bennehan-Cameron plantation, 1, 5–6, 30, 142n11; treatment of enslaved persons at, 38. See also Stagville plantation

Benson, Stephen, 67, 68, 70, 74–75, 76, 77, 79–80, 83

Bexley, Liberia, 51, 63, 66. See also Liberia

Black Baptist Association, 55, 84, 161n15

Black Laws, 84; California, 127, 129; Illinois, 5; Indiana, 55; Maryland, 129; Ohio, 54–55

Black people. See enslaved people; people of color

bleeding (medical treatment), 8, 29, 123

Bondwoman's Narrative, The (Crafts), 101, 166n3

Brown, Henry, 92–93, 96, 109

Bryant, Anthony, 85

Buchanan, Thomas, 46

California: for Black immigrants, 122–23; and gold rush, 116–17, 120, 121–22; legislation regarding testimony of Black persons in, 133; San Francisco, 119–21, 120, 124–26, 125; travels to, 118–19

calomel, 8, 29

Cameron, Anne (Duncan's daughter), 31–32

Cameron, Anne (Ruffin; Paul's wife), 24, 26, 27, 65, 111

Cameron, Duncan, 9, 10, 19–21, 20, 27; and Paul Cameron's Alabama failure, 41; enslaved labor, management of, 24–25; as executor of Thomas Bennehan estate, 36; nervous breakdown of, 107–8; role in ACS, 45–46; travels of, to Philadelphia, 44–45, 46–47, 152n17; views on Luke as personal servant,

Fells Point neighborhood, Baltimore, 113–14
fever. *See* malaria
Forman, Robert, 130
freedom, and slave rebellions, 3–4. *See also* manumission
freedom, as concept, 13, 36, 44, 90–91, 93, 101, 107, 136, 143n26, 161n17
free people of color, 105, 123; in California, 129, 130, 133; denial of rights of, 55; as passing as white, 127; in Philadelphia, 45
Free Soil movement, 54–55
friendship: of Paul Cameron and Virgil, xv, 38, 42, 61, 103; of Paul Cameron and Virgil, broken, 104–5, 107–8; interracial, 11–12, 42; loss and betrayal, 41; Virgil's interracial network, xv–xvi, 11–12, 38, 65–67
Fry, Charles. *See* Thomas, Charles "Scrub"
Fugitive Slave Law (1850), 134
fugitive slaves, 105–7, 150n31

Gales, Joseph, Jr., 52, 53
Garrison, William Lloyd, 130
Gibbs, Mifflin, 129
gold mining, 113, 116–17, 120, 121–22
"good conscience" of slaveholders, xvi, 33
Goodmanson, James, 61, 74, 88–89, 102
Grace (enslaved at Stagville), 66
Gracie (enslaved by Thomas Amis Jr.), 33, 147n5
grains, milling of, 5–6
Gray, N. B., 126
Green, William Mercer, 66, 156n11
Greensboro, AL, 37, 39, 41
Guadeloupe slave rebellion, 3
Gutman, Herbert, xiii

Hall, James, 52, 58–59, 72–73, 81, 88–89; correspondence of, with William McLain, 117–18; and *Liberia Packet*, 108; and Virgil's death, 128–29
Halleck, Henry, 116
Hamilton, Patrick, 58
Harriet (enslaved by John Umstead), 35, 36

Harris, King Joe, 47–48
Harris, Polly, 67
Harris, Samuel, 67–69, 156n14
Harris, William, 66
Harry (enslaved by Thomas Amis Jr.), 33
Haywood, William, 21–22
heroic medicine, 28–29
Hillsborough, NC, 10
Horton Grove slave dwellings, *xii*

Illinois: Black immigration to, 84; and 1847 constitutional convention, 55; and Free Soil movement, 54–55
immigration: European, to Baltimore, 129–30; of free Blacks to northern states, 55, 84. *See also* Black Laws
Indiana, Free Soil movement, 54–55
indigenous peoples: Africa, and slave trade, 47–48; Bassa people, 47–48, 65, 71, 95; Kru people, 47–48, 65, 71; land ownership of, 47; of Liberia, 65, 79
ipecac, 8, 29

Jackson, Andrew, 110
Jayne, Walter, 77–78
Jefferson College of Medicine, Philadelphia, 44–45
John (enslaved at Stagville), 103
Johnson, Jane, 100–101

kitchens as infirmaries, 8, 9, 28, 29
Kollock, Samuel, 10
Kru peoples, 47–48, 65, 71

Lane, Lunsford, 90–92
Lettey (enslaved and buried at Stagville), 15, 16
Lewis, General John N., 63, 64, 72–73, 74–75, 80
Liberator (abolitionist newspaper), 130
Liberia, 43, *66*; creation of, 45–46, 54; and Cresson project, 46–47; criticism of, 89, 129–30; dissatisfaction of immigrants to, 46, 154n43, 157n6, 163n19; farming in, 65, 79, 95, 158n24; medical practice

in, 64–65; mortality rates in, 82, 163n21; *Our Home Colony*, 135, 136; poverty in, 165n32; power structures and hierarchies of, 84–87, 160n14, 160n11; rainy season in, 73, 79, 95; reports of, in United States, 83–85; respect shown to immigrants in, 63–64; slave traders in, 82. *See also individual names of settlements*

Liberia Herald (newspaper), 57, 87

Liberia Packet (ship), 51, 57, 58, 79–80; landing at Bassa (1848), 73; management by James Hall, 108; in Monrovia harbor, 43; and space on 1848 journey, 52–53; and Virgil's return to United States, 102–3; voyages of, 81–82, 88

Lincoln, Abraham, 133

Little River Cemetery, *15, 16,* 57

lowlands: drainage of, 8; medical dangers of, 7

Lugenbeel, J. W., 72, 73, 74, 75, 77, 80, 83

Luke (enslaved carriage driver), 23–24, 66

malaria, 126, 171n28; acclimation to, 71, 72, 75, 85, 87; African fever, 71–72; Bassa outbreak of, 76–80; death rates in Liberia from, 75–77, 79–80, 88; and plantation expansion, 6–8; treatment of, in Liberia, 72, 74–75, 157n13; venereal disease and vulnerability to, 75, 82–83

manumission, 36, 44; of children of slaveowners, 141n3; enslaved persons' refusal of, 36–37; of individual enslaved persons, 32–33; legal frameworks for, 36–37; and North Carolina law, 34–35, 44, 104; offers of, 32; and relocation to Liberia, 52; and requirement to exile, 53; John Rex case of, 45–46; in slaveowners' wills, 32–33, 148n13

Margaret "Peg" (Phoebe's niece), 25, 36, 38, 57, 102, 114

Maryland Colonization Society, 52, 88

Matchett, Richard J., 115

McCorkle, A. B., 72

McDaniel, George, xiii

McLain, William, 49–53, *50,* 57, 58–59; correspondence of, with James Hall, 117–18; and criticism of Virgil, 117–18; decisions regarding Bassa, 78–79; downplay of Liberian mortality, 92–93, 163n21, 164n28; on enforced *Liberia Packet* landing at Bassa, 74; and funding for ACS, 81; as head of ACS, 79–80; and Liberian recruitment efforts, 92–93, 152n26, 153n27; and malaria in Liberia, 71–72, 83, 89–90; and management of rumors and opposition, 108–9; and opposition to slave trade in Africa, 82; and push for educated emigrants to Liberia, 53–54; refutation of Virgil, 96; role in ACS, 67, 69, 71; and "spies" and reports from Liberia, 87–88; and Virgil's request to return to Liberia, 109–10

McPheeters, Reverend William, 21–22

Meaks, Esther (Virgil's grandmother), 1–2, 14

Meaks, Mary (Virgil's mother), 2, 12, 14, 143n14

Meaks, Nelly, 26

Meaks, Phillip (Virgil's grandfather), 1–2, 12–14, 16, 16–17, 26, 33, 120, 143n24

Meaks, Virgil (Virgil's uncle), 2

Mearis, M. M., 114

measles, 26–27

medical institutions, and racism, 45, 150n5

medical treatment: bleeding or cupping, 8, 29, 123; the drill, 28–29; heroic medicine, 8, 28–29; kitchens as infirmaries for, 8, 9, 28, 29

Mexico, 54

Middletown, CT, 22

migration, forced, 34, 36, 38, 58, 103, 138. *See also* exile

milling of grain, 5–6

mill ponds and stagnant water, 5, 7–8, 142n15, 143n17

Mima (Virgil's aunt), 57

Mina (enslaved person), 103

Steubenville, OH, 55–57, 87–88
Stokes, Darius, 129–30

Tate, Mark, 66
Taylor, Zachary, 110
Teage, Reverend Hilary, 63, 87
Thomas, Charles "Scrub," 12–13, 144nn26–28
Tilly, E., 66
To Free a Family (Nathans), xiii
Trinity College, 23
tsetse flies, 79
tuberculosis, 31

Umstead, Ben (enslaved carriage driver), 66
Umstead, John, 25–26, 34, 36, 102
Underground Railroad, 100
University of North Carolina, 3, 22

Venable, A. H., 53
venereal disease, 75, 83

Walker, Mary, xiii, 32, 36, 105–7, *106*, 167n18
Walker, Moses Fleetwood, *134*, 134–36, *135*, 172n3

Walker, Moses W., 55–57, *56*, 83–84, 87–88, 122, 134, 161n17, 172n3
Walker, William, 99–100
Washington College, 23, 25, 67
Watson, Daniel (enslaved foreman), 66
Webb, James, 44
Wentz, John, 123
Wheeler, John H., 99–101; *Reminiscences and Memoirs of Eminent North Carolinians,* 99
William "Toast" (Phoebe's nephew), 25, 32, 36, 38, 57, 102, 114
wills: of Thomas Amis Jr., 147n5; of Thomas Bennehan, xiii–xiv, 31–34, 35–36, 38, 44, 148nn13–14; execution of, 44, 53; and manumission of enslaved persons, xiv, 32–33, 34, 36, 45, 93; of John Rex, 45–46; and transfer of enslaved persons, 1–2; of John Umstead, 35, 148n12

Yates, Beverly Page, 63
Yerba Buena Cove, San Francisco, 124
Young Men's Colonization Society of Pennsylvania, 46